IRON WILL

The Triathlete's Ultimate Challenge

by Mike Plant

Foreword by Scott Tinley

VeloPress
Boulder, Colorado
USA

International Standard Book Number: 1-884737-67-6

Library of Congress Cataloging-in Publication Data

Plant, Mike.
  Iron will / by Mike Plant : foreword by Scott Tinley.
     p.   cm.
  ISBN 1-884737-67-6 (pbk.)
  1. Triathlon. I. Title.
  GV1060.73.P55 1999   99-3778
  796.42'57--dc21   CIP

Printed in the USA

Distributed in the United States and Canada by Publishers Group West.

VeloPress
1830 North 55th Street
Boulder, Colorado 80301-2700 USA
303/440-0601; fax 303/444-6788; e-mail velopress@7dogs.com

To purchase additional copies of this book or other VeloPress books, call
800/234-8356 or visit us on the Web at www.velogear.com.

Photos by Mike Plant
Cover and Book Design by Paulette Livers Lambert
Edited by Lori Hobkirk

*To my wife and
children, and to the
ghosts of all the
Iron men and women,
past, present and to
come, who will haunt
the highway forever,
searching for the
perfect race they
have already run.*

When I first read Mike Plant's book *Iron Will* in 1986, I didn't know quite what to think. Here was a story...no, a tale chronicling so many aspects of this event I had come to be a part of, and it of me. In some ways, Mike had made the Ironman larger than life. Almost gushing at times in my self-obsessed competitive bubble, I took minor offense with him for putting down in black and white what I had toiled so hard to be a part of. I did not understand nor did I fully appreciate any media intrusions in my little sphere of athletic influence. If the sport of triathlon were an identity for me, the Ironman was my new birth certificate. And it seemed a little odd to read about my personal experiences in such a vivid, colorful and accurate tome as *Iron Will*.

As the years passed, and I grew and matured as an athlete, a writer and a person, the stories found within *Iron Will* became like an old roll of film that had been forgotten, and one day found, developed and treasured. In many ways, Plant's book, like the man himself, was way ahead of its time. Triathlon wasn't ready for a piece of historical latitude in 1986. Heck, the Hawaii Ironman wasn't even 10 years old. It had all the makings of great cultural significance, but not enough people had actually been there, seen the race, felt the prescience of "Iron magic." Some of us had. And while a portion of the experienced few wanted so much to tell the world of this newfound "event," others such as myself were still unsure if spreading the word would somehow spoil the feeling that one received from entering the Gates of Babylon on Alii Drive. There are mountain climbers who will spend hours or days reaching an insurmountable peak for no other reason than to be standing at the local pub, effacing a Cheshire-cat grin, telling no one of their achievement. If they were to speak even a word of their accomplishment, it would be worse than failing to summit. I must confess now that I tried too hard to say too little. Future generations of Iron men and women have fate to thank that Plant became a preacher of the multisport word.

A lot has changed in the past 13 years, though. If the only constant in this life is change, we are fortunate that the Ironman still exists in much of its same form. One cannot hold back the tide of a good thing when word gets out. Ironman is a big deal, not just in the hearts and minds of its participants, but in all those who are touched by the human performances played out on its stage. Millions of people around the world know about it in one form or another. And their impression is nothing if not a deep feeling of something powerful.

And so it is time for *Iron Will* to be presented to all the newcomers—people who can only hear the tales of epic battles fought between, but mostly within, the dark reaches of an individual's true character. And for those who have been there and back, what a great book to re-read. Because those of us who have been touched by the event in so many ways know that it can't be held in private for one's own benefit. And while some of the magic is rubbed away when it is bottled and sold, that is not the case with *Iron Will*. The best way to really feel the Iron magic is go to down to the pier at 7 a.m. of the full moon Saturday, in October.

So, go out and ride until your quads are tender, and swim until the ends of your fingers are all wrinkly. But save enough energy to pick up *Iron Will* for a few minutes before you fall asleep. Just make sure you don't have a workout planned for early the next day. You may not be able to put it down. I couldn't. And I've already read it twice.

—*Scott Tinley*

Not all that much has changed at the Ironman since *Iron Will* was first published more than a decade ago. The lava fields have greened up a bit, but hardly enough to comfort anyone willing to run or ride a bike through them. And the upscale resorts along the Queen K Highway have multiplied, elevating the value and prestige of the Kona Coast moonscape, but increasing the risk to lonely riders on the highway who continue to be targets for speeding automobiles.

The triathletes speak many more languages than they did 12 years ago. Back then, U.S. athletes set the standards of the sport at every level. Dave Scott, Mark Allen, Scott Tinley and Scott Molina shared center stage, and Scott (as in Dave) ruled the Ironman with unquestioned authority. But the Big Four long ago departed the scene, victims of time and accumulated fatigue, and it is the Europeans and Australians who now dominate the ranks of the top finishers—so much so that in 1997, the top three men across the line were German.

If you stepped out of a time machine to bridge suddenly the gap between then and now you might marvel at the technology of the bicycles zooming in and out of town during race week. And you would probably gawk at the stunning level of fitness of the competitors. If Kailua-Kona was the hard-body capital of the world in 1986, it is something else now. The bodies gleam, the muscles ripple, the eyes sparkle as never before. Nowhere else in the world are you likely to see pure, gleaming health in such volume, such numbing abundance. If there is a spot on the planet where a model for Victoria's Secret would feel self-conscious in a bikini, this is it.

You also might notice that the staging of the race is more sophisticated than it was. The rough edges have been sanded down, polished and re-painted. The Ironman is no longer just a race, it is an event, a sport marketing property of international impact. Valerie Silk, earth mother to a generation of triathletes and foundress of the Ironman movement, is gone (but never forgotten, heaven knows), replaced years ago by businessmen-athletes who are unlikely to be seen under the floodlights at the pier, Silk-like, with tears in their eyes, hugging sweaty, stumbling, half-delirious finishers. One of Silk's most endearing assets was that she never even contemplated doing her own race. She thus remained awed and somewhat baffled by the exploits of her charges, and completely dedicated to her ministry of comfort and compassion. The Ironman has owners now instead of a guardian. Its goddess has vanished and will never be replaced.

Yet for all that, the essence of the Ironman remains as it was. In the furnace of the Queen K Highway, the lava still cracks and groans under the fiery Kona sun. The temperature still soars to 120 degrees Fahrenheit at noon on the asphalt, and the art of getting to the finish line is still as important as whatever courage and physical strength you can muster.

No one has ever conquered the Ironman; some have simply survived it more gracefully than others. And it hardly matters that the athletes curse the highway now in a variety of tongues as they head toward town from Hawi, their legs and minds windblown to shreds and their visions of glory in tatters. German, French, Japanese, English. Hell, the gods speak their own language out there on the lava. They never paid much attention to anyone I ever met—except maybe Mark Allen, and it took him seven years of talking to get them to listen, even a little.

As for the technology, well, all things being equal, the machines are faster than ever, and they sure do look good—all 1500 or so of them propped up there on the pier before the race. Very slick. And maybe if you have a chance

to win the race on a perfect day, when everyone else in the field is having a perfect day right along with you, then okay, nice bike.

The fact is, you can count the perfect days in Kona since 1981 on the fingers of one hand. When the wind is really howling out there at the north end of the bike course, or when you realize too late that you took all that aerodynamic crap a little too seriously and still have a marathon to run, it's not what bike you're riding, but who you are, deep down inside, that makes the difference.

The Ironman's ability to crown heroes and humble fools is undiminished. Its disrespect for perfect bodies is as cruel and unrelenting as ever. If anything, the new technology, the superior conditioning of the athletes, and the increased intensity of the competition have merely whetted the race's appetite for destruction.

Back in February 1982, the Julie Moss saga tugged at heartstrings, mostly because she was such a…waif. Her cap was too big, her bra strap kept slipping and she ran—even at the start—more like a college girl trying to lose a few pounds than a highly trained endurance athlete. It was riveting. But when her desperate, heart-rending, wobbly kneed, crawl-to-the-finish-line performance was replicated—in stereo, no less—15 years later by Sian Welch and Wendy Ingraham, two steely-eyed, finely tuned professionals—what you mostly wanted to do was close your eyes and look away. Moss's experience was a soap opera; Welch's and Ingraham's was a car wreck. Good heavens, you thought, if this race can turn these two perfect women into jelly, what would it do to me?

This is not a book about statistics. You might note that they are quoted infrequently. This is because at the Ironman, statistics, like race strategies, tend to get lost in the shuffle, battered into nothingness by those 1500 pairs of flailing arms and legs during the chaotic spectacle of the Ironman swim start. (I'm not sure I mention it in the book, but I can hear that sound now, at my desk—all those bodies at the same time. It's unlike anything you've ever heard, and it never leaves you.) This race is about tactics, not strategy. Damage control. "Oh, God, what am I going to do now?" is a far more frequent refrain than "Gee, I wonder how fast I should run that first mile when I get off the bike?"

But I find one particular statistic intriguing. Since the Ironman introduced the 17-hour time cutoff in 1982, the winning times of both men and women have dropped dramatically. To a triathlon insider, the race times of the early years noted in *Iron Will* may sound a bit, well, quaint. And yet, despite the new, sleek machinery, the high-tech shoes, the leaner, better conditioned, better fueled muscles, the larger pool of athletes from which to choose, the times for the final finishers have not gotten...faster...at...all. The last official finisher still crosses the line at about 17 hours, and there's always someone still out there, roaming around on the highway, cursing, pleading, praying, after midnight.

The day never works for everybody. The Ironman still tests, and a lot of folks still find themselves looking for small moral victories to replace the shattered dreams they have left behind them on the asphalt.

No, when you look just below that wafer-thin veneer of aluminum and Lycra that has overgrown the race I wrote about in 1986, you realize that nothing really has changed. The Ironman is still a place where people go, ultimately, to find themselves—and that is why I feel comfortable offering up *Iron Will* a second time, with only minor revisions.

Factually, *Iron Will* is about the Ironman as it was. It's a fair and accurate history. Emotionally, it is about the Ironman as it is today and will be forever, as long as people ride and run up and down the Kona Coast in search of dreams, redemption, fame, glory, revenge and whatever else motivates the annual pilgrimage.

Something I learned during my years at the Ironman is that members of the endurance subculture grow so close to the subject they lose sight of the vastness of their achievement. Without thought or even the barest acknowledgment, they pass through mental and physical boundaries on a daily basis. Meanwhile, the public stands in awe.

If you are not an Ironman, I hope you will read this book with interest and will find in its pages a touch of personal inspiration. It's a good story. If you have done the race, I hope this volume will remind you of your accomplishment, and of your status as a hero to all the world.

—*Mike Plant*
Escondido, California
June 1999

PREFACE TO THE ORIGINAL
EDITION OF *IRON WILL*

Like so many of my friends and associates in the triathlon world, I was introduced to the Ironman by an article about the race that appeared in *Sports Illustrated* in the spring of 1979. Unlike some of them, however, I was not moved immediately to devote my life to the event. What I was moved to do, actually, was shake my head in amazement, put the magazine in a box and go on running 10km and managing restaurants.

Obviously, that wasn't the end of it. Less than a year later I was making 50 bucks a month (and spending a couple of hundred) as editor of the *San Diego Track News*, a job for which I was not in the least qualified but which I attacked with great enthusiasm. By that time I had met Tom Warren, the winner of that 1979 race, and was involved so deeply in the San Diego running scene that avoiding the fledgling sport of triathlon was all but impossible. I'd even written an article, complete with pictures, about Warren's Tug's Tavern Run Swim Run, which I submitted on a freelance basis to a little magazine called *Swim Swim*, a now-defunct journal of Masters competitive swimming that was the direct ancestor to *Triathlon* magazine. The article was returned, awash in red ink, with a rejection note attached. I still have the piece in a file somewhere. I'm not sure if I have ever mentioned it to the current editors of that publication (which is now called *Triathlete*), who in a fit (or a slip) of gushy generosity in 1985 called me "the dean of triathlon writers," a handy little bit of praise that I polish off and throw into a résumé every so often, although it is a title that reflects, I think, my endurance more than anything. How many triathlon writers do you know?

None of which has anything to do with the Ironman exactly, except to say that the event was still new and unknown when I began writing about it seriously in 1981. I did so from a distance at first, from San Diego, since the trip to Hawaii was beyond my means. I relied on photographs and firsthand reports and interviews, gradually piecing together what I thought was a pretty good impression of what the race was actually like. As it turned out, I didn't have a clue.

I finally covered my first Ironman live in October 1982, apprehensive about the load of responsibility I had shouldered. I was the official team photographer for the infamous Team J David, with an additional assignment to write the feature article for the inaugural edition of *Triathlon*, as well as the lead piece for my own publication, the *San Diego Running News*. In fact, I collected enough material for 10 articles and could have shot another 40 rolls of film. The 17 hours I spent on the course whizzed by; half of what I did, I did unconsciously, by instinct—I was too awed by the scope of the event to concentrate much on details. I ended the day standing in the dark, in the glare of the spotlights at the finish line, next to a close friend I had seen for the first time in years that very morning on the Kailua Pier. It was pouring rain and both of us were crying, staring openmouthed at the undiluted joy and anguish of the men and women who were running, walking and stumbling down that last hundred yards.

I've been back to the Ironman every year since, once as a competitor, the other times as a journalist, each year unable to resist the call of those first-year memories and the sight of those bright lights at the finish line and the cheers of the crowd along Alii Drive. Never once have I been able to look at the Ironman course without marveling at its awesome impossibility, or to take the racing there for granted, with anything even close to journalistic detachment.

From the outside, it is easy to see the Ironman as an exercise in self-indulgent fanaticism. Frankly, considering the kind of dedication required of the triathletes who compete, it *is* self-indulgent. And I suppose that swimming, cycling and running 140 miles in a single day could easily be considered fanatical. But it's not as simple as that. As I discovered in 1982, the race is more than just photographs and anecdotes. It's more than raw miles and times on a watch, and even more than wonderful athletes like Dave Scott and Scott Tinley pushing themselves beyond conventional limits of physical performance.

The Ironman, in fact, is about people who become heroes. It's about an impossible task proven to be possible year after year. It's about athletes, the fast ones and the slow ones alike, stripped of everything but the simple desire to take one step farther than they themselves believe is possible. That they do this voluntarily, some of them on an annual basis, might sound crazy, but noble is what it really is.

I guess that's what I like best about the Ironman: the nobility of the effort. I hope some of that comes across in this book. Hell, it's what this book is all about.

—*Mike Plant*
San Diego, California, 1987

1

THE SUN GOES DOWN IN KONA

THE TWO WOMEN HAD BEEN ON THE HIGHWAY THE ENTIRE day. One of them was blonde, with fair skin; the other was dark. For most of the time, they had been hunched low over the handlebars of their bicycles, the blonde one chasing the other through the furnace of the grim lava desert. In less than six hours, they'd covered 112 miles, their minds gradually numbed by the steady flow of the white line that marked the shoulder of the road and by the constant swoosh of their tires on the smooth black asphalt.

Their bodies, however, had not been numbed. Beneath a fierce sun that climbed behind them as they rode, one tiny area of pain had been added to another until a vast catalog of discomfort had been logged. The women breathed hard, perspired freely and tried unsuccessfully to ignore it all. They shifted back and forth on the narrow black seats and stood on the pedals of their bicycles to pump up the hills, but their butts got sore anyway. So did their backs, their hands, their arms, and if there had been any circulation left in their feet, those would have hurt, too.

Now they were running. The blonde still trailed, but she was gaining ground. She looked—well, not as awful as the one in front. At least she was still on her toes; her head was up, and her eyes, which were hooded beneath a white visor, flickered with optimism.

The dark-haired woman was struggling; there was resignation in her face. And either the white line was moving, or she was weaving just a bit. She walked frequently, and she was too far from the end for that. She walked from one aid station to the next, drinking, filling her mouth with ice, sponging her face and drinking again, then running on reluctantly. The blonde was drinking, too, of course—to pass up a single chance to drink at the Ironman is suicidal—but she was grabbing what she could at aid stations along the way and drinking on the run, gaining time. At a seven-and-a-half- to eight-minute-per-mile pace, she wasn't chasing the leader furiously, but rather with a kind of grim determination, whittling away at what had begun as a 20-minute lead.

The darker woman was Julie Leach, a 24-year-old former Olympic kayaker from Newport Beach, California. She had long, tanned legs and curly black hair that capped a handsome, square-jawed face. Her eyes were a piercing blue. Lost in concentration and fatigue, they stared out into nothing, and occasionally she would roll them back into her head, taking her vision and mind away from the tension of the highway.

Leach was competing in her first Ironman, aware now that the race was even more terrible than everyone had warned. She had already made the turnaround out past the airport at the 17-mile mark and was running south again, back toward town. She still had nine miles to go.

Still moving north, not even a mile behind Leach, was the blonde woman, Kathleen McCartney. She lived in Newport Beach, too, an ex-waitress and college student who had taken leave of both her job and her class schedule to train for the Ironman. Many of her friends thought she had taken leave of her senses as well. With her fashion-model skin, her golden hair and cover-girl face, she seemed an unlikely candidate for such self-inflicted suffering. What gave her away were her legs, which were strong and brown, clearly the legs of an athlete—in this case, a unique athlete, to whom 2.4 miles of swimming, 112 miles of cycling and 26.2 miles of running represented not only the ultimate physical challenge, but also the ultimate competitive opportunity. The challenge went beyond mere survival. McCartney pressed on in the hope that she could run Leach down, pass her, then move on to her second consecutive Ironman victory.

It was a reasonable goal. McCartney had looked remarkably fresh when she won the race the previous February, in 1982. In one of the most dramatic moments in the history of televised sport, she passed the early leader, Julie Moss, just yards from the finish line. McCartney had to ask if she had won, unaware of how close the race had been, unaware that Moss was on the ground just 20 yards away. The fledgling sport of triathlon was burned into the minds and hearts of the entire world when Moss crawled, in apparent agony, to a second-place finish.

In fact, Moss's agony was more mental than physical. She was helpless and frustrated when her legs simply ran out of fuel and stopped working. After 140 miles of competition, she would have undoubtedly preferred a little real pain to nothing at all—the pain might at least have gotten her across in first place. As it was, her legs failed to support her, and she wilted to the pavement several times, going to her hands and knees while spectators and media looked on out of the darkness, cheering her, willing her to get up and finish the race. Three times she did get up, wobbling forward a few steps before going down again. Physically wasted but still in control mentally, Moss finally decided that her best bet was to finish the day on her hands and knees. In so doing, she all but stole the show from McCartney.

Eight months later, McCartney came back to Hawaii hoping to win the race cleanly. The physical victory in February had certainly been hers, but she wanted the emotional part, too. Had McCartney trained properly, her chances to win again in October would have been excel-

lent. But a nagging tendon injury had kept her from putting in anywhere near the running mileage that she needed during spring and summer. Now on the Ironman road
again, in second place and gaining against Leach, she was
anything but confident. The second half of her marathon
loomed as a great unknown. She worried about her pace
(was it too fast?), about her legs (was that latest twinge the
start of a cramp?), and about Leach, whom she could see
now in the distance, moving toward her on the way back
from the turnaround.

Leach was thinking about the pass, too. She was struggling to pull her own pain deep inside because she knew
McCartney would try to assess her condition. If she looked
bad, that might give McCartney hope, and these last nine
miles would be tougher yet. Also, there was the ABC television camera hanging out of the back of the van that simply stared, and had been staring all damn day. And there
was her own opinion—the most important one of all—
because the predominant feeling of any competitor at this
point in this day of quiet insanity was that simply stopping
and walking off the course was probably the smartest
option. If McCartney looked too good, that would be just
the excuse Leach needed to quit. She could simply flag
down her husband, Bill, who was out on his bike somewhere on the course, and tell him the day was over.

About half-a-mile south of the turnaround, the two
women passed within a foot of each other, neither giving
any indication that she'd seen the other. McCartney's eyes
were screwed to the 20-foot-high inflatable beer can that
marked the 17-mile mark and the turn; Leach looked at the
pavement. Perhaps some unseen force crackled at their
elbows—it seemed strange that they could come that close
and not have something happen—but if it did it went
unnoticed. "Second place," Leach thought. "She's moving
too hard. I'll never hold up."

"She looks tired," McCartney thought, "but no worse
than me. I'm not sure I can catch her."

So they ran on, through the human wreckage of a nine-
hour day that would grow into 10, 12, 14 hours and

longer—much longer, for many. Up ahead, a quiet, intense man named Dave Scott had already won his second Ironman in record time. A handsome blond sailing instructor named Scott Tinley, the defending Ironman champion, had placed second, 20 minutes behind Scott. But out on the two lanes of the Queen Kaahumanu Highway, under the pressing weight of air so heavy with moisture you could almost feel it sitting in the palm of your hand, the rest of the field still struggled. The question of who would be the women's champion was still unresolved.

For a long time, it looked as if McCartney would do it. Still moving strongly, she made the turn and headed back toward town. For three miles, she continued to close the gap. People told her she was gaining. At each aid station, there was a spark of excitement as she arrived, a flurry of activity as the volunteers rushed to get her water, an orange, ice, anything she needed. While she couldn't actually see Leach through the long line of slow-moving cars that jammed the highway, and the slower moving line of triathletes on the shoulder, she could see a helicopter hovering above the road not more than half a mile away. Below that helicopter, she knew, was Leach. In her mind she felt that she could almost reach out and make up the distance in an instant.

But then her legs began to go. They began to ache, the twinges of pain in her thighs lasting longer and longer as the fatigue set in. The shoes that had seemed so light just a mile before were heavy now, soggy with sweat and water—like old rags left in the bottom of a bucket. The asphalt seemed to soften and hold each foot in place for an instant before grudgingly letting go, only to hold the next step a little longer. Within the space of half a mile, McCartney's aggressive style fell apart completely. She had run up that big hill outside of the Kona Surf Hotel at the start of the marathon as if it didn't even exist; then she passed a whole group of men on the second hill on the way out of town like they were standing still. But now, 12, 13 miles later, she was merely shuffling, moving like an old woman, swinging her bent arms back and forth as if she

"She looks tired," McCartney thought, "but no worse than me. I'm not sure I can catch her."

were running at a respectable pace (she thought she was), but her feet were barely leaving the surface of the road.

Finally, there came the hill just before the 23-mile mark. It isn't a hill, really, just a shallow rise you'd hardly notice in a car, but after a full day of racing in the heat, triathletes climb it as if they are trudging up the side of Mauna Loa. It was more than McCartney's under-trained legs could take. At the base of the rise, her knees buckled, and a ripple of collapse shivered across her shoulders and down her spine, as if someone had opened a valve somewhere and let out a great whoosh of air. She recovered quickly and didn't fall, but the realization of what had almost happened frightened her. She remembered the sight of Julie Moss crawling to the finish line just eight months before. "My God," thought McCartney, "that could be me!" And indeed, afraid that it *would* be her if she continued to run, she walked to the top of the hill, then down the other side, where she at last could hear the announcer's voice at the finish line echoing over the public address system. Joanne Dahlkoetter, who had been in third place for most of the marathon, ran by her quickly, without a word, into second. Two miles to go. Five, six hundred yards ahead, Julie Leach moved on, running more easily than she had all day, her exhaustion relieved by the glimmer of hope that she would, after all, be able to finish first.

In the gathering darkness, McCartney continued to walk—off the highway at last and down the big hill toward the pier. Finally, she turned right onto Alii Drive and saw the bright lights of the finish line. The cheers were loud, and she was tempted to run again, but fought the urge, fearing that she might fall. She was in fourth place now, having been passed for the last time during that final mile. The woman who passed her, a long-time endurance athlete named Sally Edwards, had urged her to run, but McCartney shook her head and smiled weakly. "I can't, Sally, I just can't," she said, knowing that she had done all she could. She would finish standing up and smiling, her dignity intact—a simple achievement that was far removed from the expectations of that morning.

Behind her, still on the highway in the darkness, more than 600 men and 150 women struggled with their personal demons of doubt and regret. A warm, sometimes heavy rain fell at regular intervals along the course; only occasionally did the full moon appear behind a bank of clouds to light their way. It didn't matter; they all knew where they were going.

2

ALONG THE QUEEN K— THE DAMN HIGHWAY

IT'S LIKE A DAY THAT'S GONE SO BADLY YOU CAN'T GET MAD anymore; you can only laugh. After all the time spent training, all the sacrifice, it looks like someone's bad idea of a joke. It sits out there like some great black monster, rolling through the lava as if it were alive and hungry. "C'mon," you think, "where are they *really* going to hold the race?" But you're in the right place, all right, and your timing is pretty good, too, because from the looks of things it's been a lot worse out there.

Officially it's the Queen Kaahumanu Highway. Locals call it the Queen K. Forty miles long and two lanes wide, scoured constantly by shifting winds and punctuated by long, gradual hills that you don't even know you're on until you're halfway up and struggling, the highway is the main arena of the Ironman Triathlon World Championship. Flawlessly smooth, sizzling hot and jet black, it's the anvil against which triathletes are hammered into Ironmen—or beaten into submission. It's an imposing physical barrier, but it's

"I despise this course," Dave Scott said bluntly, after winning the event for the third time in 1983.

9

a mind-numbing psychological barrier as well. It's an intimidating complication in an event that even in an ideal environment would transcend the most liberal definition of common sense: 2.4 miles of open-water swimming, 112 miles of cycling, and a 26.2-mile marathon—consecutively, all within 17 hours. The course record is slightly less than half that time. Twice during the bike ride, the triathletes must traverse the highway's entire length. That done, they must head back out and run 16 miles of the marathon on it as well, facing conditions that are horrendous. You don't conquer the highway—you survive it. You don't deal with the highway—you can only hope to deal with yourself.

"The highway *is* the Ironman," said Joanne Ernst, winner of the women's race in 1985.

"I despise this course," Dave Scott said bluntly, after winning the event for the third time in 1983.

"We'd better rethink this race," said a worried boyfriend/coach of a top triathlete in 1986 after he had ridden the course for the first time.

The Queen K runs through some of the most hostile-looking land on the planet. Primitive and bleak, the North Kona-Kohala coast is as far removed from the Hawaii-as-tropical-paradise travel brochures as you can get. There are beautiful beaches, but only one has been developed for public use. There are several pricey resorts scattered at wide intervals along the rugged shoreline, but they are well hidden from the highway and were carved from the lava at ridiculous expense. The huge 1243-room Hyatt Regency Waikoloa resort, for instance, was built at a cost of around $250,000 a room. Developers not only had to pipe in a supply of water from deep underground reserves but had to truck in soil for plantings as well.

Except in places where man has intervened, the North Kona coast is a desert, where not more than 20 inches of rain, and most years less than 10, fall each year; 60 percent of that comes during the "rainy" season, which lasts from October through March. Instead of graceful, shifting sands, however, the desert offers only a vista of exploded stone, a vast expanse of black and chocolate-brown volcanic rubble—lava that rushed and bubbled down the slopes of nearby Mount Hualalai or the massive and distant Mauna Loa, and then cooled slowly under the fiery sun. There are stretches along the highway where nothing grows at all, and other areas where patches of dry, brown grass eke out a Spartan existence in cracks where handfuls of windblown dust have settled. There are no houses, no gas stations, no billboards. Every hill looks the same; every inch of the highway from Kailua-Kona to Kawaihae is identical: an endless series of yellow traffic dots down the middle and a white line running along each edge, marking the narrow shoulder.

The man-eating reputation of the Queen K is part of the attraction of the Ironman. Hell, that *is* the attraction. A critical element of the race is its aura of impossibility; it was designed from the first to be an ordeal, a true test of endurance and courage. If it weren't hard, if it weren't just about the toughest damn thing in the whole world, it wouldn't be the Ironman. People wouldn't spend a year training for it, giving up their weekends and their mornings and who knows what else—including the goodwill of their spouses, their kids and most of their friends.

Still, that first glimpse is something to remember. Regardless of how well trained they believe themselves to be, rookies are usually shocked when the jet that has brought them from the mainland—probably by way of the tropic gentility of Honolulu—banks into the wind and they get their first look. Expecting to see palm trees and lagoons, they are greeted instead by a scene of impossible desolation.

Ron Smith, a Southern Californian and a veteran of five Ironman races, remembers what it was like seeing the highway for the first time: "It's got to be similar to when those guys on the Apollo took a look and said, 'There's the moon, babe. What are we gonna do now?' It was awesome."

Smith, a former Navy UDT frogman and SEAL team member, made a small fortune as one of the founders of the nationally successful Chart House Restaurant chain. He first did the Ironman in 1980. That was when the race was held on Oahu, when the main hazard to the competitors was the heavy traffic in downtown Honolulu.

Smith has been back to the Ironman every time that his health has allowed—and once or twice when it didn't. He missed the February 1982 race because of a broken hip, raced the October 1982 event in one piece, then hobbled through the 1983 edition with a dozen screws and a metal plate holding his left leg together. The previous summer, while cycling down a long, steep hill near La Jolla, California, Smith's front tire exploded and flew off the rim, jamming between the wheel and the brakes. The wheel stopped, but Smith didn't; it was a terrible crash. The doctors who cut his leg open screwed the bone together and then sewed him back up, leaving an 18-inch incision in his heavily muscled thigh. They told him to forget cycling for at least a year and to forget running forever. But he was working out on a stationary bicycle within a couple of weeks after surgery and was out on the road for real within two months. He didn't run well at Ironman that year, but he finished. Smith is divorced now from his second wife, Ronda, primarily because of that kind of obsessive behavior. "It was a stupid thing," he admitted. "If I hadn't done the Ironman that year I'd probably still be married."

Smith has trained extensively on the Queen K since 1981 and knows it about as well as anyone. A big, weathered man in his 50s, with a body many 25-year-olds would envy, he is one of the best Masters (over 40) triathletes in the world, and he can still ride with some of the top competitive cyclists in the sport. His best time for the 112 miles of the Ironman bike course is five hours, 25 minutes. Most people would have a hard time matching that on a moped. While it would be silly to describe him as a typical Ironman competitor—mostly because such a thing does not exist—Smith is representative of the kind of people who tend to get involved. He's an intelligent, financially successful overachiever who is comfortable with commitment, physical and otherwise.

"People thought those 12 people who did the race in 1978 were crazy," Smith said. "I had to have some of that. It was another challenge. It looked like fun."

Although Smith had already gone the Ironman distance once—on the old course on Oahu—he was as surprised and startled as anyone by his first glimpse of the Kona landscape from an airplane in 1981. Stepping off the plane into an oven, however, was something else again. "It was frightening," said Smith. "The first time I trained on the course, I went out about two in the afternoon and rode north for about an hour. Then I turned around and realized I could not, absolutely could not, make it back in the heat. I had to hitchhike. I thought, my God."

To this day, the blast-furnace effect is what leaves first-time Ironman hopefuls wondering about their own sanity: "What have I gotten myself into? Can I possibly have trained enough for this craziness?"

Probably not.

To make matters worse, there are other athletes on the flight who have done the race before. Their obvious confidence, the marks on their bicycle bags and the veins in their legs reveal it. As nervous first-timers wait for their baggage, a half-dozen tanned, sweaty triathletes, looking as though they've been out on the road for hours and could go hours more without a second thought, show up and loop the terminal on their bikes, searching for friends who've just landed. If they find them, they chat for awhile, leaning with studied nonchalance against their bikes, basking in their position as island veterans. They're probably from Oregon or Wyoming and flew in only two days before, but everyone quickly picks up the Ironman swagger. The conversation, which cannot fail to be overheard (it's meant to be overheard), has mostly to do with the weather: "It's been so hot!" "The winds up near Hawi have been awesome!" The rookies listen without really wanting to, fascinated, but more apprehensive by the minute.

The first close-up look at the highway comes on the drive into town, over the same route that the marathon and the beginning and end of the bike ride will follow on

Saturday. To the right, sweeping down toward the ocean, is a low, slanting plain of lava, covered in parts by wispy, brown grass. To the left is the rising slope of Mount Haulalai, greener at higher elevations, the upper portions forested and lost in mist. Ahead, the shallow rises of the road are cut off by shimmering waves of heat, which make cyclists in the distance look as if they've left the road entirely and are riding off into thin air. Finally, there are buildings and an intersection; with a right turn off the highway, the town appears, and the scene begins to shift. Palm trees appear, and there is shade across the road. There are knots of nylon- and Lycra-clad athletes standing here and there— triathletes, obviously, but somehow more familiar than the ones at the airport. There is Hawaii, at last, although the sight of all that lava out there is hard to forget.

While in 1978 the original concept of the Ironman revolved around the near-impossible distances, the extreme conditions of the Queen K have compounded the task. Training for the race is only the first step. A well-conditioned athlete must deal with a wide range of problems along the highway, from the physical to the psychological, from eating and drinking during the competition to the delicate balance between acceptable levels of physical stress and imminent collapse. The basic question for many of the competitors is "How hard and how fast can I go and still get to the finish line?" But there are many little side issues that must be considered as well. Failure can come from any direction—or from several at the same time. Small mistakes born on the highway tend to grow up quickly. Two, three, four hours after you've made them, they can come back to grab you hard.

"There's no margin for error," two-time winner Scott Tinley said in 1985. "Absolutely none. If things aren't going right, they're going wrong. There's no middle of the road. You're either awesome, or you're beat."

The main enemy on the highway is heat. Surface temperatures between the Kohala Airport—seven miles north from the start of the race in Kailua-Kona—and Kawaihae, 33 miles up the coast, soar at midday to well over 100 degrees. A thermometer placed on the asphalt will jump to 120 degrees in a few seconds. As far as what the temperature is in the shade, there's little point in wondering, because there *is* no shade.

How the triathletes deal with the sun and the heat on the highway is partly a matter of individual experience and physiology, partly a matter of common sense. Some can handle it, some can't—their bodies aren't made for it. There are accomplished triathletes who race well in shorter triathlons, or under less extreme conditions, who have never finished well in Hawaii. In fact, there are some who have never finished Hawaii at all, despite repeated attempts and several different strategies. They go slow early in the race, or fast early in the race; they eat too much or not at all; they drink two, three, four times as much as they think they need, but they still blow up well before the finish line.

Scott Molina is a professional triathlete who started his career in the small, industrial northern California town of Pittsburg, moved to San Diego in 1983 and then to Boulder, Colorado. He is known as "The Terminator" for his relentless style of racing. He, Dave Scott, Scott Tinley and Mark Allen make up "the Big Four," a group that dominated the sport from 1982 through 1986.

Molina is perhaps the best short-distance triathlete in the world. He's won more than his share of long races, too, including an Ironman-distance race based in Lake Tahoe called the World's Toughest Triathlon, which he won in 1984 and 1985. The World's Toughest featured thousands of feet of climbing, both on the bike and the run. On paper, the race looked like it might even be worthy of its name, although the beauty of the course, the altitude, and the cool—sometimes even cold—weather made it an entirely different kind of challenge than the Ironman. It certainly never attracted the large, competitive fields that Hawaii did. As Molina himself said in 1985, "What makes a race tough is the racing."

In any case, Molina learned over the years to give the Ironman a wide berth, primarily because of the heat.

"People thought those 12 people who did the race in 1978 were crazy," Smith said. "I had to have some of that. It was another challenge. It looked like fun."

Superbly conditioned, as intent a professional athlete as there is, he has never been able to handle the Queen K—at least not at the speeds at which he must race there to be competitive.

The 1981 Ironman was Molina's first triathlon, and he started well. He spent most of the race in second place—until slightly more than halfway through the run. Then the cumulative effects of the heat and dehydration hit him hard. He started getting cramps that were so intense, he was afraid muscles in his legs were going to tear. He fought the inevitable for several miles, alternately walking and jogging, then finally dropped out 17 miles or so into the marathon. They took him back to town on a stretcher. He came back and placed fourth in October 1982, but the effort was agony and the results far below his expectations.

"I accept it," Molina said about the chink in his otherwise impenetrable triathlon armor. "It's not anything that's overwhelming anymore. It used to be. I've learned to deal with it. It's harder for me to win on hot days. I think it's that way in a lot of ultrasports. There are people who handle the heat well over a long period of time and people who don't. I guess that's a subject for science.

"A lot of people think the trick is to get your body to absorb more water. I think the secret is not how much you absorb but how much you lose. If you can keep your body from losing it fast, then you don't have to worry so much about how much you're taking. I lose more water per minute or per hour than the other guys. After a while you lose so much you can't put it back. For two hours, three hours, I don't care how hot it is. But for six hours, nine hours...."

Forced each year to at least consider the Ironman, Molina can look back on his experiences in Hawaii and say no without a second thought. It was like that in 1985, when he was in first place but fading rapidly at the Nice Triathlon in France. Ironman was three weeks away. Like several other top competitors, he'd gone into the European event considering a Nice/Ironman double. Unfortunately, it was exceptionally hot at Nice that year.

"At about seven miles into the run in Nice," said Molina, "I said to myself, 'Just think, you've got 13 or 14 miles to go. Suppose you had 20 to go and it was 10 degrees hotter and you'd just come off a 112-mile bike ride. Be realistic. You're barely going to make it today!'"

Molina laughed at the thought. "I knew at that point," he said dryly, "that if I went to Ironman, I wasn't even going to finish."

Dr. Doug Hiller, an M.D. from Memphis, Tennessee, and a three-time Ironman finisher himself, is one of the few physicians in the world to study triathletes under race conditions. Since 1983, he and his partner, Mary O'Toole, a Ph.D. in exercise physiology, have been directors of LAB-MAN, a privately funded, nonprofit research group. With his own intimate competitive relationship with the highway as a backdrop, Hiller over the years has come to know well how hours on the Queen K can affect the bodies of Ironman contestants. Like people who spend their time studying sharks, Hiller is now even more respectful of the highway for its unpredictability and its dangers than he was at the beginning.

"There are a whole bunch of things that go into being able to do this race," said Hiller. "First of all, how much you sweat is genetic, and it varies by 700 percent from, say, an Irish woman to a black male. Well, 300 percent is in the literature, so that's safe, but people of different races have a ratio of one to seven in the number of sweat glands they have per square centimeter of skin. There's a tremendous difference there.

"There are also things—independent of how much you sweat, that nobody really understands—which allow some people to tolerate heat. That's one of the amazing things about Dave Scott. He has an unbelievable ability in that area. In 1984, when everybody else was dying, Dave ran an incredible marathon. A lot of good marathoners couldn't do what he did under those conditions—forgetting the swim and the bike ride. He's somebody who is genetically capable; who has trained himself, who takes care of his body, who knows how much fluid he needs—he just has the ability to deal with the heat, all the way around.

"And it just isn't mental," Hiller said. "As a matter of fact, I think the most dangerous thing is for people to take the attitude that, 'Well, I'm tough, I can do it.' Those are the people who get in trouble."

Hiller wasn't saying anything that most competitors at the Ironman don't know. Still, there is a lot of self-generated pressure to finish. Dropping out is as terrible a fate as you can suffer at Ironman, since the whole event revolves around the ability to endure, the ability and the courage— misguided or not—to shove aside the danger signals your body is sending to your brain for just another mile, and then a mile after that and a mile after that, and on and on. Usually, it's only when it becomes physically impossible for a triathlete to continue that he or she will leave the race. Cramps such as Molina suffered can finish you as surely as if you were run over by a tank. And the effects of severe dehydration and heat exhaustion are scary. Most triathletes have become familiar with the symptoms— light-headedness, goose-fleshy skin, chills, and the inability to perspire—through firsthand experience. They know that the signs can sometimes be ignored and sometimes not, although the prospect of riding or running on and doing serious damage weighs heavily—assuming they are thinking clearly at the time, which is not always the case.

As Hiller does, the official medical people at the Ironman counsel caution. Printed material distributed to the athletes before the race is full of warnings about heat exhaustion and heat stroke. A final word comes at the meeting on the Thursday before the race. But that kind of talk rubs against the grain of the general philosophy of the competitors, who are by nature somewhat reckless when it comes to their own physiology. Physical limits are frequently exceeded, sometimes with a fair degree of desperation. Athletes during the marathon can find themselves wobbling back and forth between despair and disgust with themselves, and surges of self-discipline. They take inventories of their aching bodies in the hope that somewhere there is an ache so bad that it will qualify as an excuse to fail—knowing full well they wouldn't accept an excuse even if one surfaced. Or would they? Sometimes just the promise to themselves that they would quit, given the right set of circumstances, is enough to keep them going.

Situations like that can be touching. Conditions were so bad in 1984—the heat set records all over the Hawaiian Islands—that even some of the leaders were looking for reasons to walk off the course and call it a day. Sylviane Puntous, from Montreal, who had won the women's race the year before, was in the lead, but she was right on the edge of her endurance.

"I felt worse and worse," she said in her lilting French Canadian accent. "I thought, 'Well, I will go to another mile and I will stop.' When I get there I say, 'I will go to another mile and I will stop.'"

Then she saw Mark Allen, running in the opposite direction on his way back toward town. He was having his own problems that day—to call what he was doing "running" is being charitable.

"I walk, and I feel so bad," Puntous said. "And he looked me in the eye and said, 'Finish.'" She reached across the table with her hand and jabbed her finger sternly in my direction to indicate how Allen pointed at her. She laughed. " 'Oh,' I said, 'if I don't finish he will be mad.' We train together, you know, for swimming."

On the other hand, some triathletes are simply too bull-headed to even consider stopping. Some people have made it to the end of the Ironman by getting so mad at what the highway has done to them that they refused to make any concessions at all. I've heard stories of athletes grumbling to themselves, quite loudly in fact, about the stupidity of the ordeal throughout the entire marathon, slogging through 26.2 miles like crotchety old men muttering in disgust at the state of the universe. Such sentiments are widely appreciated but are never taken seriously. The grumblers are often three- and four-time finishers who will be back again the following year.

The basic concept of the triathlon as a purely individual endeavor is stressed at the Ironman, although enforcement of the rules that define "individual effort" has at times been haphazard. Disputes over drafting and pacing and outside assistance have raged year after year. Protests by athletes and race officials have been lodged; athletes have been disqualified or penalized by race officials. The competitors' views on outside assistance range from paranoia over the possibility of disqualification to blatant dishonesty to frustration with race officials for not being more sympathetic. The elite athletes lobbied for years for technical support during the race, reasoning that mechanical failure during a 112-mile bike race is a contingency over which they have no control. At the other extreme, I've seen exhausted, semiconscious finishers fight off volunteers trying to help because they weren't sure they'd actually crossed the line. In 1983, my wife, a spectator that year, stepped out of a car to make sure a triathlete who was fixing a flat tire was okay. A gust of wind blew one of his cycling gloves in her direction. She stopped to pick it up and was startled when he screamed at her: "Don't touch it! Don't touch anything!"

Race administrators became very sensitive of charges that some of the top triathletes were skirting the spirit of the no-help rule. In 1986, when prize money was offered to the professionals for the first time, friends and family members of the athletes were restricted in how much information (pace, distance from the man or woman in front of them, etc.) they could give to the competitors and when. Instead, race officials themselves supplied the information on a trial basis. This was a token effort that left many of the competitors in the dark and ignored the women almost completely. It was a difficult situation because while the information was critical, the fear of obtaining it illegally and thus being disqualified was acute. The entire competition was permeated with a kind of vague unease. No one, neither the athletes nor the officials, was exactly sure of what was allowed and what was not.

The aid stations are obviously a necessary exception to the individual-effort concept. They are, in fact, a critical issue in a race in which competitors are allowed to eat only what they can carry or what they can pick up from official sources along the way. Beyond that, the aid stations provide help of a less definable nature. Moral support during the Ironman can be almost as important as water and bananas.

Staffed by thousands of volunteers (2500 of them in 1986), most of whom manage to maintain an extraordinary level of enthusiasm and empathy with the competitors throughout the long day, the aid stations are set up along the highway at approximate five-mile intervals on the bike course and one-mile intervals on the marathon route. On the bike especially, when the athletes are strung out in two directions over 100 miles of road, the aid stations are oases of sanity, reminders to the riders that the civilized world did not entirely disappear when the starting cannon boomed that morning.

During the marathon, the aid stations not only fill the needs for fluid and fuel but also serve as short-term goals for runners too exhausted to think about the Big Picture, the finish line. Even the better runners can find themselves shuffling desperately from one station to the next during the run, a single mile at a time, grateful for the encouragement, sympathy and psychological counseling they receive along with food and drink.

"All *right*!" scream the volunteers working the aid stations on the way out to the turnaround. "You're looking good! You're looking strong!"

"Way to go," they say more softly at the aid stations on the way back into town. "You've got it made now. Just keep moving. You're almost home."

For the first three years of the Ironman competition, there were no aid stations. The race was held on an around-the-island course on Oahu, and each athlete was required to supply his or her own support crew, which tagged along or leap-frogged over the course in a van or a car, meeting the athletes at agreed-upon intervals, passing along food, drink, advice and encouragement. Some of the crews were sophisticated and organized; there were family operations like Dave Scott's in 1980, with his manager

"I felt worse and worse," Sylviane Puntous said in her lilting French Canadian accent. "I thought, 'Well, I will go to another mile and I will stop.' When I get there I say, 'I will go to another mile and I will stop.'"

aboard along with his dad and mom. Organization was the key to Scott's success. Other groups were locally recruited and hastily arranged—a little better, but not much, than nothing at all. The system was the source of both joy and despair along the route, with support crews helping one another out or feuding, cheering the other athletes on or accusing them of unfairness, being of great service to their own athlete or leading him into stumbling, falling-down ruin by getting lost or missing rendezvous points.

The support crews worked well when only a handful competed in 1978 and 1979, but things got tight with 100 athletes on the course in 1980. When the Ironman moved to Kona in 1981 and the field got bigger still, the aid station concept was the only way to deal with the problem, although it took a year or two to work the kinks out of the system. Race director Valerie Silk was so upset over the way it was handled that first year that she hid in her apartment for months, depressed, sure that every athlete who had competed was enraged over her negligence.

"Every aid station I passed was calling out and telling me that they were low on water," said Silk, who had patrolled the course looking for problems. Since there is no water along the highway, it's delivered by truck, and the truck that year had one problem after another, including a flat tire.

"I was scared to death," Silk said. "I was afraid somebody was going to die on the course."

But no one did. The situation had never been as acute as Silk feared. The race survived, and the system for supplying the athletes became increasingly sophisticated. Considering the environment and the conditions along the highway, it remains one of the more complex support mechanisms in the world of sport. It needs to be.

The triathletes' bodies lose fluids at an incredible rate along the highway: from two to six pints an hour, depending on the level of effort and the athlete's size and physiology. That adds up to between three and nine gallons or more of water for a 12-hour race, between 24 and 72 pounds. Clearly, it's a good idea to throw as much of that back in as possible—and what you can't throw in, you throw on. The endurance athletes' adage, "If you wait until you're thirsty, you've waited far too long," carries the weight of scientific fact.

Compounding the problem is the high Hawaiian humidity. At midday along the Kona coast, simply standing in the sun is enough to make you start sweating. On the day of record heat in 1984, while I was waiting for Mark Allen, the lead cyclist, to roll into the bike/run transition area at the Kona Surf Hotel, I remember watching beads of sweat drip off the matted ends of the volunteers' hair. They hadn't moved a muscle; all they were doing was waiting, like I was. I knew the leader was Allen because 10 minutes before I'd watched him riding down Alii Drive with a big lead, drops of sweat forming at the tip of his sharp nose as he whizzed along at 23 miles an hour. Not even air moving into his face at that speed could dry him off.

In the heavy air, the cooling effect of all that sweat is minimal. The triathletes' core temperatures rise inexorably as they ride, sometimes beyond levels their bodies can deal with—even if they are drinking enough water. Most of the athletes wear light-colored clothing that reflects the sun, and they quickly learn that their heads are terrific radiators; keep a cool head and the world feels better all over.

The athletes drink mostly water, although during a race as long as the Ironman the body's fuel and chemical stores must be replaced, too. Electrolyte imbalances can short-circuit even a well-hydrated triathlete.

"Nineteen eighty-six was the third year we'd drawn pre- and post-race blood at the Ironman," Hiller said. "I wanted to look at the electrolytes because I thought it would be interesting. I didn't think there'd be any big changes. But between 10 and 25 percent of the athletes that we looked at were salt-depleted when they finished the race: hyponatremic. There were people who had absolutely bizarre sodium values, low enough to put a normal person into convulsions."

Hiller concluded that the low sodium levels were due to athletes sweating out salt and water, then replacing just water.

"It's like pouring out half a glass of salt water and then filling it again with plain water. It gets diluted. It takes a race this long for that to show up clinically. So the athletes are first dehydrated and second hyponatremic. Both of those things can make them sick, but hyponatremia is extremely dangerous. We've had a number of people who have gone to the emergency room with extreme hyponatremia. That's sodium. Potassium is something that people have always worried about, attributed muscle cramps and everything else to. Essentially no one has abnormal potassium levels after the race. In our experience so far that hasn't been a problem."

While the data is new, electrolyte replacement drinks have been around for a long time, with different athletes having their personal favorites. As a result, "The Official Electrolyte Replacement Drink of the Ironman Triathlon World Championship" has been a source of some minor controversy over the years.

For the first two years the honor went to something called ERG, an acronym for "electrolyte replacement with glucose." It was developed during the late sixties by Bill Gookin, a longtime runner from San Diego. The drink became known as "Gookinade."

Gookin, a frantic, absent-minded man with a background in chemistry and a saintly devotion to distance running, used a chemical analysis of his own perspiration to help him with the original formula. ERG worked exceptionally well for some and made others throw up; there seemed to be no middle ground. Many San Diegans, familiar with the stuff because it was a staple at 10km and marathons in Southern California, swore by it. Gookin helped Scott Tinley develop something called "jet fuel," which Tinley used to help him win the February 1982 Ironman.

For all his eccentricity, Gookin was a pioneer in an important field. His mission in life seemed to be to assure that all runners and triathletes everywhere were properly hydrated and electrolyted. Unfortunately, he was hopeless as a businessman. ERG was replaced at the Ironman when Gatorade paid the race for the right to fuel competitors in

1983. It was a move that many triathletes saw as crass commercialism, a victory of the Ironman's greed over the athletes' well-being, since the Gatorade formula was far from what experts at the time were saying was ideal for endurance events. In 1985 the contract went to Exceed, a sophisticated product developed specifically for endurance events by a large research laboratory in Ohio. The athletes seemed satisfied.

In whatever form it comes, liquid aid at the Ironman is usually cold, a classic touch that does as much for the mind as it does for the body. Along the bike course, water bottles and sponges are kept chilled in big garbage cans full of ice and then handed to the competitors as they pass on the fly, usually at high speed. It's a delicate procedure that is exciting to watch, especially since tired cyclists toward the end of the ride can get a little wild.

The best volunteers have a feel for water-bottle choreography. Their sense of timing is amazing. They work in teams of three or four to each triathlete. Running in advance of an approaching bike, dancing around the empties thrown in their direction, they hold a full bottle at arm's length, giving the passing cyclist a clear shot at the target. Correctly placed, the bottle smacks into a palm moving along at 20 miles an hour like a baseball into a fielder's mitt. Whack! goes the first, filled with water, and the cyclist leans forward and slides it into one of the bottle cages on his bike frame; then whack! goes the second, filled with Exceed or whatever, and that goes into the second cage; then swock! a cold, wet sponge hits the same palm and the cyclist moves on. When the process clicks, it's the sport's version of a smoothly executed double play; when the timing is off, the air is filled with bouncing water bottles and the curses of the passing athlete, who must now ride for another five miles only partially provisioned. That's never a good situation.

"One of the things that happens that isn't appreciated by the athletes, even by the real good athletes," Hiller said, "is that you lose a lot of water when you're swimming. An average swimmer can lose two to six pints an hour—same

"I was scared to death," Silk said. "I was afraid somebody was going to die on the course."

as a runner or cyclist. So they start the bike dehydrated. Plus, the water in this bay [Kailua Bay] is some of the saltiest water this side of the Dead Sea. It's much saltier than anywhere else in the islands. That makes you a little less likely to eat, and it makes you a little bit thirsty, but a bit nauseated too, which counteracts the thirst.

"The bike is really your chance to maintain, or even regain what you lost swimming. A lot of the inexperienced athletes aren't aware of that. Thirst is a terrible indicator of dehydration. If you wait for thirst, then you're always going to be behind."

Hiller knows from firsthand experience. You'd suppose that being an expert would exempt him from problems, but that hasn't always been the case. On race day in 1984, that day of record heat, Hiller suffered right along with everyone else.

"That was the worst experience I've ever had," he said, laughing softly. "I really knew how much I was supposed to be drinking and it didn't work. I was losing more water than I ever imagined. I got in at the end of the bicycle ride and started hallucinating. I walked to the first tent, sat down, had a few Cokes, and walked for 25 miles!"

Hiller recalled that he was far from alone. Between 250 and 300 athletes ended up in the medical tent that year—fully 25 percent of the field.

"There were some very sick people in the top 10 that year," he allowed. "Some real sick people who required IVs and who had very messed up blood counts. The medical tent has no respect for your ability as an athlete; it has respect for your ability to pace yourself. The way you end up in the medical tent is to ignore your own limits."

In addition to the water and the Exceed, there is food at the aid stations: bananas, oranges, and cookies, even sandwiches—guava jelly sandwiches, to be exact, an odd tropical touch that has to do with the simple fact that guava jelly is common in Hawaii. The sandwiches recall the first year the race was held on Kona, when race director Silk, ignorant of the needs of endurance athletes, asked around and was told that peanut butter and jelly sandwiches were probably a good thing to have on the course. The second year Silk was asked to hold the peanut butter. She did, gladly, unable to conceive that such a thing as peanut butter could be palatable during a marathon in 90-degree heat. Apparently, neither could the triathletes. The just-jelly sandwiches hung on for a while. In 1986, after receiving increasing reports from the volunteers that the sandwiches were often thrown back at them by exhausted triathletes, Silk scheduled the sandwiches to be eliminated from future aid station menus.

The food is not a defense against the heat, of course; in a race as long as the Ironman the athletes do need to eat during the competition. They use the term "bonking" to describe the light-headed, weak-kneed, sometimes overwhelmingly weary feeling of hypoglycemia, or low blood sugar, that results from being underfueled. In 1983, while fighting hard to hold onto a slim lead over Scott Tinley during the marathon, Dave Scott could barely keep his eyes open. His first thought upon reaching the finish line was to find a place to sleep. Chris Hinshaw, who finished second to Tinley in 1985, had the same problem the following year. He came off his bike in fifth place, but his marathon was punctuated with stops because he was so sleepy. "I couldn't stay awake!" said Hinshaw at the finish line that year. "I was so tired. The only reason they let me stay in the race is because I told them I was on the U.S. National Team, and I said I had to finish.

"I went way too hard on that ride. When it got to the run, I had to stop every three miles. I lost 15 minutes at mile three. I stopped and sat down. I was out of it. I kept telling myself that something was wrong. I kept saying to myself, 'What am I doing? What am I out here for?'"

The obvious answer to those questions—that he was out there to test himself, to test the limits—got him going again, until mile 10, when he had to go through the process all over again.

"I sat down and ate a whole bunch of cookies. While I was doing that, everybody passed me," said Hinshaw. "I dropped to 17th place."

But the cookies worked, and if Hinshaw didn't finish strongly, he at least finished, which is why the cookies are part of the aid station inventory. So are the bananas and, formerly, the jelly sandwiches. If hypoglycemia is the problem, anything sweet, gobbled quickly, will usually get a triathlete going again. The real trick, though, is to avoid getting to the stage where you *need* to eat. Triathletes at the Ironman must eat to prevent problems, not solve them, and a competitor who starts to feel light on the way to Hawi during the bike ride is in for a long day.

Most of the elite competitors carry their food with them, either in a fanny pack or tucked into their cycling jerseys. They take little from the aid stations during the race except bananas and perhaps an occasional orange. Some have begun to experiment with liquid food sources, concerned that taking solid food in hot weather can slow the movement of fluid from the stomach, thereby increasing the risk of severe dehydration.

Each athlete has his or her own preference when it comes to edibles. Dave Scott's longtime favorite was figs. He used them because they were moist enough to eat on the move and were "calorically dense." Joanne Ernst ate an odd combination that included fortune cookies and long strings of red licorice—a regimen she strayed from in 1986, to her detriment. She had a Hinshaw-like episode at the 14-mile mark and needed a stern, supportive word from her husband along with two "dried-out" guava jelly sandwiches, six miniature Famous Amos chocolate cookies and a glass of Coke to get her running strongly again.

"One of the most interesting things that came out of a study that we did," said Hiller, "was that when we looked at what 15 athletes—eight men and seven women—burned during extended exercise, we found that, without regard to sex, they varied from burning 95 percent carbohydrate to burning 85 percent fat."

Hiller admitted no one knew if it was due to genetic variance or to training.

"It's not very scientific in the sense that we have a big map and we can see and predict what's going on," he said. "But it's the essence of science for Dave and Joanne, who experimented and found things that worked for them. It's pure scientific method. They've got the document that shows that their experiment works. They *are* the document!"

❖

Dealing with the various physical considerations during the race, however, is only the beginning. The mental game along the highway is important, too. Among the toughest factors in that department are the winds, the northeast trades, which sweep over the plain between the 13,000-foot Mauna Kea to the south and the low, heavily eroded Koahala Mountains to the north.

The wind is a fact of life at the Ironman, but certainly not one that any of the triathletes adjust to easily. The gales that can blow up north near Hawi are frightening; they can turn that part of the bike ride into a grinding, one-yard-at-a-time ordeal. But the triathletes are prepared for those; worse are the shifting winds along the Queen K itself, which take sharp aim at the mind as well as the body.

"They're always blowing hard enough to bother you," said Scott Tinley after the race in 1984. "They're like an itch you can never get to."

"The course is mentally crippling," said Dave Scott. "It's so repetitive. The winds are so relentless. You can't get to a certain part on the course where you say, 'Good, I'm at 80 miles, now it's downhill, or it's just rolling hills—it's going to be easier.' You can get to 80 miles and all of a sudden get the worst wind of the day for the last 30 miles of the race! At that point, when you need a little respite from the race, you don't get it."

The winds are the least tangible, but perhaps most serious obstacle the triathletes face. Coming off the bike and moving into the run, you can feel how all the pushing has wasted the big muscles in your thighs and made the bottoms of your feet so sore you can hardly stand.

"It's bloody awful!" exclaimed Rick Wells, a top triath-

"It's bloody awful!" exclaimed Rick Wells, a top triathlete from New Zealand who had been hearing about the Ironman for years and finally saw the course in 1986.

lete from New Zealand who had been hearing about the Ironman for years and finally saw the course in 1986. He wasn't entered that year, and he was glad of that after his first look. "I was tired after 35 miles!" he said. "You can see why it's the toughest race in the world. You've got that heat and then you've got that wind out there. One year I'll do it, I guess, but I can see why a lot of guys are scared of this race. You're thinking you've got a tail wind, you're clicking along at 28 miles an hour and then suddenly you haven't even changed direction and you're into a head wind! And you're just creeping!"

"I know guys who say they have never taken a pedal stroke on the island of Hawaii without running into head winds," said Ron Smith. "I know grown men who say that the island is haunted. The goddess of the wind, whoever she is,'" Smith laughed, shaking his head. "I'm telling you the truth here. An intelligent friend of mine told me that. He told me that he'd never race a bicycle there again because of the wind. It's just there all the time. Don't doubt for a moment that there's not some spirit working out there.'"

Currents of the ancient Hawaiian mysticism still run strong along the highway. Stories of construction projects mysteriously halted or abandoned, or of bad luck caused by the lack of a blessing by a kahuna, or local priest, are told by many intelligent, well-educated people in Kona. Asked about it, they will catch themselves in mid-sentence, shrug and laugh the way Smith did, and then move on, admitting their superstitions. "Listen," they say, "I know that doesn't make sense, but I don't fool with it. I know what I felt in that place."

In 1986, alarmed by a rash of serious bike accidents on the Queen K, all in the same general location, Ironman officials called upon the services of a local kahuna, a Congregationalist minister named Leon Sterling. They asked Sterling to stop and take a look. Something was going on.

"The only accident we ever had during the race that I'm aware of," said race director Silk, "was in 1981—a kid was

hit by a car in that same area they're getting hit today. There's visibility all over the place out there. It just doesn't make sense."

Sterling, who regularly blesses weddings, new homes and new construction all over the Kona area, offered a prayer at the site. Chances were that the lay of the land was the cause of the problem, but there was a chance too that something of a spiritual nature had been disturbed.

It can all sound a little silly if you're sitting at the bar in the Kona Surf Hotel, sipping a mai tai. But out on the highway, frying under the hot sun, with the wind blowing in your face, it doesn't seem so strange. There are places all along the highway that can send chills down the spine of even the most oblivious triathlete. The Hawaiians call it "chicken skin," goose flesh, and why so many people get clammy in the same locations, as if on cue, is anyone's guess.

Some of the more sensitive Ironman competitors take precautions, just in case. They are private about it, their attitudes similar to those of the locals: Why fool with something you know nothing about? The night before he won the 1985 race, Scott Tinley drove out onto the course, stopped the car and walked out onto the lava, where he sat down for a moment and asked Madame Pele, the fire goddess of the ancient Hawaiians, for safe passage, carefully explaining that he didn't intend to take any of her precious lava, nor was he interested in disturbing any of the ancient spirits. "I just wanted to get up to Hawi and back safely," Tinley said, not in the least embarrassed by his concession to local custom.

The winds are at their worst over the last six to eight miles of the 18-mile climb from Kawaihae to Hawi, the northernmost settlement. The long, rolling hills get steeper and steeper. (A widely held misconception back on the mainland is that the Ironman course is flat. It isn't, not by any stretch of the imagination.) As it climbs, the road follows the coastline, curving toward the tip of the island to the east, gradually out from the lee of the Kohala Mountains and straight into the howling trade winds. In a curious twist, the environment becomes more pleasant as the winds grow grim. Up near Hawi the land gets greener, and there are trees.

On a normal day, the head winds near Hawi blow steadily at 15 to 25 miles an hour. At the Ironman in 1983 the winds howled through the town at more than twice that—gusts of up to 55 miles an hour were reported, strong enough to stop cyclists dead in their tracks, strong enough to blow others right off the road. Some competitors simply got off and walked into Hawi, and even the strongest were afraid to let go of their handlebars to take water bottles from the aid station near the top.

Ron Smith remembers the wind in 1983 well. No one who raced that year can forget. "I saw people actually crying out there," he said. "I saw people who were walking their bikes to the turnaround because they were afraid if they rode they'd get blown over. The wind was blowing so hard they could hardly walk."

The aid station at the turnaround is one of the most exciting on the course because there's always a big crowd of spectators and media people. It's a high point, a big psyche, especially after the wind and the hills. Turning to the left, grabbing a pair of bottles and perhaps a banana as they go, the triathletes are reasonably sure that for a few miles, at least, the wind will be behind them. They fly through this part of the course, spinning their pedals furiously until they run out of gears to push, hunching low over their handlebars, hissing through the warm air in a rush of sparkling chrome and blur of bright color, moving easily for the first time all day. But that lasts for what seems like only a few precious seconds before the wind starts shifting, gusting back and forth. The cyclists are still going fast, but their knuckles are white, and in their minds is the thought that if one of those big gusts catches them from the wrong angle, it's going to whip them off the island and into the ocean. The race in 1983 was the worst in that department, too.

"The crosswinds were awful that year," Smith said. "Every time you got into one of those little canyons you got a gust, a little cannon shot, in the side. Guys were going off into the bushes."

Finally, at the bottom, with their hearts settled back into their chests, the cyclists take a sharp left turn at Kawaihae, then climb a short, steep hill and turn right, which puts them back on the Queen K. From there on it's a straight shot back into Kona.

Or rather, it's a straight, long shot. The race has just begun, actually. With the exhilaration of the turnaround a distant memory, the 50 miles back into town begin to soften and stretch like taffy under the hot sun. The winds, while not as strong as they were up north, are far more frustrating, and the hills have grown bigger somehow than they were on the way out. The triathletes begin to fight not just the cumulative physical effects of the long swim and the hours of hard riding, but also the inevitable impatience to be off the damn bike. To some, first-timers mostly, or fools who have forgotten, the marathon actually starts sounding good 80 or 90 miles into the bike ride. It's a stupid thought. They regret it quickly once the run starts.

"I never thought that," laughed Smith, who has ridden his bike as much as 25,000 miles in a single year of training. He's a good runner, with a marathon best of well under three hours, but it's never been his strong suit. Looking ahead to the Ironman marathon is for him like looking forward to jumping off a building.

"The toughest part of the ride—outside the damn wind—is knowing that after busting your hump out there for five hours it's going to be 1:30 in the afternoon, you're on asphalt, and God bless America if you're going to be climbing that stupid hill and heading back out into the lava fields again."

All good endurance competitors learn that patience is a precious, irreplaceable virtue. About the worst thing for a triathlete to do during the Ironman is to anticipate the end of anything, be it the swim, the bike ride, or the run, or any segment of the three. Pacing and strategy are important, but a certain psychological calm is critical. Putting the miles behind you, one mile at a time, is the key.

Thinking ahead makes you anxious, eager to be there instead of where you are, and you have to be where you are because there's little you can do about it except keep pedaling or running. An anxious triathlete, impatient with the pace, thinks the hills should be easier to climb than they are, thinks the bike should weigh less than it feels like it does. Getting mad at the Ironman is never a good idea, but it happens frequently, and the nagging wind often speeds the process along. The final, critical step for a frustrated competitor is pushing too hard too soon—it's as sure a recipe for disaster as any.

"The winds can tease you into going crazy!" Smith said. "You have to adopt the ultra philosophy; you have to be very patient. You have to know the race is going to take eight, 10, 12 hours or whatever. If you're going to push through a long race like that, you'd better be prepared for the consequences."

3

THE MARATHON —THE LARGE PRICE OF SMALL VICTORIES

The consequences of pushing too hard during the bike ride begin to stack up during the run. The marathon is the crux of the Ironman. The advantages some triathletes have in skill and experience in the water, or in technology and technique on the bike, aren't worth a damn when it comes to the final event. Talent helps—several of the top triathletes in the world have marathon times in the 2:20s. But talent can hurt, too, because if a triathlete relies on talent, if he assures himself that when he gets to the run it's all going to get better, he might just crumble completely when he realizes after taking a step or two that at some point during the bike ride someone stole his legs and replaced them with someone else's.

There is simply no one who gets off the highway for the second time without a fight. The Ironman marathon is never "easy," not even in the parlance of endurance athletes, to whom "easy" can mean anything from a 15-mile run in a blizzard to a three-day bike ride. Nothing is assured for many of the triathletes beginning the marathon at the Ironman—not finishing, not winning. Well, that's not entirely true. One thing is assured: almost everyone will entertain thoughts of quitting, either the race itself or the pursuit of their goal for the day, whether it be a certain time or a certain place.

For a long time people said that the Ironman was a cyclist's race, that you needed to be a tremendous cyclist to win or even come close. That's still true in the sense that the cycling is critical. You can lose so much time on the bike that you'll never make up enough on the run. But with the generally high level of cycling competence that has marked the event in recent years, you can't gain enough during the ride to assure anything. The race is decided during the marathon and nowhere else. During the ride you can blame yourself, the conditions, the volunteers, or your machine, but you have to look yourself squarely in the eye during the run. Do you have what it takes? How badly do you want that T-shirt, that trophy, that time? Oh, Lord, it's still 26 miles away.

There are probably not many more dramatic places in sport than the top of the two hills at either end of Alii Drive on Ironman Saturday in Kona. The marathon begins on the first. From the changing rooms at the Kona Surf, the athletes run out through the parking lot and are cheered by the big crowd. For a brief minute or two they can forget their sore backs, their aching feet, the weariness in their legs. But the 100-yard climb back up to Alii Drive is cruel, and it sends signals to the legs that this is going to be a terrible time, actually. Seeing the hill for the first time, you half expect the first few athletes to stop, turn around, and walk back toward the hotel.

But they never do.

Some athletes walk up the first hill, trying to stretch their legs out a bit and roll into the marathon with the hope that their pace will continue to increase as the miles go by. Tom Warren, who won the event in 1979 and is as careful and methodical an endurance strategist as ever existed, always walked up as a matter of personal policy.

But that was back in the days when time was less precious at the Ironman, when even the fastest men and women changed carefully between events, spending several minutes in the transition area making sure everything was just right before heading back out. The Ironman is still one of the few triathlons in the world where the top competitors usually wear different clothes in the three segments, but the changes are furious now. The routine at the Kona Surf is tumultuous, chaotic. Volunteers grab the bikes of the competitors as they roll in, shouting directions and pointing the way as the athletes dismount. On the bikes, the cycling shoes swing upside down, still attached to the pedals, while their owners, in bare feet, dash off toward the changing area, shedding clothes as they go. Their numbers have already been relayed to the volunteers standing at the long racks of equipment bags, and so their running gear precedes them or follows them closely, fire brigade-style. "Twenty-four!" comes the shout. The number is echoed three, four times, and in response the bag containing the running shoes and shorts, the shirt and socks of triathlete number 24 comes flying back, 15 feet through the air from one volunteer to the next—once, twice, three times, and then gone, into the changing room. Within seconds the best athletes are out again, their eyes wild, their hands frantically grabbing for a cup of water or Coke or a banana. It's hard to believe they have just spent an hour in the water, five hours on the bike. They should be crawling. It's hard to believe they are as anxious as they seem to get back out on the highway. "Where? Where? Water! Water!" the athletes shout. "Right! Go right!" or "Go there, stay left!" scream the volunteers.

The seconds do count. Tinley lost to Scott in 1983 by 36 of them. After nine hours of racing, he lost by 36 seconds.

The seconds do count. Tinley lost to Scott in 1983 by 36 of them. After nine hours of racing, he lost by 36 seconds.

So now almost no one with a chance or the ambition to win, place, or show walks up the hill. Almost everyone runs, full of good intentions, thinking that if they can just get to the top in good shape they'll be well on their way to the finish line. "I'll run up this sucker if it kills me," they say, although they aren't on their way at all, not even close.

The next seven miles or so of the run is along Alii Drive, which is calm after the frenzy of the transition area, and shaded, although the trees that hang overhead seem to hold the moisture in the hot air. On television the drive looks cool and tropical, even pleasant. It is neither. Mostly it's just hot, an oven, with the occasional patches of sunlight reminding the triathletes of what it was like—and will be again—out on the unshaded Queen K. And there are rolling hills along Alii Drive, hills that look like nothing from a car but feel like mountains during the marathon. The good news is that the people of Kailua-Kona are out in force, standing in front of private homes and condominiums, cheering. Among the spectators are many friends and relatives of the triathletes, who are aware of the subtleties of the race and are eager to help. The encouragement is wonderful, especially after the hours of desolation during the bike ride. For many of the triathletes the run along Alii Drive is relatively easy (that word again). Without actually trying to, many of them run their fastest miles of the day there.

The second hill comes at the far end of town. The triathletes turn right and run up Palani Road, a long, steep climb that takes whatever spirit the run through town restored and tears it away. The climb was big in the morning, when it was the first thing the cyclists faced when they came out of the swim and off the pier. Somehow it's even bigger now, and it goes on forever. The worst part is the fact that at the top is the good old Queen K again.

Interestingly, most women competitors run up Palani Road (also known as the "Pay and Save Hill," after the discount department store located near the top), while many of the men walk. The observation was pointed out to me a few years ago, so I made a point of watching. Sure enough, it was true. No one has an explanation, although I suspect that many of the men run too hard along Alii Drive, psyched by the crowds, trying too hard to look good. The women run more for themselves, their pace measured by realistic estimates of their condition rather than the expectations of the spectators. The elite triathletes aside—their strategies, men and women both, are always intense—women at the Ironman seem to have a better grasp of the Big Picture than the men. They are less apt to drop out, more willing to accept their personal status quo at face value, instead of what they think it should be or should have been. I suspect that women are psychologically better equipped to deal with long races.

The first part of the highway is a continuation of the Pay and Save Hill, a looping left-hand turn that climbs for several hundred yards, until the road levels, then dips, and turns again gradually to the right, where another long, shallow hill begins. If the marathon is the crux of the Ironman, then this spot—near the 10-mile point of the run, right about where a green milepost reads "99"—is the crux of the marathon. This is the point where potential winning efforts have failed repeatedly, where for elite competitors and mere participants alike the feeling good or the feeling not-so-bad ends and where the death march begins. It's as if the mental sighs of relief at reaching the top of the hill go too far, too deep, expelling not just fatigue and tension but something more vital as well. It's the point Julie Leach was talking about when she started to fade in 1982; it's the point where Mark Allen's hopes for a win in 1984 were dashed; it's the point where John Howard's extraordinary bid for a place in the top two or three that same year came to a screeching halt.

"It's probably the most difficult part of the course," said Dave Scott, "going back out, running away from the finish line to a point that's nondescript and then turning around and coming back in. The design of that course is just mind-boggling."

And it happens quickly. When things start to go during the marathon, they go. By the time you come to the realization that the long day has been gnawing hungrily at your finely conditioned cardiovascular system, your talented legs, your infallible strategy, and most of all your brain, it's too late.

"It just hits you," said Howard, snapping his fingers. He won the race in 1981, and finished an unexpected sixth in

1984, the year of the terrible heat, after many authorities had discounted his ability to be among the leaders. They'd written him off as being far too old. He was 37.

"Ohhh, it's like *death*!" he said. "I remember Julie Moss standing there in '84 at the last hill going into town saying, 'C'mon, you can make it; it's no big deal.' But it is, it *is*."

Like many of the triathletes that year, Howard had ridden too hard, unaware how high the temperature was going. With the wind in his face, lost in the intensity of the competition, eager to pass as many people as he could before the ride ended, he was oblivious to the increased need to conserve. He climbed off his bike in third place, ran through town, struggled to the top of the Pay and Save Hill, and then nearly collapsed.

He was able to laugh at his predicament—in retrospect. Endurance athletes typically develop a finely honed sense of black humor about their worst experiences, and Ironman veterans have a bigger library of horror stories than most. Some competitors rely heavily on their sense of humor during the event itself, fearing perhaps that if they dwell on the actual conditions, on how bad they're actually feeling, they would simply flag down a car and take a ride back to the pier—an act they would never forgive themselves for later.

"The first thing I tried to do was toy with the reality of it," said Howard, explaining his personal disaster plan. "I went through a justification period where I thought, 'I should have consumed more water.' And then I went through a period where I hated myself for not drinking more, realizing I was finished. After I wore that one down, I started pulling out every trick in the book. My favorite, which got me past Rob Barel [a top Dutch triathlete], is a technique that Ian Jackson taught me a long time ago: to breathe, basically performance breathing. It worked great until I ran up against the wall with heat exhaustion—from lack of fluids. I started forcing it, overemphasizing my breathing. It just didn't work anymore. So I gave up on the tricks. That was my last trick. At point I just gave in: *Ahhhhohh, God, it hurts so bad! I wanna die!*

"I just...didn't...give...a...shit. That's when Tinley went by me. I said, 'Awww, let him go.' Then the next guy was Barel—just *crawling*—but I couldn't do anything. 'Let him go.' Then the next guy: 'Let him go too, I don't care.' Finally I started asking people, 'How far's the guy behind me?' I didn't care about catching Mark Allen anymore. I heard he was walking, but it didn't matter. I walked every aid station—slowly, *slowly*. We weren't runners anymore, we were pedestrians. We were history."

Howard's story is hardly unique. During another Ironman, the one in October 1982, Scott Tinley's brother Jeff, in fourth place at the time, was told by a spectator that the man in front of him, Scott Molina, was looking bad, looking worse than Tinley was. "If I'm looking better than he is," Tinley thought, "then he must be *dead*."

In 1984 Curtis Alitz, a tall, lean U.S. Army physician, did the Ironman for the first time. Alitz had surprised the triathlon world a month before by outrunning Scott Tinley for second place at the U.S. Triathlon Series (USTS) National Championships at Bass Lake, California. So unexpected was Alitz's performance that officials at the race momentarily questioned its authenticity. Had the unknown athlete cut the course? Had he cheated?

Far from it. The officials quickly learned that Alitz owned some impressive credentials. In 1977, while he was a third-year cadet at the U.S. Military Academy, he had placed fourth in the 10,000-meter run at the NCAA Track and Field Championships. The following year he didn't place as well, but still rated status as an All-American. His 10,000-meter best time on the track was an impressive 28:36; his best marathon was a 2:17 at Boston in 1979. Those were levels of pure running that no top triathlete at the time could hope to match. What was surprising was that Alitz had been able to swim and ride as well as he had, then climb off his bike and run down the more experienced Tinley. Novices— even fast ones—weren't supposed to be able to do things like that. Running people down had always been Tinley's game.

Some competitors rely heavily on their sense of humor during the event itself, fearing perhaps that if they dwell on the actual conditions, on how bad they're actually feeling, they would simply flag down a car and take a ride back to the pier—an act they would never forgive themselves for later.

When Alitz said that he had been riding a bike seriously for only a few months—since June—and that he planned to do the Ironman in October, the raised eyebrows went higher. The man was obviously a talent. Was he the elite runner many people had predicted would burst upon the triathlon scene and prove to the triathletes that they were nothing more than laborers in a non-elite sport? Was Alitz going to be a dark horse in Hawaii? Was he strong enough to ride the course hard and then put his 2:17 speed to work during the marathon?

But the Ironman was, as always, in a category of its own. Alitz himself had made it clear that he was going into the race without expectations, that he was racing only as an "afterthought." On the other hand, there was that little germ of possibility growing in the back of his mind that there might be a chance.

"After Bass Lake I had a little bit of a feeling of invincibility," he admitted.

Alitz came out of the water in good shape, three minutes behind the leaders. And he felt good on the bike, at least until he was interrupted about 15 miles out by a race official who ordered him to re-pin the number on his back; one corner had come loose.

Alitz was furious, and rightly so. The official's action was unprecedented, certainly with regard to the top competitors, whose identities were usually obvious and easily verifiable. Numbers on the back were always something of a hit-or-miss proposition at best, especially since the competitors also had plastic race numbers strapped to their bikes, and numbers written on their arms and legs for identification purposes during the swim. But the official was threatening him with disqualification, so Alitz had to pull over, dismount, and re-pin the number. That cost him precious time and several places—to athletes who he couldn't help but notice weren't wearing any numbers at all on their backs, fluttering or otherwise. Among them was Tinley. Alitz lost what was left of his temper along with his sense of perspective. When he got back on his bike he took off like a shot, hoping to regain the lost ground, but all he succeeded in doing was destroying his undertrained legs. A 25-mile USTS bike ride around beautiful Bass Lake was one thing; 112 miles through the lava fields was another. By the time he reached the bike turnaround at Hawi his legs were already beginning to tighten up. The cramps began on the way back. He didn't have a chance during the marathon.

"The run was kind of a death march for me," Alitz said, sounding like any one of a thousand triathletes you could have talked to that evening in the massage tent. "My goals were to make it to the next aid station and get a cookie and something to drink. It wasn't painful; it was kind of humorous, really. All I could do was shuffle along. I couldn't even run fast enough to get tired."

The fastest marathon of the day that year, 2:53, was run by Dave Scott, who won the race. Scott's best marathon ever—just a marathon, without the swim and the bike—is in the 2:40s. Alitz that day, his talent and his 2:17 marathon still lying somewhere out there on the highway between the Sheraton Waikoloa Resort and the airport, ran a 4:21:30. He finished 70th.

The Ironman marathon is the great equalizer. There comes a time for almost everyone when the basic motivation changes, when most of the goals have been discarded, when the only thing left to do is finish. As a spectator you can actually watch the change occur. There is a point—it varies for each individual—when the looks on the faces of the triathletes shift from a kind of curious optimism ("How will I feel? How long can I go at this pace?") to a grim, almost angry determination.

No one is immune. At no time during the competition is that more obvious than late in the day, during the run, when you can watch men with chances to finish in the top 10, top 20, running south, with five, six miles to go, then look across to the other side of the road and see men and women moving in the opposite direction, toward the turnaround, with hours left to run and no chance in the world of any recognition beyond their own private victories. You realize that both groups look exactly the same. If you had to guess, you'd say they were all running the same speed. It's a stunning scene, really, because it is so obvious that the Ironman has reduced the finest endurance athletes in the world to mere survivors.

The portion of the highway that is used for the Ironman marathon—from Kailua-Kona to about a half mile past the airport—is a depressing stretch of road. It's bleak, like the rest, but there's a weariness about it, too, a nondescript, institutional tan color, like the walls of an old post office. The road is lined with scraggly plantings of bougainvillea. The plants were added years ago, but they continue to look as if they were put into the ground the day before the race, making the road seem even more forlorn. The vast, primitive hostility of the middle of the bike course, which would at least give the athletes something to fight, is missing. What takes its place is a feeling of dislocation from reality.

This feeling is enhanced each year by the strange failure of Ironman officials to mark the miles of the marathon accurately. The triathletes are left to compute their location either from the highway mileposts ("Where did I start? Was the last one 97 or 98?") or from the mile marks on some of the aid stations, which display hopelessly complex numbers like 15.3 or 22.4. Maintaining a sense of place and pace is important in a long competition—it's a psychological anchor for even the slowest runners—but exhausted, dehydrated triathletes are simply not capable of even the most basic math. They can punch a button on a watch at a mile sign, punch it again at the next, and see how fast they're running, but that's about it. Subtracting 15.3 from 16.8, then figuring out a pace per mile is far beyond their capability. The pacing part of the problem is not even the most critical. The real need is for the triathletes to know where they are, and during the Ironman marathon they almost never do.

"You go through a point in the middle of the race, between 13 and 18 miles, that in some ways can be worse than the last six," Scott Tinley said, rehashing his win in 1985. "The last six of the Ironman can be great if you're in the lead, because you can enjoy the hell out of it. But you still have to run that five miles in the middle, even if you have a 20-minute lead. And there are no mile markers. In 1985 I didn't know where I was! I could have been anywhere from 11 to 16. I had no idea."

"It gets long and lonely," said Joanne Ernst. "It all blurs together. I remember feeling that it was going to go on forever. I was never going to get off that highway. It was going to be the highway, then an aid station, the highway, then an aid station."

The ultimate Twilight Zone nightmare for a triathlete: the highway, the marathon, forever.

Ernst is an intriguing athlete, an intelligent, strikingly attractive woman whose emotions always run close to the surface during competition. They probably have cost her as many races as her considerable physical abilities have enabled her to win. A runner in college, then a marathoner, and finally a triathlete, she entered the Ironman for the first time in 1984, placed fourth, came back to win the race in '85, then placed third in '86.

Closer in philosophy to triathletes who compete at the Ironman merely for the experience than to the elite, top-10 people she was racing against, Ernst came to see the Ironman as an annual test of her moral fiber, a test on which she finally gave herself a passing grade only in 1986—for a performance many considered to be her least successful Ironman effort. That year she went from first place to fourth during the marathon, but she was happy with herself at the finish line. She'd gone through a rough period during which she had been barely able to walk, let alone run, but she had pushed through it and ended the day running well. She was proud of the race; she would have been proud if she had finished 10th. And as if to underscore how unrelated her feelings of accomplishment were to the final standings, Ernst moved up to third place when the winner, Patricia Puntous, was disqualified for drafting.

Ernst was an adopted child, given up by her parents as an infant. Her husband, Jim Collins, who was well known in rock-climbing circles during the late 70s, thinks that the

"It gets long and lonely," said Joanne Ernst. "It all blurs together. I remember feeling that it was going to go on forever."

rejection by her biological parents has had a profound effect on Ernst's perception of her self-worth. Ernst disagrees, but not vigorously. In any case, she was bright and serious and self-motivated from the start, driven to succeed. She was also, by her own admission, difficult to deal with, mostly because she demanded as much from the people around her—her parents, her brother, her friends—as she did from herself. Judgmental and uncompromising by nature, she retreated further and further into her perfectionism as her family life, which was punctuated by a pair of irresponsible stepfathers, became less and less comfortable. But it wasn't to a secure place that she retreated. Despite so much evidence to the contrary, Ernst could not be convinced that she was anywhere other than constantly on the brink of failure. Not even her eventual graduation, Phi Beta Kappa in economics, from Stanford University in 1983 could do the trick.

What finally turned things around was the Ironman, in particular the marathon. On the surface that may sound ridiculous—that a 10-hour endurance event could have a life-changing effect on a bright, Stanford-trained economist. But physical challenges such as running, cycling, rock climbing and wilderness obstacle courses have long been used by organizations such as Outward Bound, est and New Age health retreats to enrich lives and increase self-esteem. Men and women from all levels of corporate America often pay dearly for the privilege of being run through the woods before dawn, plunged into frigid streams or frightened half to death at the top of a 200-foot rappel. Not that Ernst, a highly competitive athlete who makes her living as a professional triathlete, was in the business merely to obtain some mystical emotional benefit. But the psychological residuals of the Ironman cannot be overlooked. Ernst was at times more open about them than most of her peers, but she was by no means alone in recognizing their value.

"The Ironman is more than one thing," she said. "There's the purely athletic, and that's what involves the top people more than anyone else. But there's the whole other thing of it being a life-changing experience—which even I feel is the most important characteristic. That's what the Ironman is all about."

The Ironman brought Joanne Ernst failure more bleak than any she had known, but she knew that she could blame no one for the failure but herself. It also brought her a level of success greater than she could have imagined, and she had no one but herself to thank for that, either. The Ironman put her destiny in her hands. In an emotional sense, the marathon put her on the same kind of sheer rock wall her husband had been so good at climbing years before. It clarified the choices. She could either fall off or climb. In the end, she climbed.

Ernst's first Ironman in 1984 ended poorly. She was never one of the better swimmers, but she was a superb cyclist and a solid runner—her 2:46 marathon in Sacramento the previous spring had qualified her to compete in the U.S. Women's Olympic Marathon Trials (she didn't race; she trained instead for Hawaii). True to form, she was the second-fastest cyclist in the Ironman field that year. But she came off the bike disheartened, in sixth place, behind Sylviane Puntous, the defending women's champion. Ernst had told herself before the race that she needed to come off ahead of Puntous, whom she considered to be a stronger marathoner.

She was beaten in her mind before she'd run the first mile. She slogged dutifully through the marathon, feeling miserable, sorry for herself, appalled at the difficulty of the event. She was a failure in her own eyes, although really she was just another Ironman rookie, caught in a web of unrealistic expectations of glory and self-fulfilled prophecies of doom.

Her next season started auspiciously. She won several big events by wide margins. Her swimming had improved, her cycling had matured and was markedly better than that of any of the other top women in the sport—including Sylviane Puntous and her identical twin sister Patricia. "The Twins," as they were known, had ruled the women's professional division for two solid years; Sylviane was the only woman to have won the Ironman twice, and Patricia had been second both times. They were superb athletes, but they seemed outclassed in '85 when they raced against Ernst in short-distance triathlons. She was even beating them at their own game, running.

But around mid-season Ernst faltered badly. She came off one big short-distance triathlon victory and ran smack into a loss at the hands of Gaylene Clews, a runner-turned-triathlete from Australia who backed up her advance notices with a reckless racing style that unnerved the emotionally fragile Ernst. To make matters worse, the American was suffering from a tendon problem at the top of the hamstring muscle in her right leg. It seriously affected her training. Injured, depressed, she began to race poorly.

A combination of two terrible races late in the season almost ended her career. The first, the San Diego edition of the Bud Light U.S. Triathlon Series, greeted a large field of triathletes with cold water and huge waves. Ernst was petrified. She was not at all confident in the ocean, not even a warm, smooth one. When the gun was fired for the professional women to start, she ran into the waves with the rest of the field, but she could not—or would not—get through. Finally she broke her swim goggles trying to put them on after a wave had knocked them off. Her competitors were already far ahead. She stumbled back to the beach in tears. Collins wrapped her in a towel and hustled her away.

Ernst's dropping out of the race was widely criticized. It was seen as a less-than-heroic effort. The consensus, at least of her fellow pros, was that she should have been able to get through the waves, and that she should have swum without goggles. "Broken goggles?" they said. "Surf? This is a triathlon!"

Two weeks after the San Diego event, the Bud Light U.S. Triathlon Series National Championship at Hilton Head Island, South Carolina, was marred by numerous accusations of cheating. Drafting was the issue, a topic that could send Ernst, long a bitter, outspoken critic of the practice, into a frenzy. Infuriated by what she perceived as drafting on the Hilton Head course, she backed off and finished the race in seventh place—a mere formality—preferable by a small margin to dropping out. She subsequently threatened to quit the sport entirely.

Ernst and Collins flew back to Palo Alto to regroup. They threw around the biggest, least well-answered question a triathlete can ask: "Why am I doing this?" The answer they came up with was that Ernst was racing because she enjoyed the sport, racing to achieve personal goals. If she went to the Ironman and raced for herself, what the others did, how the others raced, was up to them—and affected only them. And what they—the other triathletes, the media, whoever—thought of her, well, that was up to them, too. For several years she had avoided becoming part of the chummy but often cliquish social scene of the top triathletes. She'd been criticized for being self-righteous and aloof. She certainly had nothing to lose in the popularity department.

"I went back to why I started in this sport in the first place," Ernst said. "When I first did triathlons I wanted to win the Ironman. That's all I cared about. The USTS was not really that big a deal in my mind. Hilton Head kind of brought me full circle."

But if she was better prepared mentally for the Ironman in 1985 than in '84, she was not at all prepared physically. Because of the tendon injury, she'd averaged just 16 miles a week of running for the previous two months. Normally, she would have been running 50 or 60. It was a critical shortfall.

There are those who say an endurance event is 90 percent mental. Mind over matter. That what you want to do badly enough, you can do. Those who say that have never been endurance athletes. If a race is long enough, or the pace is fast enough, there's no mind in the world strong enough to overcome the physical problems that will be encountered. "You can't fake a marathon," an undertrained Kathleen McCartney had said after her failure at the Ironman in October 1982. The physiological stress from nine, 10, 12 hours of racing is real. When muscles stop working, they stop working. When the blood stops flowing, nothing moves.

Cramps are a part of life at the Ironman. So many of the athletes suffer from them during the marathon you'd almost think they were required equipment, part of the checklist.

Proper preparation is critical. Triathletes talk about a thing called their "training base," a backlog of training mileage built up over a period of months or years that they use as a jumping-off point to further, more intense levels of conditioning. Endurance athletes of all sorts—swimmers, runners, and cyclists—will spend the early parts of each competitive season "building a base," training at increasingly longer distances, gaining strength as they go, and adapting their body's chemical factory to the demands of the long hours on the road or in the water. Once an acceptable base is established—once the muscles are strong and have "relearned" how to supply themselves with fuel and oxygen—an athlete begins to "sharpen" his or her training, concentrating on shorter, more intensive workouts. For triathletes, short-distance triathlons during the early- and mid-season serve to sharpen their conditioning, although those with the Ironman in mind must continue their distance training. A delicate balance must be maintained. If triathletes race every week (as many of them do), lightening their training load before each competition and resting the day after, they can actually race themselves out of shape for the long events. If they simply train over long distances and not become fast, they will not be competitive in the shorter races, which provide the bulk of a professional triathlete's income.

Unfortunately, the effective range of training is relatively narrow. The training effect lasts only so long before the level of performance drops off. In the case of a complete layoff the first thing to go is the ability to run fast. Cardiovascular conditioning can start to deteriorate in as little as three days. Next, the distance capability begins to drop. Running a marathon in, say, three hours is no longer an issue. The question becomes: "Can I run a marathon at all?"

Ernst faced that question in 1985. She was counting on her years of running to pull her through. She was counting on her base. And while she hadn't put in many total miles in the months before the race, she'd managed a couple of long runs several weeks before the Ironman that gave her confidence. Her swimming was stronger than it ever was.

Her cycling was in top form. The marathon would take care of itself.

But the marathon never takes care of itself.

It started well. Ernst came off the bike in second place, behind Julie Moss, who was making an Ironman comeback and had been widely proclaimed as a pre-race favorite—largely on the basis of a fast Ironman-distance race in Japan earlier that year. But while Moss was much improved as a runner since her dramatic triathlon debut in February 1982, she was not a real threat to win. Ernst passed her four miles into the marathon. She ran well for the next 13 miles, to the marathon turnaround, approximately 17 miles into the race. Nine to go. Then her undertrained legs deserted her. They started to cramp painfully. Ernst began to wonder not whether she could hold onto the lead but if she was going to be able to finish at all.

Cramps are a part of life at the Ironman. So many of the athletes suffer from them during the marathon you'd almost think they were required equipment, part of the checklist. Shoes? Right. Bike? Right. Shorts? Right. Cramps? Right.

Physiologists don't really know why the cramping occurs. References are made to electrolyte imbalances, calcium uptake problems and muscle tissue breakdown as a result of physical stress. What the triathletes can tell you for sure is that the cramps are excruciatingly painful. The spasms and the swelling of the muscle fibers put pressure on nerves and can leave a triathlete in terrible distress. The big, bunching cramps in the hamstrings and the calf muscles are crippling. Those are the kind that Scott Molina suffered at the Ironman in 1981. They stopped him cold. The other kind are less dramatic but equally painful—long spasms in the big muscles of the thigh that can make each step an agony, a factor that presents a special problem for an endurance athlete, to whom pain is usually of a more subtle nature—different entirely from the tangible, lung-searing pain, say, of a sprinter. Sharp pain to a triathlete is usually the sign of an injury, and the first instinct is to stop. The competitor asks, "Am I doing damage that I can't repair?"

Kathleen McCartney suffered pain in her legs like that in October 1982. For Joanne Ernst in 1985 the cramps in her thighs were a sign that the race was a long way from over. With Moss far behind her, no longer in contention, Ernst had a healthy lead and a fairly good read on the rest of the field. Who could catch her? But as the cramps worsened she began to wonder whether she was going to be able to finish at all.

During the run back toward town, Ernst stopped periodically and pounded on her thighs with her fists, kneading them, trying to coax them into working. But the desperate self-massage was painful, and it didn't seem to help. And by that time she had seen the long, lean figure of Liz Bulman gliding along in the opposite direction, toward the turnaround, running at what looked like an easy, seven-minute per mile pace. Bulman had placed ninth at the Boston Marathon the previous spring, and Ernst had been one of the few people to mention her as a dark horse at the Ironman. Now Ernst's prediction was coming back to haunt her.

The situation got worse and worse. The pain was getting ridiculous. Ernst began walking through aid stations, then stopping at intervals in between, knowing that Bulman was coming but unable to control the situation. The margin between the women narrowed from a gaping 20 minutes after the bike ride to less than four by the time Ernst reached the 23-mile mark. Her first place was fading so quickly she could almost hear it go, whooshing away from her like a dream. Perhaps, she thought, it had been no more than that all along.

She turned off the highway and ran down Palani Road—the Pay and Save Hill—headed straight for the pier. The finish line was in sight, down another small hill, just one hundred yards away. But that first look at the finish of the Ironman is a cruel tease, a taste of the end that is whisked away in an instant, for at the bottom of the hill the runners must turn left, onto Kuakini Highway, and go around, to run yet another mile. Ernst made the turn. At the pace she was running she was perhaps 10 minutes from the finish line. The spectators were thick; police at the intersection were using whistles and white gloves to reroute the heavy traffic. For most finishers this is a wonderful spot, the beginning of a long run into personal stardom. The barely restrained chaos at the intersection is invigorating. It seems that even if your legs were to stop working, the enthusiasm of the crowd would carry you down Kuakini, through the final two right turns that lead to Alii Drive and then down the last stretch to the finish line. And the noise for Ernst was especially loud because she was the first woman.

She should have been emotionally buoyed, but she was far from that. The crowd was a blur, the noise they made a mere echo in the back of her brain. The long, steep downhill had been a painful, parting insult to her aching legs, and although the crowd couldn't know it, first place—in Ernst's mind at least—was anything but assured. She gave them a hint of that when she stopped dead. She closed her eyes and rubbed her thighs and then continued, trudging toward the end.

"I'd been making deals with myself," she said. "I'd stop at an aid station and say: 'Okay, this is the last one you're going to stop at. You won't stop at the other ones.' Of course I stopped at all of them. And then I did end up stopping one more time when I was just a mile from the finish line. There was nothing there, I just stopped."

Ernst's voice trailed off as she remembered the scene. "Oh," she said, "I can't believe I did that."

She recalled that she almost stopped once more, farther down the road. "I can remember that the people were making so much noise. 'Go! Go!' they were saying. 'Don't stop now!' I wanted to stop, but I thought, 'I can't stop, because there are all these people here. I can't let them down, I can't stop now—200 yards, 300 yards from the finish line.' But I wanted to stop more than anything in the world. I thought Liz was closer than she was. I mean, I thought she was like, five feet. I thought any minute . . . Every time I turned around I could not see her. I never saw her once. I had no idea."

"I wanted to stop, but I thought, 'I can't stop, because there are all these people here. I can't let them down, I can't stop now— two hundred yards, three hundred yards from the finish line.' But I wanted to stop more than any-thing in the world."

Bulman was actually more than one-and-a-half minutes behind. Even had she stopped and walked that final time on Alii Drive, Ernst still would have won. Despite the cramps and all the walking, she finished 51st overall among the 1018 triathletes who completed the course. Her time was 10:25:22, just three seconds slower than Sylviane Puntous's course record.

❖

Goals are tossed aside frequently by Ironman competitors during the marathon. Like the paper cups at the aid stations, they litter the Queen K from the top of the Pay and Save Hill all the way to the airport and back again. Sometimes the goals seem modest: "I'm going to run through all of the aid stations." "I'm going to finish before dark." "I'm going to break 10 [11, 12, 14, 15] hours." Sometimes they're more substantial, as winning was in Ernst's case. None, however, is more valid than any other. And as Ernst herself indicated, even the top athletes have little intermediate stars they reach for—and miss.

Some of the goals go easily, rationalized away or simply dropped, unexcused: "Screw it, man, I'm walkin'." Others go hard, unwillingly, with a crushing sense of helplessness against the inevitable—although there is often a strange moment of relief attached to the loss as well. When you're running as fast as you can and there are five miles to go, and the sun is on the edge of the horizon, there simply isn't any way you're going to finish before dark. The damned highway has had its way with your dreams. But for a while, until another goal asserts itself (and triathletes will always find another goal), you are at least free of your compulsion.

The sense of failure comes only in retrospect. The memory of the pain blurs quickly, and the "I didn'ts" and "I couldn'ts" rapidly become "I could, ifs...." That's part of what brings people back each year, of course, even those who vowed at the turnaround they would never, never return. Those last 16 or 17 miles of the marathon have a strange and terrible attractiveness to them. The highway may be littered with unachieved goals, but it is lined with possibilities too, and while the goals are finally swept away and forgotten, the possibilities grow, month by month, until the pain of the Ironman is gradually replaced by its potential.

Joanne Ernst took great pride in having hung on to win in '85, but what she saw as her mental surrender disturbed her. There were moments during those last few miles when she had wished that Bulman would go by. That would have left her with a certain measure of freedom—to agonize in the security of her own failure—but it would have also left her with an emptiness she would never have been able to fill. Intellectually, she knew how hard it would be to lose the race so close to the end, which is one reason she didn't stop that last time. Physically, though, she had been willing to let it happen. She'd gone as deep into the emotional well as she was able to go. If Bulman had been close enough....

It was the failure, then, not the victory, that brought Ernst back to race again in '86. She saw the potential. She knew she could do better.

"I can go faster," she said. "I still have a perfect race for myself out there. I don't think that it means I have to win the race. I think I can feel that, 'Yeah, I hit it today. This is absolutely the best performance Joanne Ernst can give.'"

4

Who's the Fittest One of All?

The media, which were so important to the rise of Ironman popularity, have taken a great deal of license with Ironman history, and not many people within the sport have seen fit to contradict the story that gradually emerged. The scene that was set was too good: a drunken, barroom confrontation in Honolulu; chisel-jawed, crew-cut men tossing back beer after beer, shouting and pounding on a table lit by a single, fly-specked bulb; the stakes of a ridiculous challenge rising higher and higher until the sun-burned, steely-eyed Commander Collins, weaving a bit but still fierce, finally stood and roared his Ironman challenge.

It made for wonderful copy. Over the years, even the publicists for the Ironman itself got caught up in the creativity, moderating the scene somewhat but staying in a beery forest of half-drunken machismo that had little to do with reality.

Commander John Collins himself, frustrated over trying to tell the real story to a procession of eager journalists more in search of color than accuracy, began to ask his interviewers which version they preferred. "Whenever I get interviewed," Collins said, "which is normally around the August, September celebrity time—you know, background color for the race—people who do the interviewing normally have some particular viewpoint that they bring to it, and they want to see that viewpoint backed up. A lot of them don't do any review of history at all, other than just reading the last thing that was written, so you can track through the years where some of these things came from."

More than a decade after his Ironman brainstorm, Collins is a tall, balding man in his mid-50s. Retired from the Navy, he's also retired from obsessive physical behavior. At 6-foot 3-inches, he weighs in at a less-than-solid 230 pounds.

"The television people in particular want an outrageous quotation," he said. "So far I haven't given them the appropriate one, so their interview with me always gets cut. Two years ago the gal who was doing it for ABC television said: 'Now let me understand how this started. A bunch of you sailors were drunk in a bar in Honolulu....'"

Collins stopped the woman and said that wasn't how it had been.

"But there was a lot of beer, wasn't there?" she persisted.

"Yeah," said Collins, "it was from a beer manufacturer."

"Then there was a lot of beer."

"Yeah," Collins said.

"So then you were all drunk," the woman said.

"No," Collins said sorrowfully, "we weren't."

The woman, nonplused, paused for a moment. Then she tossed her head, made a nice comment about the shirt Collins was wearing, and walked away.

The single, basic fact of the event's birth usually did make it through the interviews however: the original Ironman was a one-day combination of the three most popular endurance events in Hawaii—the 2.4-mile Waikiki Rough Water Swim, the Around-the-Island (Oahu) Bike Ride, and the Honolulu Marathon. Collins, at the time a commander in the Navy stationed in Hawaii, was not initially aware that the bike ride had always been a two-day affair. Nor were most of the men who expressed interest in the proposed event. One man who did know was 27-year-old Gordon Haller, a successful military pentathlete and former Naval officer, and more recently a Honolulu taxi driver who had participated in the around-Oahu ride race himself in 1973. Haller elected not to inform the group of the oversight at the first organizational meeting at Collins's house in late 1977. Confident on the bike but a mediocre swimmer at best, Haller thought it best not to press his luck by splitting hairs on a procedural matter involving something so insignificant as a single day.

"We just kind of put it together," Haller said. "I don't know why I didn't mention that the bike race took two days. Maybe nobody cared. I was just glad the swim was as short as it was, so I didn't say anything about the bike ride. I knew I could do that. I used to do bike camping trips where I'd do as many as 140 miles in a day with full packs and everything."

Collins was a recreational runner, swimmer and cyclist when the Ironman idea came to him. He was not especially talented in any of the three sports; his involvement was at least as social as it was physical. Like many runners at the time, he and his wife Judy were devoted to the doctrine of long, slow distance. Patience and camaraderie were the stuff of their athletic world, not fierce, one-on-one competition.

❖

Collins was never under any illusion that his Ironman brainstorm was an original idea. The specific combination of the three events was his, but not the concept. That came from San Diego.

"The San Diego Track Club," he said, "Nobody ever wants to write it, but I always say that. Mission Bay San Diego Track Club Triathlon. First time I ever heard about it I went and did it."

John and Judy Collins had heard about the race from a friend, who had seen an announcement in the San Diego

Track Club's newsletter in August 1974. Two members of the club, Don Shanahan, a local lawyer who had taken to biking while recovering from his running injuries, and Jack Johnstone, a past club president and former competitive swimmer, had decided to hold a "triathlon" at Mission Bay, expanding by a third the basic, multisport concept of the David Pain Birthday Biathlon, a run-swim combination that Pain, a San Diego lawyer, had started in 1972 in honor of his own 50th birthday. Pain was something of a legend in San Diego running circles for both his irascible temperament and his patronage of running. He almost single-handedly founded the Masters (over 40) competitive track and field movement in this country during the 1960s, and so had his fingers in the germ plasma of two fairly significant athletic evolutions. At the time, however, neither his biathlon nor Johnstone and Shanahan's triathlon were seen as the first ripples of a new wave of fitness; they were intended merely as a lightly competitive alternative to the day-in, day-out grind of distance running.

The first track club triathlon was held on Fiesta Island, a nondescript, inappropriately named and evil-smelling splotch of sand that sits at the east end of San Diego's Mission Bay. The island, parts of which are used to dry sludge from a nearby sewage treatment plant, is used frequently for local running and cycling races, although it is best known for the annual Mission Bay Over-the-Line Tournament, a raunchy three-day celebration of the best and worst of Southern California beach life, just barely disguised (and less than barely clothed) as an athletic contest. As a kind of free-fire zone of outdoor entertainment within the otherwise strictly controlled San Diego park system, Fiesta Island was an ideal location for the triathlon. The track club members were familiar with the area, and it was unlikely the local police, who usually had their hands full with drunken picnickers, would object. No one expected much of a crowd, anyway; the first race attracted about 40 people.

The original order of events was complicated. Almost everyone who competed remembers it differently, most of them recalling simply that they seemed to be either swim-ming or running constantly, with the bike ride stuck in the middle someplace. Johnstone recalls that the course con-sisted of 2.8-mile run to the Sea World Amusement Park and back, a 5-mile, double-loop bike ride around Fiesta Island, then a series of short swims and runs north along the bay and back again. No one actually trained for the event; a fast runner with a swimming background was at a great advantage, and no one had much more than a ride-to-the-beach background on a bike. Still, it was a start. Collins, competing in what has since come to be widely acknowledged as the first swim-bike-run triathlon ever held, finished far down in the field, but since he'd never run more than three miles at a stretch, he was pleased. A man whom Collins would see again in a few years—a man who would play a big role in the explosion of triathlon popularity worldwide—finished second. His name was Tom Warren.

It wasn't until 1986 that the triathlon world began to look back to its beginnings and the early Fiesta Island triathlons were rediscovered. Warren had long been acknowledged as a pioneer, but where his first steps in the sport were taken had never really been explored. The pub-lic history said the sport began in Hawaii, with the Ironman, and like the tale about Collins's drunken chal-lenge, it spread and became accepted reality. Hawaii was certainly a far more dramatic location than a remote swamp in a forgotten corner of San Diego.

The retrieval of the real history was long overdue, although it is ironic that the almost obsessively conserva-tive San Diego Track Club was given credit for launching so uninhibited a sport. Indeed, there was a good deal of resist-ance to multisport competition within the club when triathlons began to gain a mass-participation foothold in the early 1980s. In the track club's eyes, triathletes were seen as less than bona fide athletes, flashy show-offs who had never succeeded as pure runners.

In fact, Johnstone himself, who served for a long time on the club's board of directors, was one of its more con-

The original order of events was complicat-ed. Almost everyone who competed remembers it differ-ently, most of them recalling simply that they seemed to be either swimming or running constantly, with the bike ride stuck in the middle someplace.

servative members, a strong opponent of growth and diversity. Neither he nor Shanahan became seriously involved in triathlons as the sport grew. The track club continued to see the activity as little more than a diversion, and doggedly resisted its incursion into the serious business of running.

Others, however, were less dogmatic, specifically Collins, who took the triathlon concept with him to Hawaii in June 1976. He proposed the Ironman six months later.

It happened in January 1977, at the outdoor awards ceremony for the Oahu Perimeter Relay Run, which had been held a week earlier. The run was an annual team competition that started near Pearl City on a moonlit Saturday night several weeks after the Honolulu Marathon and continued through Sunday. Each team was composed of seven runners who alternated with each other in three-, four-, or five-mile increments in a counter-clockwise direction completely around the island—a distance of about 140 miles. The teams were supported by vans, cars or pickup trucks, which transported team members from point to point, carrying food and water and acting as mobile cheering sections, encouraging or insulting whatever team member happened to be on the road at the time. Held annually for many years until insurance problems closed it down in 1986, the run started at night to minimize problems with both traffic and the heat. It took the fastest teams some 12-and-a-half hours to complete the entire route.

The awards ceremony for the relay that year was held at Primo Gardens (for Primo Beer, the company that sponsored the event) in Pearl City, and it was there that Collins posed the challenge. Almost a hundred teams had entered, so there was a big crowd.

The discussion that turned the wheels in Collins's head centered around the question of which athletes—runners, cyclists, or swimmers—were the most fit. Most of the people with Collins were runners, so there was a bias in that direction. Many were swimmers as well, however, and pressed the merits of marathon swimming. Run-swim biathlons were common in Hawaii at the time; there was an ongoing rivalry between the Waikiki Swim Club and the Mid-Pacific Roadrunners. An annual biathlon was held to decide the issue, with a trophy—a running shoe hanging from the inside of a life ring—passing back and forth between the clubs.

"I had read quite a bit about bicycling," recalled Collins. "The exercise physiology books at that time said that bicyclists had the highest oxygen uptake, that Eddy Merckx [five-time winner of the Tour de France] was the fittest person in the world. The runners always felt that they were at such a disadvantage in the water, and the swimmers always felt that the swim wasn't long enough and that they were better runners than the runners were swimmers, so there always was that sort of argument going on. I was expounding about the fact that bicyclists really were the most fit, and I was just sitting there thinking about it: the Waikiki Rough Water Swim started down at the Outrigger Canoe Club, then went outside the breakers and ended up at Fort Derussey. If you did that and then got on a bike and went counterclockwise around the island up over Wahiawa....

"So we got out a road map and it looked like about three miles from Aloha Tower to Fort Derussey. I said if you take the 115-mile race and you cut three miles off, it'd be 112 miles and you end up at Aloha Tower, and you just run the Honolulu Marathon course. I said that we could put all three of those things together. Whoever won that could call himself the premier endurance athlete in Hawaii."

Encouraged by the response of the handful of people around him, Collins climbed up on the stage, took the microphone, and explained his idea. "Whoever finishes it first," he announced, "we'll call the Iron Man. Anyone who thinks they can handle it, see me."

"I got a big laugh," Collins said.

But he was serious, and while almost everyone thought the idea was ridiculous, several people who heard the announcement remembered it. Over a period of some weeks they contacted Collins and asked him if he was going to go through with the plan. He was indeed; he'd been talking the proposal up at every opportunity. Finally,

Tom Knoll, one of Collins's Navy friends who had expressed a strong interest in the race, received orders for Okinawa. He was due to be transferred in the early spring.

"If we were going to do it," Collins said, "we had to do it before Tom left, so the time was fixed to be as soon after the Perimeter Relay the next year as possible."

Collins, who had always been an enthusiastic organizer, began piecing together an assortment of official permits and private, unofficial cooperation. Then he typed up several pages of instructions and suggestions, photocopied them along with several pages of maps, and began distributing the package to those who had talked to him about the race. On the cover was a hand-drawn map of Oahu with the route indicated by a dotted line. Hand-printed at the top of the page was the name of the race: "First Annual Hawaiian Iron Man Triathlon." Below the map Collins had printed:

"Swim 2.4 miles!

Run 26.2 miles!

Bike 112 miles!

Brag the rest of your Life!"

The race was held on February 18. Eighteen men signed up, 15 started, 12 finished. There was Collins, of course, and Haller and Knoll, who finished sixth. John Dunbar, a former Navy SEAL, was second. Dave Orlowski was third; Sterling Lewis, a physician, and Ian Emberson, a hotel bar manager, tied for fourth. In seventh place was Henry Forrest, a crew-cut, active-duty Marine; in eighth was Frank Day. Collins was ninth. The last to finish were Archie Hapai, a student at the University of Hawaii; Dan Hendrickson; and Harold Irving, also a student at UH. It took Irving more than 22 hours to complete the course.

Not one of the competitors that first year knew going in that the Ironman was even possible. To their knowledge, nothing like it had ever been attempted. The damned thing seemed to sit right out there on the edge of what a human body was designed to do. There were some real fears that it might even be dangerous. All the men were marathoners or swimmers or both, but few had any cycling experience, and the lack of expertise in some cases was downright frightening.

Hendrickson, for instance, went to Sears the day before the race, bought a ten-speed Free Spirit bike, then showed up at Collins's house that night and asked him for help putting it together. "Can't," said Collins, "I'm still working on the damned trophies." And Knoll, who was an experienced ultramarathon runner, was an absolute novice in the water. Like everyone else in the race he was required to have his own paddler on a surfboard alongside him during the swim. As it turned out, he needed a lot more.

"He could hardly swim at all," recalled Collins. "We had a boat that was assigned to follow along and play shepherd. When the lifeguard in the boat saw how bad a swimmer Tom was, he had the boat stay close. Tom ended up following that boat the whole way, with the lifeguard standing up and shouting instructions—telling him how to move his arms and breathe—as they went."

Collins, himself, who was 43 years old at the time, swam the 2.4 miles in 91 minutes. From then on he was in uncharted territory. He was so unsure of his ability to finish that he stopped every 10 miles during the bike ride for a drink of water and a piece or two of toast slathered with honey. When he got really hungry over on the far side of the island he stopped at a fast-food restaurant and ate a bowl of chili. Time was hardly a consideration; survival was the issue.

Not one of the competitors that first year knew going in that the Ironman was even possible. To their knowledge, nothing like it had ever been attempted.

"Is this possible?" he kept asking himself, and there were times during the marathon when he thought the answer might be no, especially about a mile or so after he guzzled half a can of beer. Then, for some reason, the last few miles of the run felt even better than the first few, a phenomenon that many Ironman competitors have experienced since, and he crossed the finish line in ninth place, 17 hours after he had personally fired the starting gun to get the whole thing under way.

"My pulse rate was 165 when I finished," Collins said. "And it was down to 100 within four minutes. It took 44 hours for it to get below that. I'd be two hours awake, and

I'd have to crash and go to sleep. I'd sleep for two hours and then I'd sit straight up in bed with my eyes open. It went on that way for a whole day."

The winner was Haller, who had been convinced when he first heard about the event that "I wasn't ever going to do something crazy like that." He'd had to run down Dunbar, the former SEAL, during the marathon.

It would be accurate to say that both Haller and Dunbar were fanatical about their level of physical conditioning.

They didn't know each other, but their paths had run surprisingly parallel: military backgrounds, cast-about employment careers, a sort of mutual evolution that put them in Hawaii at a propitious moment, in a frame of mind that made the insanity of Collins's Ironman seem plausible. Dunbar was immediately enthusiastic, Haller needed to be convinced— but it didn't take much. Both men were good marathoners, although Haller had an edge in that department. Dunbar had a strong advantage in the water; Haller was a better, more experienced cyclist. When the Ironman that first year actually developed into a race, it was Haller, gaining during the bike ride, who made it happen. Dunbar fought him off as long as he could, but ended the day in second place, more than half an hour behind.

Dunbar, whose father was a career Naval officer, joined the Navy himself right out of high school, hoping to become a frogman. The recruiter he talked to steered him in an even more demanding direction when he mentioned the SEALs. Half attempting to discourage the young man from a decision he would probably regret, the recruiter warned Dunbar that SEAL training was exceptionally difficult, that he'd be in the water day in and day out, that most of the candidates dropped out of the program, etc., etc. Dunbar thought it all sounded wonderful and signed on.

"I never was a person to sit around and do things that became boring, monotonous," he said.

The SEALs, certainly, were not boring. Formed during the Kennedy Administration as an elite offshoot of the already elite Underwater Demolition Teams, the SEALs are the Navy's version of the Army's Green Berets. Just to begin with, SEAL candidates must endure a nightmarish 18-week basic-training program that is designed to make them crumble. For four-and-a-half months they are almost continually wet and muddy, constantly harassed by instructors ("Take a Marine drill instructor and multiply it by 10," said a former SEAL officer), run day and night, push-upped almost to death, and when they aren't being pounded by something else, they are being pounded by the cold California surf. The attrition rate among SEAL trainees is something close to 90 percent—despite the fact that dropping out of the program is made to be as emotionally devastating as possible. The defeated candidate must walk to the front of a formation of men who were just a moment before his closest associates, remove his distinctive red helmet and place it humbly at the feet of the instructor. A more crushing admission of one's failure to measure up probably does not exist.

"We're looking for chinks and cracks," said one former SEAL team instructor. "There's no way you would want someone who wasn't qualified to slip through. But I'll tell you, everything after that training is a piece of cake. You can't hurt a guy like that. You can make him tired, but mentally he's unbeatable."

"In the SEALs," Dunbar said softly, "if you quit you lose. And you lose a great deal. The thing no trainee wanted was to quit."

Dunbar left the Navy in 1976 and he enrolled at Chaminade University in Honolulu almost immediately. He'd saved a chunk of money while on active duty, and he was getting a monthly stipend as part of his G.I. Bill entitlement, so he didn't have to work. And he spent little; he lived in a van so he didn't have to pay rent, and he bicycled almost everywhere he went. Or he ran. He competed regularly in running and swimming races in the Honolulu area, ran his first marathon in 1977 and stayed in generally terrific shape.

Not surprisingly, he was one of the first people to tell Collins that his Ironman suggestion sounded like a good idea. When Collins called him a couple of weeks later and told him that several more people had signed on, Dunbar said immediately, "Great, there'll be some competition!"

"I wasn't about to let anyone beat me in an event that incorporated a number of different activities," Dunbar said.

Had you asked, Haller would have given you a similar evaluation of his own abilities. Mild-mannered but highly competitive, he'd been an athlete all his life, and since his return to Hawaii in January 1976, shortly after his discharge from the Navy, he'd been running, cycling and lifting weights almost constantly. In fact, he'd flown to Oahu specifically to compete with a team in the Perimeter Relay. Unfortunately, a big storm caused a two-week postponement of the relay that year. Haller, seeing the situation as an opportunity rather than an inconvenience, cashed in his ticket for the return flight home and stayed.

Of course he didn't have a job in Honolulu. Not that he was all that particular—nor were his needs all that complicated. Anything that would keep his belly full so that he could train would do. And almost everything did. He collected a little unemployment, did some gardening, sold a weight-loss program door-to-door and even did some surf reports for a local radio station. He joined the Navy Reserve and spent a year driving a cab. "I got pretty good at that," he said, shrugging off a less-than-ambitious period of his life. "I was just enjoying everything," he said. "I was single, had absolutely no responsibilities."

Mostly, he was running, morning and evening both, putting in up to 120 miles a week, competing whenever he could. It was the lifestyle of many good but never-to-be-great marathoners at the time who understood their limitations but stayed with the program nonetheless; full-time athletes whose source of income, partial or otherwise, would never be running. One of the highlights of Haller's career came that winter, in December, when he ran a 2:29 at the Honolulu Marathon and placed 10th.

In November 1977, Haller thumbed a ride on a military hop out of Honolulu and flew off to Washington, D.C., to race in the Marine Corps Marathon. He was in the best running shape of his life, and he ran what still is his best time—a 2:27. He was back on Oahu in late December, just two days before the Honolulu Marathon. He planned to run that, but he needed first to find a job. Among the places where he went looking was a Nautilus fitness center on King Street in Honolulu where the owner, Hank Grundman, told Haller that he couldn't hire him, but that he'd let him work out for free in exchange for a few hours of work each week.

"I thought that sounded like a pretty good deal," said Haller. "I would have just turned around and spent the money to join a place like that anyway."

Grundman's offer put the last of the Ironman pieces in place. Haller was back in Hawaii and not in any immediate danger of starving. Dunbar was well-fed, too, living in his van and spending most of his time either studying, working out or arguing with various police officers who kept insisting that his sleeping arrangements were illegal. Collins and his wife were training for the next Perimeter Relay, to be held in less than a month. It was Grundman, through his three fitness centers, who would sponsor Haller's participation in the first Ironman. He would, in fact, sponsor the race itself in 1979 and '80, while upstairs in his King Street center his wife at the time, Valerie Grundman (formerly Silk), who did the books, grumbled about the incredible amount of money the clubs were throwing down the drain of a "crazy-ass" sport.

❖

The battle between Haller and Dunbar that first year was dramatic. It had never occurred to Collins that someone might want to race his event; many of his friends were telling him that not a single one of the entrants was even going to finish. But to Dunbar it was a race right from the beginning. For weeks he'd been telling himself that he could win, and so on race day he hid his second thoughts ("Maybe they're right; maybe this can't be done. Am I going to collapse and die?") behind that grim SEAL face of

"In the SEALs," Dunbar said softly, "if you quit you lose. And you lose a great deal. The thing no trainee wanted was to quit."

his and charged through the swim. It took him almost exactly an hour; he came out in second place, three minutes back, but he was in first within a few miles on the bike and pulling away from the field.

The big lead didn't surprise Dunbar at all. Nor was he surprised when he came off the bike in first place, with no one else in sight—although he was a bit concerned, because the ride had been harder than he'd anticipated.

When he started to stagger during the marathon, when the stomach cramps set in and his legs started to go numb, and most of all when he got word that Haller was behind him, gaining fast, and looking pretty strong...well, that surprised him. The only way to handle the situation—he was a SEAL, for God's sake—was to go harder.

"The bike ride was pure agony," Dunbar said. While he had been riding his bike steadily before the race, he hadn't really been training on it at all, not for the Ironman anyway. His longest ride was something like 20 miles, which he thought was probably enough because he was in great shape, although of course it wasn't near what he needed. He had learned what thousands of Ironman competitors who would follow him would learn by equally bitter experience: cycling was the key to the event; it either set you up or set you down for the marathon.

"I thought I'd just be able to cruise through 112 miles, that there wouldn't be too much competition, that I'd go at an easy pace and save myself for the marathon," Dunbar said. "But like every event I've been in where there are other people, I've gotten that competitive spirit in me that's caused me to drive through every moment of the competition."

Haller kept coming. At the end of the bike ride at the Aloha Tower he'd been some 13 minutes behind, which is either a lot of time or not, depending on how the guy in front of you is feeling. In this case, it wasn't much, and Haller knew it.

He picked up ground on Dunbar quickly, lopping 10 minutes off the lead by the time he had crested Diamond Head. But downhills are tough on tired legs, and Haller was forced to stop at 17 miles and have his cramps massaged. He too was learning an Ironman lesson: running a marathon after riding hard for five or six or seven hours or more is a bitch, no matter how much you've trained. Dunbar's lead increased again—to eight minutes. But the race was in Haller's hands now. Dunbar was through, barely holding on, and it took Haller just three miles to get close once more. Then he stopped again, this time to urinate. Finally, at mile 21 he went by for good, unnoticed by Dunbar, who was at that point well past caring about first place at all—or second or third for that matter. He had trimmed his goals to one bare essential. "When you quit, you lose," Dunbar the SEAL had said.

To hell with Haller.

The winning time was 11:46:58. Dunbar was 35 minutes behind. He'd almost passed out, and had been hallucinating, which scared his one-man support crew, Ron Figueroa. Figueroa wondered whether he shouldn't just pull his man off the road and head for the nearest hospital. As if Dunbar's exhaustion and lack of proper training on the bike weren't enough, he'd downed a couple of beers when Figueroa had run out of anything else to drink.

"I guzzled one can and thought that would do it," Dunbar said with a grin. "It tasted so good. I thought it was doing the job, and of course I was tough, I thought I could handle it, so I guzzled another can. It started affecting me within half an hour. I was delirious within thirty, forty-five minutes. I wasn't sure I'd make it."

The next day the *Honolulu Advertiser* carried a report of the event on the front page of the sports section. There was a picture of Haller taken during the run. He was smiling, so it must have been between cramps. Although 12 men finished, the last five (including Collins) crossed the line too late to be included in the story, which referred to the event as a "gut-buster." No one had died; no one had been seriously injured. No citizen of Honolulu had complained about being inconvenienced by the event. Under the terms of Collins's written instructions, that officially qualified the race as a success.

5

A METHOD
TO HIS
MADNESS

Twelve people that first year had proved that the distances could be completed. The Ironman was possible. Haller and Dunbar had shown that if you had the guts to turn a few screws, you could even go fast—for a while, anyway. By January the next year, word of the event had spread, interest had grown and there was even an official sponsor of sorts, since Grundman had agreed to pay for the T-shirts if Collins would allow him to put the Nautilus logo on the back. Grundman also wanted to supply trophies to the top male and top female finishers (he knew there would be a woman because he was training one for the race at his center). Collins agreed to both offers, and then processed applications for 50 people. He decided to charge everyone an entry fee of eight dollars this time instead of the five he'd charged the year before because he'd lost 25 bucks on the race in 1978 and wanted to make it back. He'd charged the five dollars in the first place because he was afraid that some of the entrants would be so inexperienced they might head out without the basic necessities.

The least he could do, Collins figured, was supply everyone with two gallons of powdered ERG, a product he'd become familiar with in San Diego. But he wasn't willing to do it at his own expense.

While the field in 1978 had been filled with locals—military guys and ultrarunners, men whose training goals and estimations of their own abilities were somewhat abnormal but who could walk down any street in Lincoln, Nebraska, and not be noticed—in '79 there was a fair share of oddballs from the mainland. Collins called them "professional characters." They were people who had moved beyond the realm of excessive fitness-related behavior and into a world of excessive behavior, period. Ken "Cowman" Shirk was one of these—a big, long-haired, bushy-bearded hippie and self-proclaimed philosopher from the Lake Tahoe area of California who panhandled his way from event to event and talked to anyone who would listen about his experience at the rugged Western States 100-mile endurance run. He eventually moved to Hawaii and became something of a permanent Ironman—an "Ironbum," according to a 1984 article in *Triathlete* magazine.

Like most of the characters, Shirk was more dedicated to self-promotion than performance. (The "Cowman" came from his wearing a furry headdress with horns during competition. It made him look like a skinny, two-legged buffalo.) But he was friendly and harmless—a self-parody, a kind of street-corner transient in the world of endurance sports. Not everyone was enamored of his retarded sense of personal responsibility, however.

"Cowman was very upset that I wanted eight dollars from him the second year," Collins said. "He said he didn't have it. I said that if he didn't have it he couldn't run. He went out and came back with a plastic bag full of nickels and dimes and pennies and quarters—I guess he'd begged it—and he counted out eight dollars. He also wanted me to find him a bicycle, someone to paddle for him, a support vehicle, a place to sleep and by the way, he was hungry."

Characters like Cowman became part of the Ironman legend during the first few years, reinforcing the oddball image of the event. It was an image that the serious triathletes who came later found mildly offensive, and one that gradually disappeared as the sport of triathlon and the level of competence grew. But the characters were part of the appeal in the early days, and the Ironman seemed to attract them like some weird psychic magnet. In 1980, when the field of competitors was 10 times as large as the year before, there were characters galore, soul mates of Cowman whose physical preparation for 140 miles of competition was often less important than their being cosmically in tune with what was happening. The people—and the results—were often strange, and they created a context in which even the simple, obsessive devotion to physical fitness of many of the more normal participants seemed odd. There were men who had run 50 marathons, 80 marathons, run across the country, swum across channels and cycled over mountains, all for no particular reason other than to be able to tell people they'd done it. One entrant in 1980 called himself Born Again Smitty. He listed his "earthly age" as 40 (having been born in 1939) and his "eternal age" as five. Smitty lived in a cave on Maui and said that before his rebirth he'd been a blackjack dealer in Las Vegas.

Unlike Cowman, though, Smitty was a heck of an athlete. About halfway through the bike course in 1980 he was clobbered from behind by the rearview mirror of a passing truck and knocked off his bike. Another competitor stopped, shocked at the obvious severity of the accident. "Are you okay?" he asked. Smitty, his head bleeding badly, proclaimed loudly that "The Lord will see me through!" He hopped back on his bike and sped off, completing not only the bike ride but the marathon too—in 3:34—with a total time well under 12 hours. He placed 19th.

In 1979 Dunbar got in on the weirdness himself. On the morning that the race was scheduled, on the heels of a tremendous storm that had been dropping swimming pools full of rain all over the islands for the previous week, with the skies still an ominous gray, the winds howling and gusting, and the water churning off Waikiki, he showed up in a Superman costume, ready to race. The conditions were abominable, but Dunbar's spirits were

There were men who had run 50 marathons, 80 marathons, run across the country, swum across channels and cycled over mountains, all for no particular reason other than to be able to tell people they'd done it.

high. He was psyched. This was the kind of day he liked, by God. It made the whole thing even more of a challenge. Where's Haller?

Not all of the 28 people who showed up—out of the original 50 who had paid their eight dollars—felt the same way Dunbar did about the weather, though. Haller, who was not the best of swimmers under ideal conditions, sure didn't. He wasn't much afraid of running or cycling himself almost to death, but the Pacific Ocean out there was bouncing around like it could kill you. He had already proved that he was tough; did he need now to prove that he was insane?

Collins was having serious doubts himself. Aside from the rest of his concerns, there was his liability to worry about. It was an area in which he had always been, as his wife, Judy, said, "paranoid." He'd gone so far the first year as to have everyone sign a provision on the original entry form that made all the starters members of something called the "Hawaii Iron Man Triathlon Coordinating Committee."

"The purpose of the committee," Collins said, "was to put on the event. If you sued anyone, you were going to be suing the committee and therefore yourself. I hoped that by doing that it would spread out any deep-pockets kind of thing that might have arisen."

The provision was part of the entry blank for the second year as well, but on that bleak and storm-tossed Saturday morning, its existence didn't make Collins feel any better. Not only was the ocean ugly but the winds were so bad that the bikes would probably get blown into the automobile traffic on the other side of the island. He decided to postpone the race until Sunday—over howls of protest from some of the competitors, the loudest of all Dunbar, who promptly challenged Haller to do the race man to man, one on one. Haller ignored him—ignored him so well in fact that he doesn't even remember Dunbar confronting him.

"Somebody asked me," Collins said, grinning, "what my criteria were for postponing the race. 'Hey,' I said, 'it's simple. I'm in charge, and if I'm afraid to do it, then we're not going to do it.'"

"Oh, it was a feeling of bitter disappointment," Dunbar said. "I mean, after all, it was an Ironman race, wasn't it? From two or three days before I was preparing myself mentally for that day, to do it. And they canceled it for some ridiculous reason—the weather." Dunbar chuckled softly, remembering how extreme the conditions really had been—and how extreme he must have sounded at the time. On the other hand, there is something inside that still eats at him a little bit.

"I felt more as if the individuals should decide to go or not to go. Between Gordon and myself it was competitive—along with it being an individual challenge. He had beaten me the previous year and I wasn't going to let him do it again. Unbeknownst to us, Tom Warren was in there and clobbered us both."

❖

Warren was a kind of living moral to the story that year—soft-spoken, understated proof that almost anything you could think of was likely to happen in a race as long as the Ironman, and proof that as mean and as tough and as long-suffering as you thought you were, there was always somebody who was meaner and tougher.

But if Warren's performance humbled Dunbar, it had a broader, longer-lasting impact, thanks to the presence of a writer from *Sports Illustrated* named Barry McDermott. McDermott's specialty was, and still is, golf, although the story he wrote about the 1979 Ironman, published in the May 14 issue of the magazine, did more for the sport of triathlon than any single occurrence over the next decade, including the exposure that ABC television gave the race starting in 1980. McDermott's story was, in fact, what brought the "Wide World of Sports" cameras to Hawaii in the first place.

Warren was the hero of the article, an offbeat, mildly eccentric, 35-year-old tavern owner from San Diego who seemed to take everything in stride, from the terrible weather, to Dunbar in his Superman outfit, to his modest acceptance of his own position as not just an underdog but as a total unknown-and-who-cares.

"To me it was going to be a two-man race," McDermott said, "Dunbar and Haller, the two guys who had almost killed themselves the year before. Warren was kind of around, but I didn't pay much attention to him, and I think he kind of felt that. It's as if he was saying: 'Hey, what about me? I'm going to win this thing.'" And everybody was just saying, 'Yeah, sure, just go over there and sit down and be quiet.'

"The other guys had obviously devoted themselves to it. They seemed, to me, to be unbelievable physical specimens. Back then, nobody did this stuff. But these guys had done it, they'd proven that it could be done. And Warren hadn't done it, either. Plus he was a lot older, and he didn't seem to be as committed as they seemed to be. It didn't seem to me that this guy who was 35 years old or whatever was going to be able to compete against guys who were 22 and had been SEALs."

Warren was committed, however—to a degree that caused McDermott's respect for him to soar. And the respect was reflected in the story. Not that McDermott lionized the event; he painted the race as just this side of insane. "They were all characters," he would say 10 years later. "They were all crazy, obviously certifiable. Even the guy Cowman, who is bizarre, you know, but in that group he was like normal."

Still, however, there was a lot of left-handed praise that seemed to just build and build—a broad, do-you-believe-this portrait that ended with an F. Scott Fitzgerald-ish scene of Warren walking alone down a rainy Honolulu street at 1:30 in the morning, having yet to go to bed, looking for someone who could keep their eyes open long enough to have breakfast with him.

To some, the picture McDermott painted proved irresistible. The skin on the back of their arms tingled and they flipped back to the first page of the story and started again, and then again after that. To this day, many of the top triathletes in the world recall the piece and remember it being their original inspiration. McDermott was besieged by requests for information on how to get into the race. He finally photocopied a form letter telling the people where to write for information in Hawaii. The article even prompted a somewhat awkward appearance by Warren on "The Tonight Show" and there were feelers about a movie.

"What happened," McDermott said, "was that right about that time the movie 'Running' came out, the one with Michael Douglas, one of the all-time bombs at the box office, and that ended all running, exercise-type movies for the next three or four years."

In 1980, the year after the article appeared, 108 people started the race, up from 15 in 1979, and ABC was there with its cameras, launching the Ironman star into television heaven.

"I thought it would be a good story," McDermott said, "but when I went there, I knew it would be great." He had been turned on to the race by an acquaintance who had sent him an account of the 1978 event, hoping to have it published in the magazine. That wasn't possible, but McDermott convinced his editor that the event might be worth a look in '79. What he saw left an impression that hasn't faded much in a decade.

"To me," McDermott said in 1986, "there was always this one Ironman of Hawaii contest, and there's always going to be just one Ironman—Tom Warren. These other guys, yeah, they can do it, and they beat his time by three hours and all that stuff, but so what? That's like saying Babe Ruth can hit home runs. Big deal. If you can hit home runs, you can hit home runs; if you can do the Ironman in nine hours and 30 minutes, great, but no one in my mind can ever approach the spectacle I witnessed. The way Tom Warren won that race was incredible. And to do what he did for a silly little trophy made out of nuts and bolts—that to me was special. He'll always be the Iron Man. He did it in a way and for a reason that will never exist again."

"They were all characters," Warren would say 10 years later. "They were all crazy, obviously certifiable. Even the guy Cowman, who is bizarre, you know, but in that group he was like normal."

❖

Warren himself heard about the race during the summer of 1978 from, of all people, John Dunbar. The two raced against each other in a small, informal triathlon in San Diego, which Warren won. To him, the Ironman sounded like the kind of event he would do well in. In fact, it sounded a lot like the challenges he'd been setting for himself in San Diego for years. At the time, he was probably better prepared for an ultradistance triathlon than just about anybody in the world.

"I didn't train for that first one," Warren said. "I could do it anytime I wanted. I'd already swum a 15-mile ocean race. I'd already done a 75-mile run in the mountains and I'd already done a 1600-mile bike ride in two weeks."

Warren is a handsome man with a full head of curly hair and a big walrus mustache. He looks somehow like the kind of guy who would have done something like the Ironman back then, although seeing him in his running shorts, you'd never believe he could actually win the thing. But he was somehow right for the part, an original, something of a loner who has always seen the world from a perspective just over the horizon from most of the world. He is unique.

"I like 'unique' better than weird," Warren said. "Most people say I'm weird."

It was early in 1986. He was sitting at a popular surfside restaurant in San Diego's Pacific Beach, eating breakfast. From the big windows he could look out over the piled up sand that guarded the cement boardwalk and the front of the restaurant from the high winter tides and see the waves breaking out around the end of the pier. Warren was dressed in his "business suit," a beat-up sweater, a pair of sweatpants, white socks and leather sandals. His hair was long in back, brushing his shoulders, and his eyes were almost hidden behind a pair of prescription glasses with photo-gray lenses. As he did most mornings, he'd driven his motor home to the beach and parked. It would be his base of operations for the day.

"My girlfriend told me I was weird again last night," Warren said almost petulantly.

"Weird about what?" came the question.

"Pretty much everything," Warren said. Then he looked up and grinned a toothy, Teddy Roosevelt grin. He never minded being a little different at all, really.

He owned a tavern in Pacific Beach called Tug's (an early nickname of Warren's), which sat on the corner of Mission Boulevard and Emerald Street, just steps from the ocean, a block-and-a-half from Crystal Pier, and just a short walk from where he was born. It had been a lesbian bar when he bought it for $10,000 in 1969, $2500 down. The place became a perfect reflection of Warren himself, who had been raised at the water's edge with a surfboard in one hand and the other curved perfectly to accept a can of beer. Like Warren, Tug's seemed comfortable with the full range of Southern California beach life. It attracted an impossible mixture of mean-looking, black-jacketed bikers who clanked like old cowboys when they walked, punked-out surf rats, transients who had managed to scrape enough change together for a taco, and clean-cut athletes in jeans and running shoes and freshly laundered T-shirts. Tug's served wine and beer and cheap Mexican food, with a special on Thursday nights where you could get three rolled tacos, a bean tostada and a green salad for $1.15.

"I like 'unique' better than weird," Warren said. "Most people say I'm weird."

"If you wanted extra cheese on the tostada it would be $1.25," said one Tug's regular. "I haven't had a square meal on Thursday night since they closed."

Warren sold Tug's in 1982, thinking that he might be ready to retire, but he bought it back six months later. The new owners had wanted him to take it back after two. Business was bad, the staff was unhappy.

"I don't think anybody, including myself, realized that I had a job," said Warren. "Everybody always thought that all I did was sit around and collect money. They all of sudden realized that things didn't get done. There wasn't that energy level. In all honesty, though, it was never the same after I bought it back."

He got rid of Tug's for good in 1985, mildly offended over the creeping yuppification of Pacific Beach, disgusted with city officials who weren't willing to grant him the full liquor license he needed to compete with the new, upscale bars that had opened all around him. The authorities seemed to want his dignity as well as his money. It was too high a cost. The night Tug's closed, the place was jammed so tight there were people standing on tables to make room for the others who were flooding in the door. All three local television stations were on hand to record the demise of a San Diego landmark. Warren, as delightful and as baffling as ever, mentioned on camera that he was probably going to invest in property up north in Oceanside, where there were more derelicts.

To Warren, how he got to a place was always as important as getting there. If he marched to a different beat than the rest of the world, he did so with precision. His life was well defined, singular, perhaps, but well ordered and efficient. Even the off-the-wall athletic goals he set for himself were accomplished methodically and analytically. He liked goals; his life was a series of goals being set and then almost regretfully achieved, with each being rated not just for difficulty, but for feel and setting.

"You should never really think about yourself," Warren said. "You can't go forward if you do. If I was going to talk about myself it would be what I'm going to do."

He had a callous on his tailbone from doing sit-ups in the sauna, because he could never simply do one thing at a time. The stories about him exercising and making business calls from a phone in the sauna made him sound peculiar, but it was Warren's way. About the only time he ever let someone else's opinion affect him was during a competition, when he was starting to hurt. He'd never let you see that he was straining, pushing his limits, because if he looked tired, then you might get it in your head that you could beat him the next time out. He might let someone have the physical edge on him—he might even enjoy the contest more if you did—but he always liked to keep one leg up in the psychology department. If there were a hundred ways to beat you, Warren would know 99 of them and be halfway to having the hundredth figured out. He didn't like to lose, ever.

"He was so smart," McDermott laughed. "He could be marooned on a desert island and somehow he'd build a jet runway and build a jet and fly off it. Or when you got there he would have colonized the place somehow, and he'd have this great setup with a bar—Tug's Tavern West."

Some of the endurance adventures Warren launched himself on he trained hard for, others he didn't. To him, the goals he achieved without really being in good enough shape for them were the most satisfying, because he had beaten longer odds. And far from buying the best equipment to achieve his goals, Warren preferred to use the worst—at least when he was competing casually, or simply against himself—because that, too, made it tougher. He'd take long bike rides on his single-speed Huffy bicycle, racing against anyone who tried to pass him. One time, while he was riding north along the Pacific Coast Highway, a large group of competitive cyclists did just that, flying by in the kind of superior, everyone-else's-a-slob way that cyclists are apt to exhibit. To their amazement Warren stayed with them for miles, riding in the middle of the pack and forcing the pace, teasing them, until he was pedaling his under-geared bike so furiously that he finally threw the chain and had to pull off the road.

To Warren, how he got to a place was always as important as getting there. If he marched to a different beat than the rest of the world, he did so with precision.

More important than beating the other guy, however, was beating himself, or at least what he perceived to be the structure of the problem that confronted him. If he bet you a six-pack that he could do more sit-ups than you could, he wouldn't stop just because you stopped. He'd keep going, perhaps because he'd secretly set for himself a number of sit-ups that you would never have agreed to, almost as if he'd used you to get him going in some new direction. If things went too smoothly, if he achieved whatever he was trying to do without what he deemed to be sufficient difficulty, it was worse for him than never having done it all.

So the conditions even on that Saturday in 1979 didn't bother Warren a bit. In fact, he pretty much agreed with

Dunbar when the SEAL raised the point that this was, after all, the Ironman and shouldn't be canceled for anything short of a major volcanic eruption.

As it was, only 18 of the 28 people who had shown up on Saturday returned to try again on Sunday. Most were enthusiastic, some were not, but the options were limited since many of them had plane tickets back to the mainland or jobs they needed to return to. It was either do it now or do it not at all.

The situation was less clear for Collins. Almost all of his volunteer help had evaporated. Most of them had signed on for Saturday only and had other commitments. Or they had looked out their bedroom windows on Sunday and simply rolled over.

Then there was a boat problem—another complication caused by the postponement—and Judy ran off a second time to find someone at the Outrigger Canoe Club willing to pilot a substitute safety boat. While that was being done her husband called for a vote on whether or not to move the swim west to the Ala Moana basin, where a break wall cut even the biggest waves down to mere ripples. Dunbar, dressed again as Superman, his hair blowing in the strong wind, demanded that the swim be held in the ocean. Warren agreed and so did most of the others. Collins gave his assent. When he did, a friend of Debbie Anderson, one of the two women who had entered the race, began protesting loudly, threatening to sue Collins if he didn't call it off and offering legal assistance to anyone who competed and was subsequently injured. Anderson, the woman who had been trained for the race at Grundman's Nautilus center, was a good cyclist and runner, but not much of a swimmer. There wasn't any way she was going to step into the raging ocean.

Collins by this time had had all he was willing to take. His fun little adventure was turning into a massive pain in the ass. Friends of his who had volunteered to help on Saturday were pissed off because the race had been postponed. The competitors were upset with him for the same reason. Dunbar was running around like a madman in his

Superman outfit raising hell. The damn weather was screwing up the entire deal and Collins was so woefully short of help that he couldn't even race in his own race. He was worried about liability as it was; now this crazy woman was screaming at him, threatening to sue. This was fun?

Collins gathered the entire group around—it was chilly and windy, so everyone huddled close in their rain gear— and in his loudest and deepest and most commanding Commander's voice explained the situation. He could barely be heard over the howling wind.

"This woman over here has informed me that if I run this thing and anybody's hurt, that she'll sue me for everything I've got. I want you to understand that in accordance with the piece of paper you signed that this is voluntary, that you are the sole judge of whether or not it's safe. If anybody wants to reconsider, I'll give you your $8 back right now."

Two men took him up on his offer. So did Anderson, of course.

"To give the money back right there I had to come up with a lot of dimes and nickels and quarters," laughed Collins. "Coming up with $24 on Sunday morning was tough."

But the controversy was resolved. Collins fired the starting gun and sent 14 men and one woman into the rolling dark gray ocean. It was a little past eight o'clock in the morning on February 14, about an hour past the scheduled starting time.

"I seriously thought that someone might get killed," McDermott said. "You cannot believe how bad the weather was. The ocean was the most threatening thing I'd ever seen. It was a life-threatening situation."

Open-water swimming is not like swimming in a pool. Navigation is a real concern. To make sure they are headed in the right direction, triathletes must lift their heads repeatedly to sight landmarks or buoys, a procedure that uses a tremendous amount of energy. Choppy seas and big swells make navigation more difficult; they made it almost impossible on this occasion. The winds and currents threatened to blow the swimmers off course and turn the 2.4 miles into 2.7 or 3 or more. A good paddler was invaluable, for he or she could do all sighting, set a straight line, and make it unnecessary for the swimmer to look up at all. Neither Warren nor Dunbar had any special problems. They had experienced people with them and they knew the ocean well themselves; they had seen it at least this bad before. Others were not so fortunate, including a petrified Gordon Haller.

The only athlete in the group with anything close to a sponsorship, Haller had the most sophisticated support of the day waiting for him on the beach, a team from the Nautilus Center eager to take him smoothly through the bike ride and the run. But he had chosen his paddler himself—for all the wrong reasons: the guy was Haller's buddy; Haller was staying at his house. Unfortunately, the man's swimming ability was not equal to his hospitality. If Haller's apprehension of the rough weather that day ranked eight on a scale of 10, his paddler's was up there around nine. Less than halfway through the swim he panicked, stopped paddling and was blown out to sea.

There was no alternative but to rescue him. Judy Collins, who was bouncing around in the substitute safety boat she had commandeered at the Outrigger Canoe Club, was nervous about leaving the swimmers, but she had no choice. On the other hand, perhaps it was for the best, since the pilot of the boat, an old salt who didn't seem to believe in life vests and insisted on zooming all over the course at full throttle, was causing Judy Collins to wonder if he might be more of a hazard than a help. The whole incident greatly annoyed her husband, who was standing on the beach with nothing to do but wait for the swimmers to come out of the water, hoping against all his fears that no one was drowning.

"I figured the goddamn paddler could sit out there and bounce up and down for as long as he needed to," the Commander fumed. "The boat was out there for the swimmers."

Meanwhile, Haller floundered along, his nearsightedness not helping the situation at all. When the boat that had fetched his friend passed him on the way into shore, Haller tried to tell the crew in between gulps of salt water that he would like someone to guide him. "I'm drowning!" he said. They told him he looked great and zoomed off.

"I just wanted someone to get back in the water and guide me," said Haller. "I had no idea, outside of the general direction of the waves, of where I was supposed to be going. I was in the middle of nowhere—a mile behind me, a mile from the beach, a mile in front of me and three thousand miles in that direction," Haller pointed west, toward Japan. "Of course, that was the way the wind was blowing. I would have gotten there quicker."

Finally another swimmer came by with his paddler—a woman who obviously knew what she was doing—and Haller followed them in. He came out of the water well behind, 49 minutes down on the leader, Ian Emberson, 45 down on Warren, 42 on Dunbar. His time for the 2.4 miles was an hour and 51 minutes. It had been an hour and 19 the year before. When he finally staggered up the beach, mildly hypothermic and dizzy, his eyes glassy, there was a mixture of concern and relief on his sponsor Grundman's face. The good news was that Haller was still alive. The bad news was that he looked as if he might fall down and die right there in the sand.

"Do you want to quit, Gordon?" Grundman asked.

"Hell no," mumbled Haller. "The hard part's over."

The race had been billed as a rematch between the two former Navy men, Dunbar and Haller. They were the only two people who had actually raced the year before, and they had both trained specifically for the event in '79. Having learned a long list of logistical lessons the year before, Dunbar had recruited a sophisticated support crew. The team's yellow Volkswagen van was filled with food, water, a spare bike and four helpers, including Kent Davenport, a local orthopedist.

Now that he was out of the ocean, Haller was in good shape, too. The Nautilus Center van was loaded with sup-

"I seriously thought that someone might get killed," McDermott said. *"You cannot believe how bad the weather was. The ocean was the most threatening thing I'd ever seen. It was a life-threatening situation."*

plies. Grundman himself was on board to help, along with several of his employees.

"It was like one camp against the other camp," McDermott said. "The Big Confrontation."

Warren, on the other hand, was working with a Honda Civic and a pickup crew, having scrounged both from Grundman, who reluctantly lent two of his employees, but only after extracting a promise to have them back by midnight—whether Warren had finished by that time or not. Warren figured that he was likely to beat the deadline by about five hours, but he didn't tell Grundman that. When the gun went off to start the race, his two helpers were still somewhat skeptical but they had already been impressed by his intelligence and enthusiasm. By the time the bike ride was several hours old, with Warren grinding away into the winds along the north shore, building his lead as the day cleared temporarily and began to get hot, they became true believers, as confident as the man they'd been assigned to, and even more enthusiastic. McDermott called them Warren's "Katzenjammer support crew."

The Oahu bike course was quite different from the present Ironman course on the Big Island, where the Queen K highway is so nasty that foul weather would probably make things easier. The Oahu route was beautiful and green, climbing and falling as it twisted along the rugged coastline, following in a counterclockwise direction the single highway that runs completely around the island. One drawback was that the road was narrow in places, with barely enough room for both a bike and a car moving in the same direction.

Dunbar had been run onto the shoulder by local residents twice during the race in '78. Several other competitors had similar experiences. The highway was also exposed in portions, and the terrible weather in '79 made things much worse. Each breathtaking vista along the eastern coastline gave the wind another chance to blow the cyclists completely off the road, which was slick and wet and covered by debris from the storm.

The worst part of the ride, though, was the climb inland from Haleiwa on the north shore, through the pineapple fields along the King Kamehameha Highway. It's a hard pull—a long, five-mile, thousand-foot grade made all the more difficult that day because the wind was blowing in the cyclists' faces.

It was certainly the toughest part of the day for Warren. He slowed for food just outside of Haleiwa and for a moment looked a little rocky. He lost time during this segment because some of the triathletes inadvertently took an alternate, and what turned out to be a more sheltered and thus faster, route, taking the Farrington Highway south instead of the King Kam. It was here that the only woman in the race, a competitive cyclist named Lyn Lemaire, gained a lot of ground. She had already passed an astonished John Dunbar into second place, waving as she went. Now, on a flashy chrome bike, and unlike most of the competitors wearing her own (not borrowed) cycling clothes and cleats, she had her sights set on first place. By the time the two roads merged nine miles later, she had closed from more than a half hour back to within 20 minutes.

Warren, however, was never even aware of Lemaire's presence. With the long climb over and just 15 miles left to ride, his mind was beginning to change gears, beginning to focus on the marathon. After almost six hours of on-the-job training his makeshift team was working like a clock. Once again, Warren was beating the odds. He had taken a bargain basement operation and turned it into a gold mine.

"They were perfect," he said of his crew. "They couldn't have been any better."

❖

The Ironman run on Oahu followed the route of the Honolulu Marathon, a course that accommodates thousands of runners on marathon day, but only because the streets are closed to automobiles. Without road closures, which the Ironman certainly did not merit, the last event was something of a free-for-all. The runners shared the sidewalks and intersections with Sunday evening traffic, both pedestrian and automotive. That was not unusual, since the route was one that recreational runners normally took through the city. And the traffic was relatively light because of the bad weather. Still, it was confusing to someone who wasn't familiar with Honolulu. And there was certainly no one for Warren to follow, since he'd headed east toward Diamond Head with a 20-minute lead over Lemaire. After seven-and-a-half hours of competition, he needed to deal not just with his fatigue but also with the difficulty of following an unmarked course.

"He didn't know where he was going," McDermott laughed. "It was rush-hour traffic in downtown Honolulu—five o'clock in the afternoon, and here's this guy in running shorts and no shirt dodging among the cars. He was running across crosswalks, pushing people out of the way. We're following in a car and he's beating us because we have to stop for stoplights."

Warren never wavered. He didn't flinch from the pace he'd set during the first few miles, although he did begin to tilt a bit. Warren's running style, his tilt, was well known back in San Diego. To this day it's a trademark, like his mustache. He broke his right leg when he was two years old, and it didn't heal cleanly. So he shuffles when he runs, his head and upper body listing farther and farther to the right as he tires, his right foot pointing out. In the heat of competition he looks more like a wounded great blue heron than a marathoner. Unless you know the history, you'd think he was about to collapse and die.

So as Warren ran, the word went out that he wasn't going to make it to the finish line. McDermott, who empathized and had watched the best efforts of the well-equipped Haller and the well-equipped Dunbar fail miserably while Warren's ragtag forces moved on and on, was by this time unabashedly partisan. He threw his journalistic impartiality to the winds and jumped in and ran with Warren.

"The other guys, Dunbar and Haller, had guys running in front of them to break the wind." McDermott said. "I thought it was so unfair. Everybody was rooting for these two guys to beat this poor, misshapen, weird little guy from San Diego. Everyone was predicting his demise, how he was going to collapse. That's why I jumped in and started running with him. It was more out of compassion than anything, to kind of urge him along. It was the most fantastic thing I'd ever seen."

For his part, Warren was weary, ready to end it. He'd been getting word of where Dunbar and Haller were, then calculating how fast they had to run to catch him. About 10 miles from the finish it finally got to the point where he could have walked in and still won. So the challenge faded. And he was a little irritable. A runner not connected with the race whom Warren didn't know, who was concerned, like McDermott, about Warren's condition, had started running with him. "Just don't run in front of me," Warren told him. With a big lead and what looked like a sure win he didn't want anyone to think he hadn't done it by himself.

So the man stayed behind, and other runners joined the first as they moved along the beach. A pack formed, and that frustrated the hell out of Warren's competitive instinct, which after a full day of competition was still racing. His instinct was to surge ahead and drop the whole bunch, or at least to push the pace hard enough so that they'd have to stop talking, but he was just too tired.

Finally it was over. Remembering a promise he'd made to Grundman when he'd borrowed his employees, Warren pulled a Nautilus T-shirt over his head for the big finish.

Finally it was over. Remembering a promise he'd made to Grundman when he'd borrowed his employees, Warren pulled a Nautilus T-shirt over his head for the big finish. The T-shirt was white, and so from a distance you could see him coming, listing. There was a crowd of perhaps 30 people standing in the rain under the Nautilus banner along Kalakaua Avenue. ("I had no idea why they were there," deadpanned McDermott.) They cheered and applauded when Warren crossed. His time was 11:15:56. Despite the terrible weather, he'd broken Haller's record by more than half an hour. He removed the shirt and the sweatband he'd been wearing, then sat for a while in the grass, talking with a reporter. Then he walked across the sand and down to the water by himself, his head low, his hands on his hips.

"Maybe I ought to take a swim," Warren thought. "Maybe a swim would feel good." But he didn't go in. He just stood there calf-deep in the water for a while.

McDermott: "He's such a . . . I don't know if egotist is the word, but he's so strong-minded he didn't want to fall over or collapse. It was important for him to stand up and look as good as he could. When the other guys crossed he wanted to be standing there fresh."

Another time that might have been true, for it was like Warren. This time, though, all he wanted was to get a shower, find something to eat and drink a beer, as many beers as he could. It had been a long day. "I felt kind of empty," Warren said, as if he'd beaten his family at Monopoly or something. Winning was terrific, having won was a bummer. But he knew he should stay, for the sake of sportsmanship, at least until second place arrived.

He waited 45 minutes, getting bored. The second finisher finally appeared. It was Dunbar. He was in pain, a too-hard bike ride having once again taken everything but the SEAL out of his legs. He was humbled, no longer a superman. Before they wrapped him in a blanket and carted him away, Warren asked him if he might be interested in going bar-hopping. At least Dunbar, who was dazed at the time and unable to respond, remembered it that way. So did McDermott. Warren, who has an accurate memory, doesn't. He was uncomfortable talking about the scene, as if he'd kind of removed it from his mind. Besides, Dunbar hadn't impressed him that much. Of all the people on the beach that morning, Warren had thought less of Dunbar's Superman outfit than anyone. To him it was a sign that Dunbar could be beaten. "It's like a boxer who smiles at you when he gets hit," Warren said. "Like maybe you should see how many times you can hit him to see how long you can keep him smiling?"

In any case, Warren didn't feel a need to say too much. He wasn't happy with the idea that he might have rubbed his victory in, even a little. "See," he said with that sly grin, "after I win a race, I really don't have a whole lot to prove, do I?"

He didn't. After Haller finished, in fourth place, then Lemaire in fifth, surviving a courageous cramp-filled marathon that had taken her an agonizing five hours and 10 minutes, Warren hitched a ride with McDermott over to the Nautilus Center on King Street, where he and the writer and Haller sat in a Jacuzzi for a couple of hours and talked. Finally, McDermott, convinced that neither man was going to admit to the other that he was ready to go off to bed, suggested they call it a night. So they stepped outside and he watched Warren wander off into the night, "cursed to win so that he will not lose, the bright-eyed mariner, all alone," McDermott wrote.

But not alone for long. Though neither man could know it, the warm, gentle rain that Warren walked through on the way back to his hotel was just the calm before another storm. Beneath the hissing sound of passing traffic on the shiny wet streets of Honolulu was the distant whirring of well-oiled chains and the thinner hiss of thinner tires. A new sport had been born. The high-tech Super Jocks were coming.

6

THE SURVIVORS —RUNNING THROUGH THE GATES OF HEAVEN

The race seems beyond comprehension. Forget the conditions; the distances are enough to kill you. Why would anyone want to do that to themselves?

The triathletes are not unaware of the general perception of their foolishness. Most got into the sport after thinking the same way. They read the article in *Sports Illustrated* back in 1979, or watched Julie Moss crawl across the finish line in 1982. "That's crazy," they thought, just like everyone else. "Those guys are nuts."

Still, there was something. The sport of triathlon intrigued them, and their gradual involvement escalated until the Ironman began to look like a more realistic goal. In fact, as the Ironman itself got bigger and more popular, and other, mostly shorter distance, triathlons began to spring up all over the world, doing the Ironman began to sound almost like a requirement, as much a necessity as having a bike or several pairs of running shoes. You're a triathlete? Have you done the Ironman? When are you gonna do the Ironman?

So they did the Ironman.

Not that some triathletes ever stop asking the question: "Why?" Mostly they ask it during the marathon, when the day has gotten longer and harder than they could ever have imagined. They ask the question of themselves—silently, rhetorically, not really expecting an answer. If you pressed them for something concrete, though, they'd probably take you to the Ironman finish line and simply point. It would clear up a lot.

It probably wouldn't surprise you that the triathletes who compete at the Ironman are all in terrific shape, well-defined and pared down to the bone after the long months of training. They're tanned and thin-skinned, tight as drums, and if their faces are a little weathered, their eyes are bright and their smiles wide and white. The young ones look ageless, the old ones look much younger than their years. They seem to have found a kind of eternal youth.

But while they may look alike, the competitors are different from one another in one important aspect: how they will approach the 140 miles of the race itself. By their third day in Kona they have seen what they're up against. They've felt the heat of the midday sun out on the highway; they've begun to acclimate to the oppressive humidity. Strategies have begun to take shape, formed with help from past experience or hearsay, or by a healthy dose of apprehension. There's bravado to spare at the Kailua Pier, but much of it is for show. The true confidence is quiet and restrained; the veterans have already put themselves into a trance of physical and emotional conservation. Everyone else is just faking it.

Basically, triathletes come to the Ironman for one of two reasons. Some—first-timers especially, even those who might have experienced a fair degree of success in shorter races—are simply looking to become a part of the experience. They have more questions than answers—about themselves as well as the competition. The smartest among them have embraced a single goal. Their hope is to get from the start to the finish in one piece. The speed at which they do that has little bearing on their own perception of success or failure. What you or I or anyone thinks is irrelevant.

Others actually race—against the clock, against their own expectations, against other athletes. Some hope to win the race itself, while others are looking for age-group awards or simply to improve a past performance. The true members of this group—not those fools whose dreams lie far beyond their actual capabilities—know that the Ironman distance is not the major obstacle. Given a certain pace, they have no doubt they can finish. The trick is to take the pace beyond that level of assurance and into the area of uncertainty.

In their approaches to the event, the Survivors and the Racers are distinctly different. There are overlaps, of course, and the motivations of both groups tend to converge toward the end of the race, congealed into a common lump of fatigue by the extreme conditions of the highway. But that comes later. Initially, they live and breathe in different worlds.

The Survivors' approach is the more sublime. While their single, tangible goal is the Ironman finish line, a vast realm of personal achievement and motivation lies before that. The Survivors come to Hawaii looking for something mystical, and they usually find it. One Japanese competitor in 1985 referred to the finish line as "the gates of Heaven." If that sounds a bit overly dramatic, it's not that extreme in context, nor is it visually far off the mark. Most Survivors finish in the deep dark—12, 14, 16 hours after the start of the event. Running down the final stretch of Alii Drive toward the pier, they make the final turn and find themselves squinting into the surrealistic glare of television lights mounted high above them on scaffolding. There are crowds of dimly lit, mostly unseen spectators lining the street, hands clapping in the dark, haloed heads obscuring the finish line itself, and the disembodied voice of the announcer booming out over it all. Usually the rush of adrenaline that comes in response to the crowd and the simple joy of being done with the ordeal fuels the triathletes' legs and they run faster than they have all day.

The Survivors' approach is the more sublime. While their single, tangible goal is the Ironman finish line, a vast realm of personal achievement and motivation lies before that. The Survivors come looking for something mystical, and they usually find it.

Dehydrated, light-headed, and often dealing with the pain of leg cramps or blistered feet, the Survivors are sucked magically to the end, into a world of achievement few even imagined existed. For most, it is indeed an experience that transcends the physical. The Ironman surpasses its reputation for misery, but it also surpasses its reputation for reward.

"I guess you could say it's the ultimate goal," a first-timer in 1985 named Wally Buckingham said. He'd been a well-known marathon and 10km runner for years back in San Diego. He began doing triathlons after he stopped seriously competing on the road in 1982, exploring whether there was, for him, life after running. The answer was a definite yes. At age 30, he became an age-group national champion in short-distance triathlons back on the mainland. But the Ironman was different.

"When I was doing short triathlons," Buckingham said, just before the 1985 race, "I looked at the Ironman and thought, 'That's insane. That's a long way to go. That's a 10-hour day, a *17-hour* day for some people.' I wasn't sure I was ready for it, or even if I wanted to do it. But it became more believable as I got deeper into the sport. This is it, the ultimate!"

For Buckingham it was the ultimate in more ways than one. When he finished that first year he was wasted; his time was an hour and a half slower than what he'd hoped for. He was shocked at how hard the race had turned out to be. Before they led him away to the massage area, all he could do was shake his head and say, "Man!" But he was glad that he had finished, happy to have qualified to return and try again in '86. The next day, responding to the question of whether the race was still the ultimate, he answered without hesitation: "You bet!"

In an article I wrote about the 1985 Ironman, I compared the race to the legendary quest for the Holy Grail, and I wasn't surprised that most of the competitors I talked with—even many of the top competitors—liked the comparison.

According to one of the most popular versions of the Grail legend, only the strongest and purest of King Arthur's knights could even hope to succeed in the Grail Quest. A knight's confidence that he was qualified—whether he was or wasn't in the end—was critical; it was in itself something of a reward. The fabled existence of the sacred chalice gave credibility and purpose to the entire concept of chivalry. It was a goal that validated an ideal.

The Ironman is a lot like that. Simply being able to say that you are training for the race is an achievement in itself. Being part of the pre-race action in Kona—arriving at the airport with your bike bag in tow, checking into a condo along Alii Drive, showing up for a swim at the pier in the morning—is like riding out over the drawbridge and off into the mists of the enchanted forest. You haven't slain a single dragon yet, but you're a knight, by God, and that's a start.

In a world in which many outwardly successful people often find themselves striving for ill-defined satisfactions, or achieving things they aren't quite sure they deserve, the Ironman can serve a Grail-like purpose. It's a heck of a lot simpler and more clearly defined than the day-in, day-out struggle to succeed in corporate America. No one is claiming that the Ironman is easy, but the path is refreshingly direct: swim, bike and run your brains out for the better part of a year, then fly to Hawaii and get from point A to point B on race day. The Ironman may seem at first glance to be a goal of Olympian proportions, impossible to achieve, but people do it every year. The obvious question arises: "Can *I* achieve it?" Sure enough, the Queen K highway is lined each October with ordinary people—Survivors—who were too intrigued by their own unwillingness to answer, "No, I could never."

Ordinariness is a trait common to the Survivors. Indeed, John Collins, who started the whole thing, describes himself as a barometer of the ordinary.

"I've been called the Jim Jones of the exercise movement," Collins says with a laugh. "Able to convince hundreds of people to go to a tropical setting and kill themselves. But you know what I really am? I am Mr. Average Man. I'm 50 years old now and whatever in hell I get inter-

In an article I wrote about the 1985 Ironman, I compared the race to the legendary quest for the Holy Grail, and I wasn't surprised that most of the competitors I talked with— even many of the top competitors—liked the comparison.

ested in, you better put your money there, because I'm right in the middle of any trend. It's kind of a humbling thing to think about, but it's been that way with everything."

But the ordinariness of the Survivors is only skin deep. True, they come from all walks of life. They are dentists and teachers and doctors and tree surgeons. Some have a long background in competitive athletics, some don't. You can pick up an Ironman program from any year and find ordinariness galore: computer programmers, interior decorators, fire captains, busboys, salesmen, pilots and engineers. That's just from a single page. But the element you can miss in the type—the obvious hidden in the forest of the obvious—is that each individual listed in the program not only has succumbed to the urge to tackle the Ironman, but has fleshed out the desire during the long months of training. Some, lucky to be well established in their own businesses, are able to integrate the time it takes to train into their lives with relative ease. The majority, however, as if the physical effort wasn't enough, must make drastic changes in their daily routines, changes that usually are not understood or even sympathized with by friends and family. The Ironman is a heroic challenge, but the commitment to complete the thing goes far beyond just one rather nasty day of competition. Whether the Survivors are heroes, fools or fanatics depends on your point of view, but at the very least they are not ordinary.

"I watched five minutes of the Ironman on TV in 1980," recalled Elliot Robinson, a retired real estate developer. "I remember saying to myself, 'These people are the craziest people to ever walk on the face of the earth.' I turned the set off. I thought it was some kind of put-on."

At the time, Robinson had been a runner for more than 15 years. He'd done several marathons, including Boston and New York. Three, four hours of competition was something he could imagine. Twelve, 13 or more was not.

"The idea that it was impossible," Robinson said, "that it was something no sane person would want to try to undertake, stayed with me for a long time. It's probably still with me!" He said this a week before his fifth Ironman.

"See," he said, laughing. "I said no sane person. That gives you an indication of how I feel about myself and the rest of my comrades."

Robinson was 50 years old at the time, but he looked 35. He is small, 5 feet 7 or 8 inches, 145 pounds, and he's hard as a rock. He once weighed 208 pounds, but he was drinking and smoking a lot then, living the good life while working for his father in the real estate and construction industry in Georgia. When he was 28 he was drunk one night and got involved in a barroom brawl. The next morning he dragged himself out of bed, stiff and sore, stared for a while into the bathroom mirror, and decided to change his life. He walked into his dad's office and quit. "No offense, dad," he said, "but this isn't working." He went off to dig ditches.

"I finally began to like myself," he said.

Robinson remembers the day he started running: July 4, 1965. The day before, an Army buddy of his, American middle-distance running great Jim Beatty, came to visit and asked Robinson if he wanted to run eight miles with him. "I can't run eight, but I'll run two," Robinson said. So he ran 200 yards and threw up. He was so embarrassed he embarked on his new program the next morning. Within a couple of years he was running four miles a day—for no other reason than to stay in shape.

Meanwhile, the ditches got deeper. He became a successful builder in his own right, and in 1975 he was able to sell the business at a great profit and move to Aspen, Colorado, effectively retired. In Aspen he began to run more seriously, and he did his first marathon in New York in 1978. He did the Ironman for the first time in October 1982, and he's never been the same. In 1985, thinking that he might be ready to live a normal life, "with a house and a car and a dining room," he went back to the South and bought a beautiful house on an island off the coast of Georgia. He lasted six months. Unable to relate to the lifestyle, to the people, he sold the house and the new furniture and moved back to Aspen. He now needs the company of his fellow athletes to be happy.

Triathlons are Robinson's life, with the Ironman the major focus. Financially secure, he can afford to train and travel when he wants, so he frequently does both, preferring, say, an early morning run in Paris to the Paris Opera. He comes to Kona each year in August, two months before race day, rents the same room in the same complex, and puts the finishing touches on his conditioning—swimming in the bay, riding along the Queen K, and running up and down Alii Drive with his regular Kona training partners.

Robinson has never won an award in Hawaii. The first time he did the race it took him 14 hours. He whittled that down to 11:54 in 1985. Going into the race in '86 he had five goals. The fifth was to place in the top five in the 50-54 age division. The fourth was to break 11:45 so he would automatically qualify to come back in '87. The third was to break 12 hours, the second to break 13. His first goal?

"My first goal," he said emphatically, "even though I've done the race four times, is to finish. The Ironman is such an awesome event, so unpredictable, that anywhere along the 140 miles it can bite you. I will be happy as long as I cross the finish line before midnight and I'm an Ironman."

❖

Robinson's devotion to, and respect for, the event is by no means unusual. It's reflected in most of the other competitors, and it certainly is reflected in the fascination so many nonathletic people have shown for the sport of triathlon. Why? And why the Ironman? After all, the sporting world is filled with outrageous physical challenges. There are many well-established endurance events in a variety of sports that require an equal amount of training and discipline. There are ultra-endurance running and cycling events, odd races in strange, faraway places throughout the world that might have captured the imagination of the public and the media the way Ironman has.

The Tour de France bicycle race, for instance, is certainly of Ironman proportions (and beyond). But like the

World Series or the Super Bowl, it is an elite event—the kind of thing we can only watch and fantasize about. Greg LeMond and Bernard Hinault are as remote from the average recreational, or even competitive, cyclist as movie stars; the likelihood of ever bumping up against them at a starting line is infinitesimal. But close contact with the stars is a fact of life in Hawaii. The sport of triathlon owes its existence to the concept of mass participation, and the Ironman, which is widely acknowledged by the athletes to be the sport's World Series, Super Bowl and Olympic Games all rolled into one, is so difficult for even the best that a bond of participation between the fastest and the slowest finisher is inevitable. Tinley and Scott and the Puntous sisters get their trophies, but their finishers' T-shirts are no different from the one worn by the accountant who stumbled across the line in sixteen hours.

At the other extreme are the famous ultra-endurance running races, such as the Western States 100-Mile Run. Many people perceive Western States to be an even bigger challenge than the Ironman. But while it is mass participation-oriented (or rather, average *competitor*-oriented—a "mass" of a thousand runners at Western States would not only be a logistical nightmare, it would send the old-timers snarling and swearing back into the woods, never to return), it's a low-profile affair, and most of the competitors would scratch and claw to keep it that way. Few other than friends and family members of the competitors participate as cheerleaders and spectators at the Western States, contrasted to the week-long hoopla that engulfs the entire town of Kailua-Kona at the Ironman. The rugged, inaccessible nature of the Western States route through the Sierra Nevada mountains has a lot to do with that, granted, but the rugged individualism of the runners contributes substantially. Ultramarathoners as a group are known to pride themselves on their quiet, carefully preserved eccentricity. Triathletes would rather train through the winter in front of a television set tuned up loud to MTV and then go shopping. No self-respecting ultrarunner would be caught dead in a pair of white Vaurnet sun-

"My first goal," Robinson said emphatically, "even though I've done the race four times, is to finish. The Ironman is such an awesome event, so unpredictable, that anywhere along the 140 miles it can bite you. I will be happy as long as I cross the finish line before midnight and I'm an Ironman."

glasses. No self-respecting triathlete would be caught *without* them—or something stylishly comparable.

"I think we triathletes laugh more," Elliot Robinson said simply.

That's a pretty accurate assessment. Not that the Ironman didn't have its share of grumbly old-timers who groused when the event began to grow up and lose its hard-core, seat-of-the-pants flavor. But from the beginning there was a more upbeat pace to the race than was ever seen in pure endurance running. Triathletes wore their egos a little farther down their sleeves, in plain sight. There was an undeniable hang-it-all-out, daredevil zaniness to the race even in 1978. You could have easily imagined that if a fourth event had been added—skydiving or bridge-jumping perhaps—everyone in the field might nod their heads, widen their wild eyes a little and go for it, grinning like fools all the way down.

Certainly one of the big original attractions of the Ironman, of triathlons generally, was the aura of both physical and technical excellence. Whereas the ideal in pure running had been the appearance of near emaciation, triathletes started talking about *total fitness*—and they looked as if they meant it. Between the swimming, cycling and running, with weight-training programs often thrown in for good measure, triathletes began to take on a classical appearance. The California look—bronzed and volleyball-ready at all times—spread as the sport did, and as the muscles sprouted, so did the style and technology. Triathletes started wearing clothing few other athletes would risk: wild, skin-hugging tights, tops, and "tri-suits" in fuchsia and Day-Glo blue, in stripes and polka dots and God knows what else; patterns that made the basic black shorts and white socks of traditional cycling look hopelessly stodgy. Speed through aerodynamics became all-important, so the need for the latest technology joined with the call for high fashion. Triathletes turned themselves into human Barbie dolls—new outfits and accessories sprouting at the drop of a credit card—with a gusto that reflected both their obvious desire to look like international caliber athletes and their generally impressive bank accounts. Not merely had the pursuit of the finish line become a Quest of Great Importance, but there was also a suit of armor to wear into battle. Even the survivors could look like heroes—going in, at least.

But before the style and the speed, before the race became a popular athletic goal, before Julie Moss sacrificed her body to the asphalt, something else about the race was working, something that was not so easy to identify. John Collins, Ordinary Man, insists the world was ready for the event, for the entire *sport* of triathlon.

"You had all these people who had gotten involved in the exercise movement," he said. "An awful lot of people like myself who were never, never going to be fast. First of all, you can't possibly run a mile, then you can *run* a mile, then you can run a mile faster, and at that point the selection is made of those who are truly fast—those who are willing to kill themselves for an extra second—from the rest of the world. Well, the rest of the world, if they're going to progress at all, if there's going to be hope, have to have some kind of goal. And the time was right for a goal that was not necessarily faster but which was longer and longer and longer. For the average person, the time was right for a person who gets better at three different things, than any one thing."

Considering the triathlon's tremendous growth, Collins is probably right. Good timing was a factor. But there is more to the Ironman than just a social impulse. More than likely its attraction lies in an intangible combination of factors that simply fit.

Perhaps most important of all, the Ironman is doable without a career investment in skill or experience. That's not to make light of the kind of training that's necessary, nor of the achievements of the top professional and age-group triathletes who race up and down the Queen K each year, shattering not just records but also long-held concepts of human physiological limits. The levels of performance that are required to excel at the Ironman are far beyond the reach of average people.

But the three events of the triathlon are at least familiar to average America. Triathletes learned to swim as children at camp or at the local YMCA, and getting along on two wheels was part of what being a kid was all about for most of them. And running? By the time word of the Ironman started to spread in 1980, *everybody* was running. The fact is, a majority of triathletes worldwide—Iron men or not—came into the sport from running. They were chronically injured or bored with weekly 10km, eager to take a step beyond the marathon.

The familiarity accomplishes two things: first, it allows the Baker family in Connecticut, sitting in their living room and watching ABC's coverage of the Ironman on television, to appreciate to some degree the effort required. Watching a team of climbers move up the north face of Mount Everest is exciting and dramatic, but who can appreciate what it feels like to lump along in the snow, one step at a time, at 21,000 feet? Who knows what it takes to ski jump 300 meters? You can't relate. But when you're talking in terms of a 112-mile bike ride, and then a marathon on top of that, well.... "My God, Bob," says Mrs. Baker, "I can't believe they *do* that!"

Second, the familiarity imparts a glimmer of possibility to the race, perhaps even a twinge of guilt here and there. Like most great accomplishments, the Ironman invites the Walter Mittys of the world to fantasize, but unlike most it offers a chance, just a chance.... It's likely that the first step in becoming an Ironman is at this very moment leaning against the back wall in the garage—a little rusty, perhaps, and it has only three speeds, but what the hell. It's unlikely there's an unlimited fuel dragster propped up back there, or a four-man bobsled.

In the end, though, the familiarity of the three events is not an attraction at all; it's merely the absence of a barrier. Few people can honestly look at the Ironman and say, "Gee, wouldn't it be *fun!*" What they say (or mean) is: "Wouldn't that be amazing!" Then the mental wheels start turning and the logical step to "I'll bet *I* can do that" is taken. Six words. The smart money is always bet against them ever coming to anything.

Clare St. Arnaud, for instance, wouldn't have fit most people's preconception of a triathlete when he flew off to Hawaii to do the Ironman for the first time in February 1982. He was a big, handsome man, a full-blooded Chippewa-Sioux Indian who lived on the Santee Reservation near the Niobrara River in northwestern Nebraska and worked as a farrier, a blacksmith. He wore his shiny black hair Indian-style, well below his shoulders and in a pony tail. Before he became a blacksmith he'd been a successful businessman, with two degrees from Mankato State University and a style of living that looked great but wasn't feeding anything but his own expanding girth. Like Elliot Robinson he was starving in the midst of plenty. So he took up running and moved back to the reservation. He ran marathons and ultramarathons. Then he read McDermott's story in *Sports Illustrated* and decided that the Ironman was worth a try.

St. Arnaud was a Survivor right from the start. He is six feet tall and weighed well over 200 pounds that first year—and he looked even bigger than that; he was built like a truck. There wasn't a chance he was going to *win* anything out there on the highway. His reward, outside of a finisher's medal and a T-shirt, would be knowing that he could go the distance.

The problem was St. Arnaud could barely swim a stroke. He lived far from the nearest pool or open body of water. There weren't too many miles of paved roads to cycle on where he lived, either. If you translated St. Arnaud's total experience in swimming, cycling and running into a list on a sheet of paper, then laid odds on whether he was going to make it to the Ironman finish line, you couldn't have found a drunk in all of Las Vegas who would give you a nickel for his chances. But St. Arnaud was confident. He figured that if he was man enough to shoe a mean horse, he ought to be able to swim a lousy 2.4 miles.

The cycling came quickly. In August 1981 he was sent as a tribal representative to a conference in Yakima, Washington. He brought along the big, heavy touring bike he'd just bought and stayed in the Northwest for two months to train, sleeping outdoors on a picnic table in a

... the familiarity imparts a glimmer of possibility to the race, perhaps even a twinge of guilt here and there. Like most great accomplishments, the Ironman invites the Walter Mittys of the world to fantasize, but unlike most it offers a chance, just a chance....

campground and running and riding through the mountains—10, 15, 20 miles a day on foot; 30, 40, 50 each day on his bike. By November he was in Arizona, near Tucson, for more training, sleeping outdoors again, shoeing horses when he could to keep his belly full. He even found a cycling coach. When he finally packed his bike in a box and flew off to Honolulu, he was in terrific shape—for a duathlon. He still couldn't swim and the race was less than five weeks away. He had $200 in his pocket and he didn't know where he was going to sleep.

Details like that had never bothered St. Arnaud. "I'll figure out something" was his motto. He's a friendly, articulate man. People sometimes didn't know what to make of him, but they always liked him, they always helped.

Sure enough, he almost immediately hooked up with a friend of a new friend and was invited to stay in Nanakuli, a community some 35 miles up the coast from Honolulu. The only way he could get there, of course, was on his bike, which was not a problem, but the only way he knew *how* to get there was on the highway, H-1, a full-blown, limited-access freeway—no pedestrians, bicycles, motor-driven scooters, etc. Could he make it there without being stopped?

No way. He was spotted by a state cop in Pearl City, just a few miles out.

"You must be *lost,* man," said the cop, a huge Samoan.

"Yeah, I am," St. Arnaud said, trying to sound contrite. "I'm trying to get to Nanakuli."

The cop eyed St. Arnaud's face and long hair. "You an Indian?" he asked.

"Yeah, I am," St. Arnaud said.

"You here to do the Ironman?" asked the cop.

"That's right, How'd you know?"

"'Cause only you crazy bastards would ride your bikes up here on H-1," said the cop, shaking his head. But he let St. Arnaud stay on the highway. He even gave him one of his cards and told him that if anyone stopped him along the way he should show them the card and tell them Sergeant So-and-so said that it was okay.

By the time St. Arnaud flew off to Kona for the race two weeks later he had compiled a long list of friends and supporters in Honolulu. He had even met a man who arranged a guest membership at the Outrigger Canoe Club at Waikiki. Not only did St. Arnaud get some help with his swimming at the club, he was able to eat for free as well. And he encountered the same kind of help in Kona—athletes who were willing to meet him at the pier and swim 400, 500 yards with him one day, then 800 or 1000 the next. "Everybody pitched in," St. Arnaud said. "I just kept plugging away." By race day he still wasn't fast, but he was strong. He started at the back of the pack and finally climbed out of Kailua Bay two hours, 39 minutes later, almost in last place.

But he was in good shape for the bike. He'd been riding long and hard every day for the previous six months, up and down every mountain he could find. He was as strong as a bull. Unfortunately, the man who had put together the new, sophisticated bike St. Arnaud had been lent by a bike shop in Santa Barbara (which is another story entirely), hadn't glued the tires properly. St. Arnaud kept spinning the tires off the rims—six in all. Luckily, he wasn't hurt. Having a tire come off and then jam between the brakes and the wheel is a great way to put a dent in your head, but he spent hours sitting by the side of the road trying to put things back together. He didn't start his marathon until after eight o'clock that night, and he didn't finish the race itself almost two o'clock in the morning. Most of the spectators were gone, of course, but the banner was still up, the announcer was still on the mike, and a handful of St. Arnaud's new friends were standing there clapping and cheering.

"It was great, I'll tell you," St. Arnaud said. "It was fantastic, the best finish I ever had."

In the years following that race, St. Arnaud became an Ironman regular, missing only the race in 1983. His best time was the 13:41, in '85, but that was just a cruise, a warm-up. Two months later he was one of 50 or so competitors in an event called the Big Island Ultraman triathlon. The Ultraman featured distances twice those of the Ironman, stretched out over three days. It began with a six-mile swim and a 90-mile bike ride. Day two involved a 160-mile ride, day three called for a 52.4-mile run.

"The Ironman is too fast for me," St. Arnaud said. "Too stressful, too. It's too hectic. Psychologically you don't get time to change gears. I mean, it takes an incredible effort to swim six miles and bike 90 miles up the volcano on the first day, but at least you get to change gears."

To each his own.

❖

Beyond the fact that the Ironman seems to have bounced along at the right time, incorporating three of the most recognizable recreational icons the world has ever known, the race has also been blessed with a tremendous amount of visibility. The media have been excited from the beginning. Then again, the media have been excited at times about figure-eight demolition derbies and motorcycle racing on ice, as well. If there's a difference it might be that in the Ironman the attention has been rewarded by real and consistent drama. The Ironman has been lucky. By and large, ordinary athletes chosen for special attention by newspapers, magazines and television have been fascinating characters, articulate and sensitive. The Ironman has been "discovered" time and time again, sucking ordinarily dispassionate reporters into an emotional involvement that often left them sounding (and writing or editing) like public relations professionals.

"I couldn't get over Tom Warren," Barry McDermott said. "I became intrigued with the guy. I just thought he was the neatest guy I'd ever met. I was so impressed with his physical output, what he could do.

"If the little elements of the story hadn't fit the way they did—if Warren wasn't the character that he was, if Dunbar and Haller weren't the young guys that were going to fight it out, and then Warren comes in and beats 'em— maybe there wouldn't be a story in *Sports Illustrated*. Maybe

I would have gone there and maybe a Scott Molina type would have won, and it wouldn't have been any big deal. When these guys finish now, sure they're tired, but I don't think it's a life-threatening situation, like it appeared to be back then."

What McDermott started, ABC expanded, beaming their coverage of the race worldwide and causing interest and participation to soar. Three times as many triathletes entered the race in February 1981 as had entered the previous year, and the field almost doubled again in February '82, the race in which Julie Moss ran most of the final mile on the verge of collapse.

Despite its obvious positive effect on the visibility of the sport, ABC's annual coverage of the Ironman has caused many triathlon insiders to bristle. Top triathletes, who would have liked to have seen the race covered as a bona fide athletic event, the way the network covered baseball or even golf, instead of as some odd, masochistic ritual, are especially critical. The ABC productions are snidely referred to as "puke-and-crawl shows." They reached their depth—and the height of triathlete scorn—with the melodramatic coverage of Millie Brown, a 48-year-old suburban housewife from Connecticut who seemed marginally trained (at best) for the '83 race, and whose agony during the competition seemed magnified significantly for the cameras. Brown wobbled through the bike ride, then stumbled embarrassingly through the marathon, collapsing at almost predictable intervals until she finally crossed the finish line just short of the 17-hour cutoff.

The following year, ABC produced a made-for-television movie about the Ironman. It featured Penny Marshall playing the role of a previously unathletic housewife who not only trains for the Ironman but actually wins the race, crawling to the finish line in a scene reminiscent of Moss's finish in '82. The story was broadly drawn for the mass audience, of course, and not very accurately portrayed, despite the use of Moss and Dave Scott as extras. Triathletes as a group were embarrassed by the production. When Moss was asked during the filming to outline

"I couldn't get over Tom Warren," Barry McDermott said. "I became intrigued with the guy. I just thought he was the neatest guy I'd ever met. I was so impressed with his physical output, what he could do."

the plot, she described it with eye-rolling sarcasm as "The Millie Moss Story."

The coverage of Brown at the 1983 race was probably the best example of ABC's continuing confusion over what the Ironman and the Ironman competitor represented. Even as the broadcasts were trying to tell the story of the average triathlete, they were missing the thrust of the average effort. Contrary to what the Millie Brown story suggested, real middle-of-the-pack triathletes at the Ironman were highly motivated, well-trained and put a lot of thought into their races. Most of them suffered at some point, certainly, but they did so quietly, with dignity, trying at all times to make the most of their situation. In its grasp for human interest, ABC consistently reached too far; in doing so they missed both the intensely athletic nature of the Ironman and most of its real heroes.

But if the triathletes were critical of the coverage, it seemed to work for the mass television audience, who saw it simply for what it was: an attempt to show ordinary people doing extraordinary things. The ABC coverage made it clear, if at times clumsily, that the Ironman was a race not just for high-level competitors but for Survivors, too. Not only did it make their struggles public, make them seem heroic, the broadcasts actually suggested the possibility that certain members of the audience could one day find themselves in the middle of the action. It was like walking out of a movie theater after watching *Top Gun* and being picked on the spot by a man in a leather jacket and a pair of aviator sunglasses standing in front of an F-14 fighter. "You there," he'd say, poking a finger into the middle of your chest. "You've got what we're looking for. Climb in."

A lot of people, like Clare St. Arnaud, did just that, naïve but also incredibly willing. For a couple of years the only requirements for entry into the Ironman were that you could afford the $80 entry fee (now $100) and get your body and bike to Kona in time for the race. The veneer of athletic refinement was thin; the gates of the asylum stood open. Competitors were cautioned in the literature they received from the Ironman office to train themselves adequately—and most of them did—but who was going to check?

A 73-year-old laborer named Walter Stack took more than 26 hours to finish the race in 1981. It was a record. Stack had already achieved a measure of fame in the running world as a profane, beer-guzzling marathoner who trained with his chest bared through the worst of his hometown San Francisco's cold, foggy winters. A long-time member of that city's Dolphin Club, Stack took delight in his daily swims in frigid San Francisco Bay. He was another of Collins's professional characters. Before he crossed the Ironman finish line on Sunday morning that year, he made a point of stopping for breakfast at the Kona Ranch House.

But if Stack paraded his goofy lack of triathlon expertise publicly and rather joyfully, thumbing his nose at whatever conventions were available, there were dozens of people who came to Hawaii with even less of a background than he had, and either completed the course or dropped out in total anonymity.

By early 1982, triathlon was no longer just a California sport. Julie Moss and ABC had seen to that. The race was moved to October to allow triathletes from all over the world to train for the Ironman in warm weather, and the increased demand for race numbers became immediately apparent: the 850-person quota for the first October race in '82 was quickly met and then surpassed. For the first time, the Ironman actually turned away competitors. By 1984, the toughest triathlon competition of the year was not racing in the Ironman, but simply getting to the starting line through the lottery; despite the fact that the field had been enlarged to 1000, only a third of the people who applied were accepted, and security procedures to protect against numbers being sold or traded were well-defined and strictly enforced. It was a situation that boggled the minds of guys like Collins, Warren and McDermott, none of whom could imagine the insanity of those first couple of races on Oahu being emulated on such a broad scale.

That first October race in '82 also saw the introduction of cutoff times for the swim, bike and overall finish. Race director Silk levied the restrictions reluctantly, realizing that the times would automatically eliminate some of the race's favorite characters. However, she knew that safety and logistical realities made them a must. That year triathletes had two-and-a-half hours to complete the swim (later dropped to two hours, then extended to 2:15); 11:30 hours to be off the bike (later 10:30 hours) and 18:30 hours for the entire race (now 17 hours). If it took you longer than any of those times, you were history. Walt Stack's record was safe for all time.

Additionally, qualifying times for Ironman competitors who hoped to return the following year (and thereby avoid the lottery procedure) were established by age group and based on a cross-section of previous performances. As the race became more competitive, those times plummeted, and the fight for age group awards became increasingly fierce.

"I'm 50 years old and I have to do an 11:45 to qualify for next year," Robinson said. "Eleven forty-five! A few years ago a person over fifty had to do only 14 hours."

Eleven forty-five. Gordon Haller won the first Ironman in 1978 with an 11:46.

But while they took some of the unrefined flavor away from the event, the standards increased its stature and only added to the Ironman's grass-roots appeal. It was now an elite race, closer than it had ever been to being, as it claimed, a "world championship." And still, the lottery still presented the wild card possibility of a triathlon novice stepping into the water on race day. The chances weren't good; of the 1000 starters in 1986, only 150 of the 4000 people who had applied had gotten in through the draw—but at least it was a chance.

The mix of elite athletes and wild, sometimes unrealistic dreamers is not unique to the Ironman field, but it is rare, and is surely one of the factors that has allowed the race to retain its emotional clout. Each year brings more pressure on the race to eliminate the lottery, to remove the Ironman completely from the list of life's long shots. But the pressure comes mostly from triathletes who have forgotten what it feels like to cross the finish line for the first time. They should somehow be reminded. It has become too easy for some of them to answer the question: "Why?" They have too many tangible answers to a question whose answer should never make absolute sense.

The Racers at the Ironman set standards that stretch the boundaries of physiological credibility. Their contributions are recorded, engraved, typeset, photographed and filed. The contributions of the Survivors are less tangible, but who can say which contribution is more valuable?

7

THE RACERS —WALKING THE THIN LINE OF SURVIVAL

You could have gotten a feel for where the Ironman was heading when John Dunbar showed up at Kapiolani Park on the morning of February 14, 1979, wearing his Superman outfit and publicly challenging Gordon Haller to a one-on-one duel in the raging Pacific Ocean. So much for item number two on the information sheet that Commander John Collins had distributed to all the competitors: "This event should be considered a personal challenge as opposed to a competition. The purpose is to finish without personal injury and without disruption or inconvenience to the public."

Unfortunately for Dunbar, he was trying to pull a psyche job on Haller when he should have been worried about Tom Warren. To Warren, the Ironman *was* a competition, and his one regret to this day about his experience that year is that it wasn't a closer race. Over the last 10 miles of the run he was tired and sore, but he was mostly bored.

But Dunbar had made the point. Like Warren, he was on the beach that morning to *race*. The distance had been already covered the previous year—and he and Haller had raced that one, too. He was among a handful of people in all the world who knew they could get through 140 miles of continuous swimming, biking and running and live to talk about it. The thing now was to win. To go faster. To race the sucker right to the end.

Which wasn't all that big of a shock to Collins. He wasn't as poor a judge of human character as item number two might lead you to believe. He knew as well as anyone that if you put two people on a starting line, one of them was going to have to win—and probably both of them would want to. Collins was merely being cautious. He didn't want to have to take the blame for the death of some poor fool whose competitive instincts overcame his need to survive. If Collins was guilty of anything, it was of underestimating the resilience of the human body. He can easily be forgiven for that, since no one at the time could have imagined how far the Ironman would go in coaxing athletes to extend their physical limits.

As the sport grew and financial opportunities began to present themselves to the triathletes who emerged as stars—most notably Scott Tinley, Dave Scott, Scott Molina and Mark Allen—the physical horizons expanded. More accurately, they exploded. The "Big Four" carved a niche in the world of professional athletics despite a raft of scientific opinion that said triathlons were not the kind of events that could be raced and recovered from with a frequency that would pay anyone's rent for more than a month or two.

Molina, who has a knack for cutting to the core of an issue, said in 1983, "I think money is a big factor in being able to recover."

Within five years of Warren's Ironman victory on Oahu, Molina and Tinley, undisputed leaders of the endurance parade, were racing two dozen times a year, on several continents, raking in prize money and performance bonuses, sponsorship fees and endorsements—all of which spurred them to train more and harder so they could continue to race. By 1985, both men were making a reported six figures a year—counting prize money and endorsements—and they were training 40, 50 hours a week, not having let up for a minute since both had participated in their first professional races back in 1982.

Both men trained with recovery in mind, which meant long mileage and carefully parceled intensity that incorporated even long races right into the training schedule. In 1985, Molina estimated he spent approximately 20 hours a week not involved directly in some aspect of his triathlon training. An average week for both men included 20,000 to 25,000 yards of swimming, 60 to 70 miles of running, and 400 to 500 miles a week on the bike. And while the pace of the mileage varied slightly at certain times, the time spent training was consistent year-round, for both men agreed that it was only through consistent training that they would continue to improve.

And they did improve. Not only did they get faster in all three events, but they got faster in the way most important to a triathlete: Each succeeding year, they could push the bike harder, then come off the bike and run harder. What had been in 1982 a wobbly 6:45 a mile pace after a 23 mph bike ride was in 1985 a strong 5:45 pace after a ride five miles an hour faster.

The rest of the sport had no choice but to chase them. Allen and Scott, who raced less frequently than did Tinley and Molina, were with them from the beginning when it came to competitive performance, but it took a few years for everyone else to get the point. By the time they did, the definitions of "good" and "fast" at ultradistance triathlons like the Ironman had been pushed out of sight.

Anyone who has not seen the event close up cannot understand how hard the top triathletes race in Hawaii. The level of effort is sometimes a source of amazement to the athletes themselves. In order to stay with their competition, or simply in response to their own sense of pace, they push through the swim and the bike ride with ferocious intensity, often at or near levels of top performance in both individual sports. How aware they are of the consequences of that speed depends on several factors: experience or lack thereof, blind faith, stupidity or a kamikaze-

Dunbar was among a handful of people in all the world who knew they could get through 140 miles of continuous swimming, biking and running and live to talk about it. The thing now was to win. To go faster. To race the sucker right to the end.

like neglect for their own well-being. Regardless of what drives the competitors, the goal is the parking lot of the Kona Surf Hotel at the base of Alii Drive, the start of the marathon. That's where the race begins, really, and while the pace during the third event is nowhere near the elite standards of pure running, the conditions during the marathon combined with what has gone before make the six-minute miles of the best triathletes seem inconceivable.

The pace of the competition can be mind-boggling. Watching it is an experience in itself, but being involved in it, especially when the level of competitive intensity is just slightly over your head, is another thing entirely.

Chris Hinshaw was just 21 years old when he placed second to Tinley in the 1985 race. He came back to Hawaii the next year as one of the favorites. The difference in 1986, however, was that the field was packed more tightly with talent than it had ever been. Prize money was being offered to the Ironman professional field for the first time, and Hinshaw had not only Tinley to deal with but an out-of-retirement Dave Scott and Mark Allen as well, along with several top Europeans.

Hinshaw is one of the best swimmers in the sport. He was out of the water in second place, a couple of minutes behind his brother Brad. Soon he was among a group of four—Scott, Allen, and Rob Barel from Holland—chasing the leader. The question was not whether they would catch him, but when. The question for Hinshaw was how long he could stay with the group. He was hanging on for dear life.

"I was going way too fast," he said, just minutes after he finished the race. "I got so *nervous*. I couldn't set my own pace. Everybody was going so *fast!*"

Hinshaw belongs to a family of triathletes—father, mother, brother, and sister. They are a happy, tight-knit group, and the closeness is reflected in the kind of fresh-faced, all-American gee-whiz excitement that Hinshaw brings to almost everything he does. He was caught up in his story now, his face animated.

"I did a five-oh-three and came off [the bike] *eighth!* And I was second out of the water! I just panicked out there! It was insane!"

Five-oh-three. That's five hours, three minutes for 112 miles. The first 25 miles had taken Hinshaw 58 minutes. And he had lost seven places.

Rarely have top competitors from any of the three individual sports entered the race and dominated in their specialty. There have been those who tried, like Curt Alitz in 1984, but their predictable failure to comprehend the scope of the Ironman effort has always led them to join the parade of shuffling also-rans during the marathon. Their participation has merely confirmed that the top triathletes are on top for the best reason of all: they're good; they are among the best conditioned, most talented athletes in the world.

For a number of years the course record for the 2.4-mile Ironman swim was 47 minutes, 48 seconds. It was held by Djan Madruga of Brazil, a three-time member of the Brazilian Olympic team who competed in the United States for Indiana University. Madruga won an Olympic bronze medal in the 400-meter freestyle in Montreal in 1976, and was a finalist in Moscow and Los Angeles.

It was after the close of his Olympic career in 1984 that he set his Ironman course swimming record. He'd been competing successfully in triathlons for several seasons, and he was a more than respectable cyclist. His running was a big problem, though. He came off the bike in '84 within 30 minutes of the leaders, but he wound up in 126th place, having all but staggered through the marathon in 4:47:04.

The point is that Madruga, for all his experience and success as a distance swimmer, and despite being so recently in peak condition for the Olympic Games, did not overwhelm the Ironman field in 1984. Hinshaw, who would finish the day in eighth place, was less than a minute and a half behind him after the swim. Two other top men, Dave Scott, on his way to a record fourth win, and Mark Allen, who ended up fifth, were less than three minutes back.

(Madruga's record was broken in 1986 by Brad Hinshaw, Chris's brother, who suffered a Madruga-like fate when he finished the bike ride in good shape, then dropped to 179th with a 4:48 marathon. His time for the swim was 47:39.)

As Chris Hinshaw's experience indicates, the level of expertise on the bike is as high as on the swim. It's the portion of the Ironman that has profited most from the growing experience and technological awareness of triathletes. In 1979 Tom Warren rode the Oahu course in a T-shirt, cycling shorts, socks and a borrowed pair of cycling shoes—on a piece of equipment that would look right at home leaning against your neighbor's back porch. The state of the art at the time had more to do with an athlete's state of mind than with lightweight aluminum frames and aerodynamic wheels.

Things were a bit more sophisticated the next year, but not much; there were still athletes hoping to place well whose bikes had nylon touring bags hanging over their front wheels. One entrant did the race on a bike that had a plastic radio mounted on the handlebars and solid, puncture-proof tires. He was afraid that if he got a flat with regular tires, he wouldn't be able to fix it. Even Dave Scott's effort was rudimentary. His equipment was better than Warren's, but his technique was raw; he looks at photos of himself on the bike that year and just laughs.

But the third-place effort of John Howard drew a lot of attention. It was a revolution of sorts, although it took Howard's win the following year to hammer the point home.

Howard at the time was just coming off a 10-year reign as America's top road-racing cyclist; in the years before John Boyer and Greg LeMond, he was the flagship athlete of America's underfunded and overlooked competitive cycling fleet. Four times a U. S. National Road Race champion between 1968 and 1975, Howard became the first American to win a gold medal in cycling at the 1971 Pan American Games. Five years later he made his third U.S. Olympic cycling team, a record. He considered a bid for a fourth in 1980, but rejected it. He had heard about the Ironman and thought he'd take a chance.

"I thought I could do well in it," Howard said. "I had an attitude that I would win the race as a cyclist. I was totally wrong, but I didn't *know*. It was a humbling experience, a rude awakening."

Howard was a dismal swimmer and not much of a runner, especially in 1980. He nearly drowned during the swim that year, despite the fact that it was held in the placid Ala Moana Basin instead of the ocean, a spot so calm and shallow that 61-year-old John "The Incredible Huck" Huckaby walked most of the way in 2:41. It took Howard a little under two hours to swim it.

He was much improved when the race moved to the Big Island in 1981. He still wasn't great, but he dropped his swim time 30 minutes, which meant that when he climbed out of Kailua Bay the leaders were out of sight but not out of reach. And the rolling hills of the new course were a prescription for Howard's success. Hunched low in the saddle of his red and black Raleigh, his eyes fierce and his long, gnarled fingers draped crab-like over the brake hoods, he flew past the other cyclists as if he'd been shot off the pier by a cannon. He took over first place at around the halfway mark of the bike ride, then ran a 3:23 marathon to win by almost a half hour, just about the length of time by which he had outridden Warren (who placed second) and Scott Tinley (who was third). A new era had begun: the second event of the Ironman was no longer a bike ride; it was a bike *race*.

Howard, a native Texan whose involvement in triathlons brought him to live in the San Diego area, is one of the more remarkable figures in American sports history. A pioneer in American competitive cycling, he was committed to competition wherever and whenever he could find it. He had a cyclist's fascination for speed—he raced motorcycles and cars as well as bikes—but he was also emotionally intrigued with endurance events, which he approached with as much intellectual curiosity as physical preparation. In 1983 he placed second to Lon Haldeman in the first Race Across America. Two years later he set a world land-speed record for human powered vehicles, racing across the Bonneville Salt Flats on a specially designed bicycle at a speed of 152 miles an hour. During the trials leading up to the attempt, Howard set another, unofficial, record of sorts; he had a flat tire at 151 mph but managed to keep the bike from going down.

The pace of the competition can be mind-boggling. Watching it is an experience in itself, but being involved in it, especially when the level of competitive intensity is just slightly over your head, is another thing entirely.

Howard wears the scars of many of his physical achievements, and he seems always to be adding more. As gentle and soft-spoken a man as he is in a social context, he has a fierce, dare-devilish competitive nature that lets him make an instant choice between his body's safety and a chance to win or improve his position in a race. During the Race Across America in 1983, he lost 10 hours to the other three men in the field on the first day of the ride when he became dehydrated in the California desert. He was advised to quit, but he climbed back on his bike and didn't get off again until he rode into Texas, by which time he was in second place. During the final stages of the ride, he was gaining a lot of ground on the winner, Lon Haldeman, but he couldn't gain it fast enough to make up the early deficit.

Howard was 33 when he won the Ironman. In Dave Scott's absence he'd been heavily favored, although what few people realized at the time was that he was suffering from a tendon injury to his right foot. He almost didn't race.

"It was severe, " he said. "It was so bad I couldn't run at all a week before the race—could barely walk."

He went to a doctor in Kona, who took a look and told him the only thing that was going to cure the injury was rest.

"Great," Howard said, "but I need to be able to run. I've got a good chance to win this race."

"Well, the only thing we can do under the circumstances," the doctor said, "is to use cortisone."

Over the next six days Howard had some 50 injections of cortisone, and treated the foot with ice, five or six times every day.

"It worked," said Howard, whose marathon time that year was the seventh fastest in the field. "I got through it, but I couldn't walk the day after the race. You could still see the needle marks six months later. I don't think I could ever do that to my body again. But at the time it was either that or not race."

It was appropriate that Howard needed to take that kind of chance to win the Ironman. It's not a chance that most born and bred triathletes, whose competitive philosophies

are more rooted in fitness than in win-at-all-cost reckless-
ness, would take. The only top-caliber cyclist to venture
into triathlons and succeed, Howard is rare, too, in that he
moves easily between the world of endurance and the
world of speed. It's a change that requires as much philosophical adjustment as physical. It gives him a unique perspective on the sport of triathlon.

He refers to bicycle racing as a contact sport. His knees
and elbows, which are masses of scar tissue from countless
crashes during competition, are a testament to the accuracy of his description.

"Most of the triathletes I know," he said, "wouldn't be
very good at bike racing. The feeling of going fast and mix-
ing it up with another rider, or riders, is a feeling that I
don't think many triathletes could be comfortable with. It
isn't the same mind-set at all. The British Formula-One
driver Mike Parks once said that bicycle racers would make
excellent Formula One drivers because they have the same
mentality—of aggressiveness."

The difference lies in the way triathlons are conducted.
Triathletes compete in what is known as a time-trial format: one rider alone, against the clock. Triathletes come
out of the swim and take off on their bikes as soon as they
can throw on a pair of shoes, but they are required to ride
alone. Triathlon rules say they must maintain a minimum
distance from other riders. Since the main obstacle to a
cyclist's progress is wind resistance, riding in the lee of
another competitor, a practice called drafting, is not only
helpful in terms of speed but it also conserves energy.
That's an important concern in a triathlon because fresh
legs on the run can mean the difference between a win and
10th place—or worse.

At the Ironman in October 1982, when charges that certain athletes had drafted were being thrown around like
confetti, one long-time cyclist who was serving as a bike
mechanic said that a triathlete who drafted consistently
throughout the 112-mile ride could save 45 minutes. "And
that's not counting the wear and tear they'd save on their
legs, " he said.

No issue in the sport has caused as much bitterness and controversy over the years as drafting. The problem has been aggravated at the Ironman by a consistent softness in the definition of rules and enforcement procedures. Julie Leach's win in 1982 was bitterly protested by many of the other women, several of whom had been accused themselves. All the protests that year were disallowed, but the tide was hardly stemmed. Each subsequent year brought new protests and new controversies as the level of skill among the top triathletes escalated, and as the sport as a whole became more widely recognized and prestigious. The prevailing philosophy among some of the competitors seemed to be to take whatever they could get away with. Since the Ironman officials never seemed sure of what they were trying to prevent, the athletes usually got away with a lot. "We don't think anyone out there is actually trying to *cheat*," said marshals coordinator Dennis Haserot in 1986, a statement that reflected a tragic level of naiveté, especially in a year when $100,000 in prize money was on the line.

Unfortunately, the Ironman could not look to the sport of cycling for guidance. Not many pure cyclists ever have to deal with the problem for the simple reason that time-trialing is not the most popular form of bicycle racing. In Europe, road racing is king, a format in which pack riding, teamwork and drafting are essential elements. In the United States, the preferred format is criterium racing, where cyclists ride multiple laps around a short, closed course. Packs and teamwork are essential here as well, and criterium racing in particular is both exciting and dangerous. As Howard suggested when he talked about cycling being a "contact sport," criterium riders use their knees and elbows almost as effectively as basketball players. You can be safe or fast in a criterium, but it's very hard to find a middle ground.

While there is a strong element of endurance to pure cycling, the focus is more on the volatile nature of the competition, the split-second shifts from a relatively pedestrian pace into sprints or high-speed drives that simply can't be sustained for long periods of time. "I don't think," said Howard, "that I've ever gone so deeply into anaerobic debt as I have in a bike race."

By contrast, the fierceness of the triathlete must be controlled at all times, tempered and sustained, even in short-distance triathlons, but especially in the Ironman. Responses to the competition must be measured carefully. Usually it's the triathlete with the best sense of himself who wins the race, not the one who continually breaks concentration to respond to someone else. "A time trial requires concentration," Howard said. "You can't let your attention lapse at all. Noncyclists frequently ask me questions like 'What do you think about?' That's almost a silly question because anyone who has ever done a ride like the Ironman knows that your mind is totally engrossed in the ride the entire time. To lose focus is to lose time; it's that simple."

The biggest difference, of course, comes in the area of training. Cyclists are sprinters, relatively speaking, and train that way, while triathletes are in for the long haul—mentally and physically.

"Bike racers hardly ever train hard alone," Howard explained. "They seem to gravitate more toward competitions. That doesn't lend itself well to time-trialing, which has always been looked down on in this country because it isn't pure wheel-to-wheel competition. Most bicycle racers are not good time-trialists. Their idea of hard training is to go out and do a race, whereas triathletes are concentrating on a pure time-trialing activity, focusing on that one event, going fast for long distances."

❖

The first few years Howard did the Ironman there was no one even close to his ability on the bike. He was 35 minutes faster than Dave Scott in '80; 34 faster than Warren in '81—although he did notice that year that some of the competitors had taken the hint. They'd smoothed off some of the rough edges.

"So tell us, Scott, what was the difference in your performance this year from last?" asked ABC's Jim Lampley, who had almost had to strong-arm Tinley into standing in front of the camera for an interview. Tinley was upset at ABC for having been a distraction during the race.
"I learned how to ride a bike," Tinley said curtly.

"There were a few skin suits, more serious equipment," he said. Then he laughed. "They'd taken the...the *racks* off the bicycles."

Next to Dave Scott, Tinley was Howard's most serious student. Howard wasn't formally teaching anyone, but they were watching him like hawks. Tinley, especially, had a lot of room for improvement—he'd placed third in '81 riding a touring bike that weighed about as much as a Volkswagen. He was back the next year on a green Bianchi racer. He'd removed the tool kit from beneath his back seat, and he'd trained a lot more. On race day, panicked by what he thought was a slow swim (actually the entire field was slow on a rough, choppy course that measured long), he threw both caution and his pre-race strategy to the winds and hammered off wildly toward Hawi in pursuit of the leaders. On the same course that Howard—Olympian, Pan American Games gold medalist, *legend,* for God's sake—had ridden a 5:03:29, Tinley clocked in at 5:05:11.

"So tell us, Scott, what was the difference in your performance this year from last?" asked ABC's Jim Lampley, who had almost had to strong-arm Tinley into standing in front of the camera for an interview. Tinley was upset at ABC for having been a distraction during the race.

"I learned how to ride a bike," Tinley said curtly. He then turned and walked away, leaving Lampley standing there with his microphone and his forced smile, egg dripping from his face onto the lapels of his "Wide World of Sports" blazer. Lampley thought Tinley was a jerk. Tinley returned the sentiment, unaware at the time of the value of national television exposure. He would be later, but by that time the triathlon spotlight was pointed at someone else.

As undiplomatic as Tinley's response was, however, it was an accurate assessment of what had made him the Ironman champion. If anything it was an understatement, considering that he had taken 42 minutes off his 1981 time in that one segment alone. An improvement of such magnitude has much more behind it than just better equipment and stronger legs. Tinley's reckless abandon on the ride, spurred by his concern over being left out of the action after the swim, was a revelation, a mutation in the evolution of the Ironman. It told Tinley and everyone else that there was life out there on the highway after a red-line bike ride. Sure, the Ironman could eat you alive, but you could press the limits much closer than anyone had thought. John Howard's performance was no fluke. Nor was Howard's ability on the bike something of impossible proportions.

Future races supported that conclusion. The bicycle course record at the Ironman continued to drop: Tinley went 5:02 in '83. In '84 Allen became the first man to break five hours when he came off the bike in first place with a 4:59:21, but 14 minutes later Howard took the record back. His 4:56:49 had taken him from about three-millionth place after the swim into third. Unfortunately for both men, the fast times were recorded at terrible expense. On a day of record heat, a dehydrated Howard wobbled through the marathon and finished sixth. Allen, feeling even worse, blew a 12-minute lead and ended up in fifth.

Twelve months later it was Tinley's turn again, and the rapid advance in Ironman technology and philosophy was strikingly evident. Riding an eye-catching, state-of-the-art bicycle equipped with aerodynamic handlebars and cage-less pedals, he broke Howard's mark with a 4:54:07. Chris Hinshaw had come off the bike several minutes before him with a 4:57:50. The following year there were eight men under five hours and Dave Scott yanked the course record down to 4:48.

"It's a bike race," Howard said. "I go pretty much flat out. You can't afford to lose a second. I think the really fit athletes in Hawaii all do the ride as fast as they can do it. I don't think they could go much faster if they were doing just that event. And that's really amazing, because *they've got a marathon to run!* I think that sheds some light on how fit these people are. They are *masters* of cardiovascular endurance."

The sum of distance plus speed can add up to spectacular failure. Not even success feels all that terrific. Tinley once compared the anticipation of doing another Ironman to looking forward to being in a car wreck—with the memory of a previous wreck fresh in his mind. Allen, who has a reputation for being able to handle pain, called the Ironman "the limit of sanity" in 1984.

The triathletes who race at the Ironman play a frightening game with themselves and their abilities. They play the distance and the conditions of the event off against a certain calculated level of effort—calculated, of course, to fall just short of reality. Like a jet plane flying 3000 miles with fuel enough for 2999, the best athletes leave themselves little room for error. "I know I can get that far going like this. I'll worry about getting from there to there when I get there." That kind of thinking draws a thin line between success and failure, especially if the competition during the ride has been close, or the conditions especially harsh. And the competition is always close, because you never know if the guy out in front is there because he's really that good or because he's a fool; you never know if the guy behind you is just waiting for the right time to start coming hard after you. In an event that requires nine hours of competition in three sports, errors are always made. The race almost never goes as planned.

❖

In 1985, Scott Tinley came to Hawaii hoping for an "easy" win. He'd had a long season, with triathlons almost every week for the previous six months. Two of those had been races of Ironman length, one as recently as September. He'd finished that one with what he called a "comfortable" 2:45 marathon.

But beyond the sheer volume of racing, he'd been beaten up badly three weeks before at the Nice Triathlon. He'd taken two hard falls on the technically difficult downhill part of the bike course, and then been forced to run 20 miles in under two hours to take second place to Allen. Back home in San Diego, just before his flight to Kona, Tinley was exhausted, bruised and scraped raw on both hips, and so sore he was wincing at the effort it took to sit down in a chair.

Still, it looked as if there was no one in the Ironman field who was capable of giving him a race. There was an ongoing political battle between Nice and the Hawaii event, with the former race offering big money and trips to the French Riviera for the list of invited pros and the Ironman offering nothing but heat, lava and a lot of prestige to whoever won. Neither of Tinley's old training partners, Allen and Molina, were racing. His archrival, Dave Scott, was retired. Then came the best news of all. The conditions on the morning of the race were going to be ideal: cloud cover and light winds, temperatures in the 80s and low 90s. For the Ironman, that's about as perfect as you'll ever see. Easy?

Tinley knew better. The pressure of being a "sure winner" was killing him. He knew the Queen K highway as well as anyone; he knew what a laugh the idea of being a sure winner actually was.

"But man," he kept telling himself, hoping for what he knew was next to impossible, "wouldn't it be great to have the lead by Hawi and be able to lay back just a little, not have to push the body too far? Maybe I will have an easy race. Please?"

Not a chance. Skinny little Chris Hinshaw came out of Kailua Bay with a six-minute lead and then went for broke on his bike. For a while out there on the highway he was pulling away from Tinley at the rate of a mile every two minutes.

"Damn," said Tinley. "I knew it!"

And so off he went on his strange-looking machine and chased down most of Hinshaw's lead before the start of the run. He was in first place, finally, by mile three of the marathon, with 23 to go. He'd needed to break Howard's course record on the bike to get there. What he needed from that point on was a new pair of legs.

"Easy, my foot," grumbled Tinley as he ran, resenting the fact that he'd had to cycle as hard as he had, resenting the heat and the highway again and the nine hours of racing, resenting the fact that Dave Scott wasn't racing while being glad at the same time that he wasn't. He was resenting, too, the ideal conditions that were going to make less

Tinley once compared the anticipation of doing another Ironman to looking forward to being in a car wreck—with the memory of a previous wreck fresh in his mind. Allen, who has a reputation for being able to handle pain, called the Ironman "the limit of sanity" in 1984.

of his performance while being glad about them at the same time.

So much for easy races. There was even a point during the marathon where Tinley had to walk, at about mile 13. He was light-headed, out of fuel. He crossed to the other side of the road and grabbed some food and recovered. He finished strongly, in record time. He was experienced. He hadn't panicked. "When did you get your legs back out there, Scott?" asked a journalist after the race.

"They didn't come back," Tinley growled. "I *made* 'em come back."

But it was Hinshaw's effort that day that underscored the go-for-broke attitude, an attitude that had forced Tinley to respond.

"I'm very, very competitive," Hinshaw said the day after that event. "If I see an opportunity to pull off a victory or improve my position in a race, I'll take it. I knew I was going to fall apart sooner or later, but when you're feeling good you have to take advantage of it. In this race I knew I was getting tired on the way out, but I had to build a commanding lead over Tinley. If I didn't . . . well, I knew I couldn't break him physically. I knew he was tired and everything, but it wasn't enough. I felt if I could get a large enough lead on him, say 15 minutes, that's got to play a big game in someone's head."

Of course, the game Hinshaw was playing was actually with himself, and it didn't come close to being enough. He needed a huge margin off the bike and he managed only three minutes, after leading during portions of the ride by more than 11. Tinley blew by him on the run like a blond Porsche, and Hinshaw was left with second place. Even that got tough near the end, when he neglected a couple of aid stations and finally wobbled to the finish line looking strong enough to the cheering spectators but surprising the hell out of Valerie Silk, who reached to put a lei over his head and found herself with a double armload of limp, sweaty triathlete. Hinshaw's legs were gone.

"See, that's the thing about this race," Hinshaw said. "You've got to think about what you're doing the entire time. You can never learn enough. I've done it four times and I still made a really bad mistake that could have cost me second place. But that's what I really like about this race—you're pushing your body to that extreme limit, that threshold." He held out his hand and fluttered it gently back and forth to illustrate the delicate balance, sounding like a stoked-out surfer who had just ridden the perfect wave. "You just hover up there and play with it, toying with it, knowing how far your body can go. I enjoy that a lot."

Tinley, who had been in the game longer than Hinshaw, had less affinity for riding the endurance crest. He was just glad the race was over. The Ironman that year was his 26th triathlon of the season. Even with the bad spot, he'd run a 3:01:33 marathon, the fourth fastest at Ironman up until that point. Two weeks later, when his friend Scott Molina called him on the phone and tried to talk him into racing an Ironman-distance event in Australia, Tinley refused.

"I can't," he said. "Look, the only thing that kept me going in Hawaii this year was the promise I made to myself to take a break. If I went to Australia I'd never be able to trust myself again."

Molina knew. He wanted company in Australia, but he knew.

❖

The variables, the chances to make mistakes—or have them occur—at the Ironman are numerous. The heat, the wind, how much to eat and drink, and mechanical failure during the bike ride, are just the most obvious. Harder to put a finger on are things like how you "feel" on race day—and how you will respond to that during the race. Ultra-endurance triathlon competition is an inexact science; some athletes have elaborate training, tapering and nutritional rituals that prepare them for race day; almost all triathletes keep fairly comprehensive training diaries, but few (I've never met even one) have arrived at an accurate method to predict whether they will be "on" or "off" on any particular day. Sometimes the best training and the most careful pre-race regimen will leave an athlete flat and not quite his best when the gun goes off, while the worst situation will leave another feeling like a million bucks. Before her win in February 1982, Kathleen McCartney spent the Thursday night and most of Friday in the hospital with an IV stuck in her arm. She'd been suffering from cramps, diarrhea and vomiting after eating dinner on Wednesday evening. It was a disaster. But on Saturday she felt terrific, stronger and stronger as the day went on. When she climbed off her bike at the Kona Surf and started up the hill she was shocked; it felt as if she hadn't biked at all.

But while feeling good (strong, well-rested, optimistic and enthusiastic), is nice, it's dangerous stuff, because in the course of the day a top competitor is going to bounce back and forth between feeling terrific and terrible a dozen times. A hundred times. Take that "good" stuff too seriously too early and you might not finish at all.

In 1984 Mark Allen raced the first two segments of the Ironman better than anyone had before him. He was in sixth place after the swim, right on the heels of Dave Scott. Then he went into first like a shot and stayed there, rocketing through the lava fields up to Hawi and back as if he'd been told secretly that the race would end when he got off his bike. It didn't, of course, but many people standing at the Kona Surf who watched Allen run out for the start of the marathon thought that it might as well have. No other competitor was in sight.

"Before the race, all I was thinking was that I wanted to stay with Scott," Allen said after the event. "I wanted to swim with him, bike with him, then go for it on the run. But when I got on the bike and I saw that I was gaining time on him pretty fast, I thought that maybe he's having another lousy race."

Scott had had a bad season. Many people said he was washed up. In a couple of events in which Allen had raced well that year, Scott had finished far out of the money. As Allen began to pull away from him at Ironman, the concern in Allen's mind grew. Was he worried about the wrong man? If he did hang back, would Tinley catch both him and Scott on the run?

"Am I going too fast?" he asked himself. He looked down and tried to feel his body work as he watched the chain sliding smoothly, quickly, like a snake, the crank arm glinting in the sun as it turned. His legs felt strong. His elbows rode low and relaxed, his shoulders loose, the heaviness of the swim already gone. "I feel great," Allen thought. "This feels easy." He glanced back and saw that Scott was 50 yards back, maybe more. Then he looked back down at the chain, settled a little deeper into his position and rode on.

Allen is a lean, handsome man who manages always to look as if he's just awakened from a nap. Exceedingly bright, exceedingly talented, there is a puppy-like awkwardness to him that is evident during a race only when he runs. Seated on a bike his body seems as hard as the metal frame, as well-defined as the alloy components. In the open water he's a knife, with his big hands scooping quarts of water at a time, moving him long at the rate of a mile every 18 minutes or so.

He rose to prominence within the triathlon world in his first year of competition in 1982, quickly becoming known in the San Diego triathlon community as a low-mileage, high-intensity trainer whose physical limits were beyond those of most. He acquired a curious nickname: "The Grip," which was short for "The Grip of Death," a reference to what it was like training with the guy. When NBC television's John Tesch met Allen before the 1983 Nice Triathlon he dubbed him "The Zen Master" for his cerebral approach to that race.

His legs felt strong. His elbows rode low and relaxed, his shoulders loose, the heaviness of the swim already gone. "I feel great," Allen thought. "This feels easy."

Allen trained alone more frequently than with his friends and teammates. Without a running and cycling background of any kind, he was unable to handle the day-to-day megamileage many of them could and stay uninjured. His friends tended to depend more on the social aspect of the sport to get them through the day, and they sometimes found Allen's constant emphasis on quality tough to handle. Tinley once said that Allen was too competitive in training; that he had to be half a step in front all the time.

Allen's approach to competition was on the aesthetic side. He raced much less frequently than the other top men, and each time he raced, it seemed, he was looking for perfection. He was also looking for his own physical and psychological limits. He was fascinated by the concepts of concentration and pain management. And he was able to put certain basic principles of endurance competition into words better than anyone in the sport.

"Training enables you to feel comfortable with pain," he said. "Your body is telling you to stop, but your mind is pushing you through that. The more you get accustomed to being in that situation during your training, then when you get to it in a race, it's not foreign. You're able to push all the way to the finish line because you know you've done it before and you've recovered from it. That's the biggest fear—that it's so intense it's never going to go away. But it goes away—15 minutes after you stop. I'm sure that there are plenty of people who could be at the top of this sport, or any sport, who aren't at the top because they haven't learned to push through the pain. It's something that once you accept, you work with instead of fighting. For me, I push until I've reached that pain level and that's when I know I'm going the speed I should be at. If it's below that I know I'm not going hard enough. In that sense pain becomes almost a friendly thing instead of an enemy."

Allen seemed to have far less apprehension of pain than most of the other triathletes. He was uniquely capable of separating the physical side of competition from the mental, as if he was somehow able to put them each in a separate compartment and move them around like blocks. "Here," he seemed to say, "this is how I feel right now, physically. Let's ignore that—put it over here. Now, here's what I'd like in my mind to *do*. I wonder...?"

"Why limit yourself to having as hard as you can go be as hard as the next guy can go?" Allen wondered. "It seems like this sport is so new that we must be a long way from the point where every race is going to be close—where we've reached the limit of what a body can do. So I'm thinking of my races as being chances to go beyond that first barrier of barely beating people. Maybe my potential is way out beyond where the next guy is."

And there were times when Allen's potential *was* way out there. In '83 and '84 he won several big races by startlingly wide margins. But there were also times when he took himself too far, usually in races where heat and distance were factors. At the Nice Triathlon in 1983, with a big lead after a mountainous bike ride, he actually had his legs go out from under him with five miles left to go in a 20-mile run. He almost went to his knees. Dazed and dehydrated, suffering from the heat, he wobbled to the finish line and won the race, but it had been a near thing. Another mile and he might not have finished.

So in 1984, even with Allen out in front at the Ironman by 12 minutes, there were doubts. He had the skill to win by that much; on a good day he might be capable of winning by 40 minutes. But had he left himself enough for the marathon?

Not even close. He had ridden too hard. Not that he wasn't physically capable of riding the course as fast as he did, but on that day, when the temperature in Kona was something like 98 degrees in the shade, he would have needed a truck moving alongside of him with a Kathleen McCartney autograph model IV tube pumping glucose and saline directly into his arm for him to keep up the pace he'd set for 112 miles. As it was, he hadn't even drunk or eaten enough to keep himself going on an ordinary day. He ran into town along Alii Drive with no problems, although his skin had started to get a little goosefleshy. Then he felt dizzy going up the Pay and Save Hill, and by the time he reached the highway he was weaving. At about mile 12 or so he ran smack into a volunteer who had his back turned, watching for cyclists, and Allen went to his knees, stunned. He'd never seen the man. A hundred yards later, his equilibrium shattered, he went down again. For a second time he got up, more out of reflex than determination, and continued on, shuffling.

"At 10 miles into the run I felt like I did with six or seven miles to go in Nice that year," Allen said the day after the race. "I thought, 'How am I going to run fifteen or sixteen miles feeling like this?'"

But he kept on. Finally, about four miles after Allen's first fall, Dave Scott went by, on his way to his fourth Ironman win. The 12-minute lead was gone. Allen had blown up. Crashed and burned. Gone for broke and lost.

He had strangled himself in his own Grip of Death. His talent as a cyclist, his training and his unique ability to concentrate for long periods of time at high levels of performance actually worked against him. "That's part of the game," he said philosophically. "It's not just the training, it's knowing what to do during the race. And Dave knows what to do during the race. Same with Tinley. You can be in the greatest shape in the world, but it's what you do with yourself while you're out there that dictates how you're going to do. If you make a mistake it's going to cost you."

8

LOSING IT IN KONA

When Mark Twain visited the Hawaiian Islands in 1866 as a young reporter for the *Sacramento Union,* he was entranced by the little town of Kailua. He described it in a letter dated in July of that year as "a little collection of native grass houses reposing under tall coconut trees—the sleepiest, quietest, Sundayest looking place you can imagine. Ye weary ones that are sick of the labor and care, and the bewildering turmoil of the great world, and sigh for a land where ye may fold your tired hands and slumber your lives peacefully away, pack up your carpet sacks and go to Kailua! A week there ought to cure the saddest of all of you."

That description still fits 120 years later. The grass shacks are gone, but coconut palms still abound. The pace of life is still slow, the climate sultry. Along Alii Drive, the condominiums and hotels are sheltered behind curtains of foliage. Private homes along the drive range from the discreetly sumptuous to the ramshackle. The beaches are small and uncrowded, the night life is so subdued it's almost nonexistent, and the local residents, a mixture of Polynesians, Chinese, Tongans, Samoans, aging mainland hippies and semi-retired, affluent Caucasians, are for the most part calm and friendly. With a permanent (and very scattered) population around 20,000, Kailua (now Kailua-Kona or simply Kona, which refers to the entire district) is a paradise for escapists.

But for one solid week in October each year, life in sleepy Kailua-Kona is far from its usual mellow self. October brings with it the triathletes, the high-tech super jocks, more than a thousand well-muscled, self-admitted fitness fanatics armed with gleaming, state-of-the-art bicycles and cardio-vascular systems of heroic proportions. They fly to the Big Island as predictably as the trade winds. Most have spent the better part of the previous six months training for this one event, dreaming of this place. With veins popping and wristwatches beeping, they flood into town from the air-port in rental cars and taxis, their necks craning and their eyes wide as they catch their first glimpses of Mecca. Americans, Europeans, Japanese, New Zealanders, Australians—they all speak the common language of obses-sion, and they are alike in at least one other respect: after an entire day locked in the cabin of an airplane, they are ready to move. No sooner do they check into their rooms than they are out again on the street, dressed for a workout—a run, a bike ride, a swim, it doesn't matter—wound so tight-ly around the thought of finally being in Kona they could burst. "The energy here is incredible!" they'll tell you. And indeed it is. The air crackles with it.

Most of the triathletes arrive a week or so before the race, and some come even earlier, hoping the extra time will give them an advantage on race day. Sometimes it does. When the crowds arrive they are through with the hardest part of their training, they know every inch of the course, and they can sit back, relatively unfrenzied, and bask in their status as old hands. The strategy can backfire, though, because knowing too much about the course can make you stale; you can lose that keen mental edge many of the new arrivals will enjoy. And knowing the Ironman course well only makes you more aware of the hazards. No matter how much time you put in, there's no way to tell what the conditions will be when it counts. During the restless days just before the race, when your body is trying to slow itself down and prepare, your mind is becoming more and more active, anticipating and dreading the competition at the same time. Unfortunately, it's usually the "dread" part that grows and gets nasty, while the "confidence" part wilts in the face of all that could go wrong. Hell, if you've been on the island long enough, most of it probably already has.

So a week is the norm. It's safer, and it's a lot cheaper.

Mostly, the triathletes come early in order to "acclimatize" to the conditions, the heat, and the humidity—and they do so religiously. For the entire pre-race week, Alii Drive is awash in muscles. From dawn to dusk, a steady stream of well-defined brown bodies moves up and down, running and sweating in the heat, flashing by on their bikes. They move alone, or in pairs or in groups, but they move endlessly, serious about their final preparations for the race, but serious about being part of the action, too— part of The Procession, in which everyone with a washboard stomach and good pair of legs is a star. Strides are firm, heads are squarely to the front, but the eyes are always busy, glancing from side to side, checking out the fitness of the competition, evaluating it, comparing it to their own. Neither self-satisfaction nor despair ever lasts more than a mile or two. There are always those who look just slightly less fit than you do, and always those who look leaner and meaner than anyone you've ever seen.

Eating is a big part of race week, too. It's what triathletes do, mostly, when they're not training. They have enormous appetites, even the women, who put down plates of food that might embarrass a longshoreman. Their husbands and wives shop, lie on the beach, snorkel; the triathletes eat. They shovel into their bodies almost anything they can find, from big breakfasts with side orders of pancakes at the Kona Ranch House, where the wait for a table is always long and the waitresses are endurance athletes in their own right, to lunches at Drysdale's and dinners at Tom Bombadil's, all washed down with pitchers of water and topped off by extra desserts. Snacks in between are anything from cookies to rice cakes to snow cones at Island Style, the little shop at the corner of Alii Drive and Palani Road, adjacent to the pier. A dedicated few actually stick to the stuff you read about in training books—whole grains and fruits and nuts—but most give only lip service to quality. Quantity is what's needed: fuel for the bike ride and the run tomorrow, fuel for the Ironman. Pack it in, man. Drink plenty. Get *strong!*

The whole town joins in. During Ironman week, you can't take a step in Kona without seeing an Ironman poster or an Ironman banner, without overhearing an Ironman conversation. Beneath the big banyan tree by the pier, in front of the King Kamehameha Hotel, the Ironman souvenir stand is busy from the first day, four, five customers deep. Few of them are athletes, but rather athletes' families and friends, or tourists caught up in the frenzy. Traffic in town is almost at a standstill. The village has been transformed: the "Sundayest place you can imagine" has become the Hard Body Capital of the World.

"I've heard stories about everything here," said one first-timer (sounding like every first-timer) before the race in 1985. "I feel like I've been here before. Everybody told me what to expect, how the course goes, the town. There's so much electricity in the town. You can feel it! I haven't seen a sour face since I've been here. It's more than I thought it would be. A lot more. I get goose bumps just thinking about it. I try to relax and stay loose, but I can't."

The locals deal with the transformation of their village generally well. The airlines, hotels, restaurants, and retail industry are understandably ecstatic. Tourism on the Big Island dipped during the 70s and 80s, and the Ironman brought needed funds into the economy when the race moved from Oahu in 1981. Each year the take has been greater. Not only has the number of competitors increased, but the race itself has achieved greater prestige and international visibility. Triathletes grew more likely to drag friends and family along, and an ever-expanding horde of press followed in their wake. According to figures proudly circulated by Ironman publicists, the Kona economy benefited to the tune of $7.5 million in 1985; the figure was expected to be even bigger in '86. The race was the single biggest moneymaking event in the island's history.

It is the stuff of dreams for local businessmen—although the joy is not unanimous. Many locals like Kailua-Kona for the same reasons Mark Twain did, and some of them see the triathlon invasion as a massive pain in the butt. Unlike the just-married couples from Japan, or the middle-aged tourists from Minnesota, the triathletes do not spend their days wandering goggle-eyed through town or cruising the bay on one of Captain Bean's big catamarans. Unlike the game fishermen, to whom Kona is another kind of paradise, they do not lease charter boats and throw $20 bills around like confetti. The triathletes tend to take over, as if the keys to Kailua were included in, what was back then, their $100 entry fee. Lost in the pursuit of their own dream, the triathletes have a tendency to forget that the dream is not always shared by the locals.

The triathletes affect the game fisherman now less than they used to, when charter boats still used Kailua Pier as a staging point (the action all takes place now up the coast a bit at Honokohau Bay), but the race is still seen by that group as an annoyance. One charter boat owner was so upset in 1982 that he zoomed into the harbor early on the morning of the race, anchored his boat near the end of the pier directly in the path of the swimmers, then roared his defiance and passed out, drunk. In the flurry of activity before the start of the race, no one noticed the boat until it was too late; a small Coast Guard craft attempting to drag it free of its anchor succeeded only in turning it broadside to the beach. Dozens of triathletes ended up swimming into the hull, some of them hitting their heads with such force that the large crowd of spectators standing on the pier winced. The owner of the boat was arrested and heavily fined.

The next year saw what many assumed to be a protest of another kind: stretches of the Queen K highway 15 to 20 miles outside of town were strewn with black carpet tacks, completely invisible from the seat of a bike on the smooth black highway. Large numbers of triathletes suffered punctures; many had two or three, which left them without spare tires and therefore put them out of the competition. It was a bitter end to months of training—the race that year is still referred to by many triathletes as "the year of the tacks"—and there was an outcry from embarrassed local residents for an investigation and swift punishment for the culprit. But the guilty party was never found, an unlikely thing in a community as small as Kona. In 1986 a more logical explanation was offered by Mike Kasser, a successful New York investor and serious triathlete who had moved to Kona in 1984. He suggested the tacks had merely fallen off a truck headed out to one of the resorts along the highway, or perhaps to a real estate development in Waikoloa.

Tacks aside though, the biggest source of controversy each year at the Ironman is the roads, where the triathletes and the locals compete, sometimes fiercely, for space. During race week, Kailua-Kona is a tiny, tropical version of the San Diego Freeway at rush hour. Triathletes are urged to ride single file along Alii Drive, and they do most of the time, but the steady procession of riders and runners, combined with the increased flow of rented Toyota Tercels, assures congestion. The letters section of the local newspaper, *West Hawaii Today*, is filled each year with pleas from race officials, triathletes, and residents for mutual restraint and courtesy, although the quickest solution is one that some of the larger and more aggressive locals are apt to use: leaning over the passenger side and yelling out the window: "Get da fuck outta da road, you dumb haole!"

The response to that is usually immediate.

But while the bikes are merely an annoyance in town and along Alii Drive, they became targets along the Queen K, where traffic moves along at 50 to 60 miles an hour, sometimes faster. When resort development along the highway began to rise dramatically in 1983 and '84, and both private and construction vehicular traffic increased as a result, the number of triathletes knocked off their bikes and injured, or even killed, also increased. By 1986 the list of injured cyclists had grown long, and there was talk that perhaps some of the accidents had been not altogether accidental, that a few of the locals driving back from the construction sites along the Queen K, with perhaps a beer or two under their belts, had gotten fed up. True or not, the rumors made triathletes think twice about straying from the white line, and the brisk business that year in rearview mirrors that attached to the handlebars with a Velcro strap was evidence they had gotten the message.

The negative incidents, however, are relatively rare. By and large, even most of those among the Kona citizenry who do not see a direct financial benefit seem to embrace the Ironman enthusiastically. Between two and three thousand volunteers are needed to staff the event each year; between two and three thousand respond tirelessly, with a fervor that often astounds the competitors. On race day volunteers are everywhere, from dawn to dusk and long, long after that, cheering, consoling, supplying the triathletes with water and food, logistical support and offhand psychological counseling.

The locals will tell you with a straight face that it's all due to the "Aloha spirit," and there is more reason to believe that than doubt it. In 1981, the race's first year in Kona, race director Valerie Silk, apprehensive about being able to enlist enough local help, was overjoyed when the volunteer quota was not only met but surpassed."

The fella who was in charge of all the aid-station volunteers just didn't think it was going to be possible to get the number of people we needed," Silk said. "But then he called me a few weeks before the race and said, 'Can you get volunteer T-shirts for another couple of hundred?' then he'd call and ask for another couple of hundred, then another. We ended up with about 950 volunteers and I finally had to turn off the faucet. We didn't have enough money to pay for any more shirts."

Silk, an attractive, six-foot blond, is an unlikely mother to one of the cruelest endurance races in the world. Indeed, while she acknowledges the long hours of training that are necessary for the Ironman, and sympathizes with the triathletes in their painful struggle to get to the finish line, she doesn't seem to understand the process any better than any of the millions of Americans who sit in their living rooms and watch television coverage of the race. The race is her life's work, but the racing isn't. "I think of it as throwing a party for 1000 of my good friends," Silk says softly.

Silk's perception of the race delights some and infuriates others. She is loyal to her staff, and they to her, intensely so, which over the years has made for a strong race organization, but also one that at times is insulated and defensive, overly sensitive to criticism and remote from current trends and philosophies in the sport as a whole. As the Ironman became more successful as a business and increasingly complicated to administer, Silk stuck to her decision-by-committee management style and her guardian-angel philosophy. "Instinct is all I have to draw on," she once said. And, indeed, instinct served her well for years, although many of the business people from outside the sport often wished she would blend the instinct with a touch of reality.

In 1984 Silk turned the direct, day-to-day operation of the race over to Kay Rhead, a longtime staff member, kicking herself upstairs to the position of race chairman. It was a job that kept Silk in charge of the operation, which had expanded into areas of product merchandising and foreign licensing, but removed her from much of the race-specific details. Still, she continued to attend personally to things such as writing birthday cards to past finishers and answering letters from athletes, personal touches she felt were critical to the maintenance of the character of the Ironman. She preferred to leave the hard negotiating, the wheeling and dealing, to others, although any arrangement that was struck had to pass the emotional and philosophical Ironman muster; practicality or profitability were not always the bottom line.

Silk's favorite moments were those that she spent standing at the Ironman finish line, placing leis over the heads of the finishers, or standing on stage at the lavish Ironman awards ceremony, gazing out at what she clearly considered to be the fruits of her long and tedious labor of love. She reveled in her position as surrogate mother to the triathletes who raced in Kona, although even there she seemed to make a philosophical distinction; while she embraced the slowest and least skillful of them, she was cool and uncomfortable with the fastest and the best.

Silk took over the operation of the Ironman in early 1980, after it had become apparent to both her and her husband, Hank Grundman, that the event had far outgrown the resources of Grundman's three Honolulu-area Nautilus fitness centers. The race that year had been a success on the surface, especially with ABC on hand to cover it, but it had been an organizational struggle, a near debacle. There was clearly a huge public interest, but the event was draining the clubs financially. It needed full-time attention, a full-time race director. As bookkeeper for the clubs, Silk had been a severe critic of the race, but her marriage to Grundman was on the rocks and she saw the race as an emotional escape. Perhaps if she threw her energies into making the thing work, she would be able to ignore her own problems.

"I was the race's biggest detractor for the first three years," said Silk. "I hated it. I couldn't understand why we were spending so much time and money to put the thing on. And it took two or three months for the clubs to recuperate after it was over, all for 15 guys who showed up on the beach one morning to do an event that anyone in his or her right mind would never want to do. Plus, I had to run all three of the clubs while they were running around with this crazy-ass sport."

But she took the job. In fact, she took the race; it was hers: The Nautilus International Triathlon. Grundman, making one of the worst marketing decisions in the history of sport, had dropped John Collins's magic "Iron Man" title, hoping to maximize the exposure of his clubs. It wasn't until February 1982 that the original title reappeared, this time written as one word: "Ironman."

❖

Silk's first job was to find a new course. The old one on Oahu was beautiful, but it just wasn't practical. For the handful of men who had finished the race in 1978 and '79, running through the streets of downtown Honolulu, and cycling on the narrow perimeter highway had been fine. The field of 108 in 1980, however, was a different story. Silk scouted locations on several islands, but was drawn to the Big Island by that long, lonely road that sliced through the lava fields: the Queen Kaahumanu Highway.

Silk had never been an endurance athlete herself, so she had no understanding of how terrible the conditions along the highway were. In fact, had she been a triathlete, it is likely she would have looked elsewhere, for no one who was knowledgeable—and sane—would have suggested such a place. The race almost went in the opposite direction anyway.

"We checked Maui, we checked Kauai," Silk said. "Then we came over here and saw that big stretch of highway along West Hawaii. Back in those days there was very little traffic. It just looked like the ideal course. But we almost didn't go out there. I was looking for a course that was going to be interesting, with some color and some flowers. I think it was maybe only about three weeks to the race in 1981 when the northbound course along the Queen K was finally decided on. Up until that point I was determined that the course was going to go south, to the City of Refuge."

The City of Refuge is a popular tourist attraction. The road south from Kailua is paved and smooth, but the route would not have been easy on a bike. Winding along the lush cliffs south of Kailua-Kona, above KealakeLua Bay, where James Cook was killed in 1779, the road is narrow, with steep climbs and descents. That was not a problem from a difficulty standpoint, but there was no shoulder at all.

Silk looked and looked. She weighed the hazards against the undeniable beauty of the route. What a difference between the road south from Kailua-Kona and the road north! Finally, she drove back and forth to the City of Refuge twice in one day and understood the dangers.

"It was just too dangerous," Silk said. "Where were we going to put the aid stations? We would have had people standing on the edge of cliffs. There were no time limits in those days so we were going to have bikers on the road after dark—and tired."

Details still had to be worked out, but the general course was set: it would be the Queen K. It was a stroke of genius, arrived at by default perhaps, but arrived at nonetheless. Silk had settled on more than just the cruelest 60-mile stretch of road in all the islands. Unwittingly, she had given the growing sport of triathlon its Yankee Stadium, its Madison Square Garden, its Soldier Field. The Ironman had come to the Big Island.

Silk based the race at the Kailua Pier, which sits beneath the King Kamehameha Hotel at the intersection of Alii Drive and Palani Road, smack in the middle of town. Logic dictated that she locate the start, the swim-bike transition and the finish line there. But the pier quickly became much more. If Kailua-Kona was to become the Hard Body Capital, then the pier was to be the capital's State House. Along with the tiny beach that abuts its southeast side, the pier became the focus of Ironman action, the center of attention the entire triathlon world during race week. If you were a triathlete, the pier is where you wanted to end up.

To triathletes in Kona for the first time, the little beach is a surprise. They expect something…well, more majestic. Indeed, at high tide the beach hardly exists at all; it's a mere 20 yards of hard-packed sand, buffeted and often completely covered by the waves that crash against the sea wall. But this is indeed the place where the Ironman Triathlon World Championship will start on Saturday, the place they've been dreaming about, the place that has scared them half to death for the previous month. It seems impossible that more than 1000 bodies could squeeze themselves into an area so small.

The pier and the beach together have come to be irreverently known as Dig Me Beach. No one seems sure where the term originated, but the description cuts right to the core. While the athletes gather at the pier primarily to swim all or part of the 2.4-mile Ironman swim course, a considerable amount of energy is spent in the pursuit of simply being part of the Ironman. There's a great deal of camaraderie and a lot of strutting. Egos bounce around like beach balls at the pier, so exposed you can almost reach out and touch them. Dig Me Beach is where the check-out scene along Alii Drive is packed tight.

If you're looking good, it's wonderful.

The routine is sharply defined. There are no rules, but the drive to congregate at first light seems almost instinctive. Each morning, starting at about 7 a.m. and continuing until 9 a.m. or so, Dig Me Beach is the social hot spot. Friends who met the previous year get reacquainted. Veterans of past races tell tales of bravery or great failures. Newcomers stand in self-conscious awe. Conversations on the pier reflect lives that by choice and subsequent necessity revolve around the physical: training mileage, injuries, diet, resting heart rates, body-fat percentages, paces per mile. The language of the endurance triathlete is spoken in Kona with an expertise that belies the fact that training for the race is a boggle of hearsay, personal experimentation, and guilt (there's always someone doing something more or better—the way you would be doing things if you weren't such a slug).

What is taken for granted is that a tremendous amount of dedication and sacrifice has been necessary to come this far. Little has been allowed to stand in the way; nothing is going to stand in the way from this point on. In 1986 one woman laughed about a talk she had with a reporter. "He said to me that I must have had to give up a lot," she said. "I said, 'Yeah, as a matter of fact, that was my ex-husband I was just standing here talking to.'"

Self-confidence is something you'd expect to find in abundance at the Ironman, but you don't. It's rare. The race is too big, the competition too keen. The unscientific nature of the training and the complexity of the event make triathletes psychologically fragile, open to doubts and suggestions that can tear their best-laid plans to shreds. How much training is enough? How much is too much? What should I eat, what should I drink? Am I doing what I'm trying to do correctly? Everyone has been looking fruitlessly for magic answers all season long, and the search continues at the pier—despite the fact that deep down, everyone knows there aren't any magic answers. The key is to just keep doing what you've been doing, to somehow make yourself feel satisfied with that. Besides, even if you've been hopelessly wrong, what the hell are you going to be able to do about it at this point?

Getting your head around all that isn't easy, though. The most experienced triathletes learn to control themselves during race week. They don't talk much, nor do they listen too attentively, either.

"There are two things I don't do," said one veteran, a retired high school teacher in his late fifties named Ken Cates, who went as far as any triathlete can go by actually moving to Kona from San Diego in 1984. "I don't talk about my time, and I don't train with someone in my own age group. I get too crazy. I'll go until this explodes." He patted his chest over his heart and laughed.

Cates is a droll, likable man who describes himself half-jokingly as a "triathlon junkie and an endorphin addict." He first came to Kona in February 1982 and surprised himself by finishing second in the 50-54 age division. He crossed the line in just over 13 hours, hand-in-hand with two friends from San Diego. "It was a wonderful, wonderful thrill," Cates said.

He applied too late to do the race the following October, but in 1983 he was back, bringing with him his two sons, Michael and Brian. Both men had been introduced to running and then to triathlons by their father. Cates's second wife, Lark, whom Cates lovingly refers to as "the big blonde," was on hand to be proud of the whole gang. That was the good news. The bad news was that Cates had retired unexpectedly that summer when his superintendent refused him the unpaid days off to race in Hawaii. He told Cates that he could "see no benefit that would accrue to your students from your having done this."

"What he didn't realize," Cates said, "was that at my age, being able to do what I could do, I was a hell of an example. I agonized over the decision; I was 54 years old and I didn't have enough money to retire, but I figured it was a once-in-a-lifetime chance. I may never have gotten the chance again to have that experience with those two young men. Finally I said screw it, I just have to do it."

So Cates resigned. All three men finished the race, and Lark was proud. A year later she and Ken moved to Kona. They struggled a bit financially, but they were happy. Cates has done the Ironman every year since, and still takes the race seriously, still feels the pressure mounting as race day approaches. Somewhat of an elder statesman now on the island triathlon scene, he writes a regular running and fitness column for *West Hawaii Today,* waxing dryly philosophical in print over exercise and competitive motivation.

Cates couldn't give you a good business reason why he moved to Kona, but he admits that the Ironman had a lot to with the decision—and a lot to do with his current lifestyle. "I'm not exactly adverse to the kind of weather that's here," he said. "I'd have to say it was a matter of timing from several standpoints, and then I've always had a good streak of lunacy in me. The idea of being here was kind of neat, and the only thing I could think of that was crazier than doing this race once is doing it twice and three times."

Cates at least knows enough to avoid the pier when he feels the pressure starting to mount. The Ironman rookies don't, however, which makes them especially vulnerable. They've read the books, put in the mileage, spent the big bucks on a decent bike. They think they're ready. Or they thought so once. Back home in Waukesha, Wisconsin, or Gainesville, Florida, or Paris, Illinois, they were minor celebrities, training for the legendary Ironman in faraway Hawaii. Friends and family shook their heads and told them they were crazy, but they trained with a sense of pride and felt the grudging admiration of their severest critics, especially when articles about them appeared in the local newspaper. They were stoically, magnificently, alone in their determination and they'd flown off to Kona like heroes.

But now? Well, the scene at Dig Me Beach gives them pause, to say the least. Surrounded by the best triathletes in the world, surrounded by a level of fitness they'd come to believe was their own private domain, they are suddenly average—perhaps not even that. They have stepped into a world in which they had believed they could excel, only to find that they might not even be able to survive. Their carefully constructed shells of confidence grow thin, and can be shattered in a moment. A single conversation at the pier can do it, sending the poor wretch fleeing to the highway for futile and often self-destructive last-minute training sessions. People like this can be seen on their bikes, two days before the race, 40 miles out from town on the Queen K, past the Sheraton Hotel at Waikoloa, grinding up the long hills under the hot sun trying to make up ground they didn't know they'd lost until that morning. The extra mileage is going to hurt them physically on race day, of course, but at least it will make them feel better in their minds. Until the next day, at least, when the talk at the pier turns to the dangers of overtraining.

The rookies aren't the only ones who get spooked. Not even the top athletes are immune to last-minute doubts. As a result, most of them avoid the pier altogether. Any information they get there is bound to be bad. Dave Scott and Scott Tinley were both known for their reclusiveness during race week. You are as likely to see them at Dig Me Beach in the morning as you were to see Michael Jackson doing a free concert on a Captain Bean's Catamaran Cruise.

"You can get caught up," Tinley warned, way back in February 1982. "You can spend too much time hanging out with the boys. You can start to think that you haven't done enough, that maybe you've tapered too much."

"I wait until later, eighty-thirty, nine o'clock, when people have started to leave," said Juli Brening, who finished among the top 10 women at Ironman for the third time in 1986. "It's the big flex scene. Everybody's out there strutting their stuff. It gets so tense and nerve-wracking. I don't like it."

Brening is an attractive, enthusiastic woman whose sister, Nancy Harrison, placed fourth in Hawaii in 1985. Brening was eighth. Harrison's was a stunning, out-of-nowhere performance that shot her credibility in the triathlon world sky-high and confused the two sisters in their perception of each other's talents. Going into the race, Brening was supposed to have been the triathlon star in a family whose all-American good looks, togetherness, and athleticism are almost clichés of the American dream. Dad, Mom, and a brother do triathlons too, although none of the three have ever done the Ironman. In 1986 the parents were both in Hawaii to support the sisters' second combined effort. Harrison wound up 10th, and Brening seventh in a field much stronger than they had competed against the year before.

What amuses Brening is her dad's reaction to the event. "He gets so wound up, he can barely talk in the morning."

"Yeah, he's down there every morning scoping out everybody in his age group," her sister added.

"Well, when you think about it," Brening said. "here we are, people that the age-groupers read about in the magazines, and they get to go and swim with them and rub elbows and talk with them. I think that's really exciting to a lot of the age-groupers."

As if to underscore her own modesty, she recalled her first time in Kona. "I know that when I first started in the sport and I was reading about Dave Scott and Julie Moss, when I first saw them I remember being so excited. I remember telling everyone, 'I swam with Julie Moss! Oh, wow, I swam with Julie Moss!'"

While that kind of attention and recognition can be gratifying, it can also be exhausting during race week. Some of the top athletes, trying to keep themselves focused, go so far as to avoid Kona itself, staying far outside of town, where the atmosphere is less intense. In 1983, the high-rolling Team J David rented an entire condominium complex 25 miles up the coast at the luxurious Mauna Kea Resort. The team and support staff, which included bike mechanics, masseuses, coaches and cooks, stayed in a compound of villas that rented for about $500 each a day.

Rank-and-file triathletes back in Kona thought the whole arrangement was disgustingly elitist, although few of them could fail to be impressed when ABC television actually went to the Mauna Kea to film their pre-race interviews with the J David stars, among them former Ironman winners Tinley, Howard, and McCartney. It was a stunning reversal in the Ironman pecking order. Up until that time, being chosen for an interview was a sign that someone had noticed you; you responded to the summons gladly.

In 1986 Joanne Ernst and her husband, Jim Collins, stayed far up the coast, too, although in far less luxurious accommodations than Team J David. They figured the privacy was worth the 45-minute drive into town. During the two weeks they spent in Hawaii that year, Ernst, the defending women's champion, swam at the pier just twice. Both times she tried unsuccessfully to maintain a cocoon of anonymity, undressing discreetly to one side, then moving directly to the water flanked by Collins and a friend. But her face was too familiar. Everyone wanted to talk, to ask her advice, to have their spouses take a picture of them next to the champ. Besieged, Ernst ended up walking away from the pier the second time with a towel draped over her head, Collins leading the way to breakfast like a seeing-eye dog.

"Hanging out is just not a positive thing for me," Ernst said. "I try to stay away from the pier as much as possible. And if I go to the pier to swim, it's worth it, for the swimming; it's the best place. But you can't get involved in all that stuff. It's just a big drain, an energy sink. Actually the whole town is. You don't go to any other race all year where it's so pervasive, where that's what the whole town is doing, thinking about."

The race week tension builds and builds. That "incredible energy" off which the triathletes were able to feed at the beginning of the week becomes unbearable by Thursday. Registration, which most of the competitors put off until the last minute, the big pasta dinner on Thursday night, the pre-race meeting on Friday morning, and then the final act—bike check-in at the pier on Friday afternoon—all combine to tighten the psychological noose. "What's out there?" ask the first-timers, growing less eager by the minute. "I wish I didn't know," grumble the veterans, some of whom have committed themselves not just to survive, but to race hard.

But nervousness about the race is only one factor that begins to get under the triathletes' skin. Cutting their accustomed long hours of training down to almost nothing—"tapering" is the term—is worse. With time on their hands for the first time in months, they grow restless and irritable. Their bodies, recovering from the long hours on the road or in the pool, are literally tingling with pent-up energy. The athletes need to move, but at the same time they're afraid to move far, because every last shred of energy has to be saved for the race. Not even the fact that they are in Hawaii, many of them for the first time, helps. They go nowhere, see nothing. They steer clear of even a two-hour drive in a car because that would tighten their legs. Dave Scott didn't once leave the Kailua-Kona area, except on his bike, in his five trips to the Big Island. Volcanoes? Nope. Hapuna Beach? Nope. Captain Cook's anchorage at Kealakekua Bay? Not that either. And he was far from alone—and more fortunate in that department than most, because Scott tapers less than almost any other triathlete on the island. He and Tinley and some of the other top men put in what many people would consider a solid training week before the race.

The large majority of the triathletes, however, are as obsessive about being sedentary as they were about their training; as the race approaches, their withdrawal becomes almost absolute. They simply sit, sprawled on floors and couches and beds in condos and hotel rooms all over Kona, bouncing emotionally off walls and ceilings, hoping that something will take their minds off the fact that Saturday is coming, slowly coming. "It seemed so incongruous," said a first-time spectator in 1983. "Here are these incredibly healthy people, in the middle of paradise, sitting in their dark hotel rooms for hours, for days. It's weird."

"As long as we can do something, as long as we can run and bike and swim," Brening said, "that's fine. But those last two days, three days, when you have to cut way back on your training, you don't have anything else to do but eat. So you eat, and you feel like you're getting really fat, and you're afraid that you're getting out of shape. You start having dreams about the race. Wednesday, Thursday, and Friday are terrible."

❖

Finally, the waiting is over. Saturday arrives quietly, warm and humid. Alii Drive is a strange place on Ironman morning. There's no place to park near the start, and the triathletes' bikes are already on the pier, so the race organization provides shuttles; some athletes hitch rides with journalists or friends, who will drop them close to the pier, then park elsewhere. Those who are staying close enough walk. All along Alii Drive the triathletes wait for their rides in the dark, standing at the side of the road with their equipment bags slung over their shoulders, like children waiting for a bus that will take them off to summer camp. The air is heavy and still; it's five in the morning and the sun won't come up until seven, so there's not even a streak of dawn on the horizon. No one says much, not even if the car is packed with people. The athletes' faces are drawn and tight, their eyes blank, their minds turned inward. When they smile or talk or laugh, it's with an eerie vacancy.

The entrance to the pier is lit brightly by the television lights and the lights of the race staff. By 5:30 a.m. there are hundreds of spectators jostling for position along the sea wall, and there is a crush of bodies at the entrance to the pier, where security guards are busy in the dark, haloed from behind by the lights, checking credentials, turning spectators away, ushering triathletes and journalists beneath the rope barrier.

It's a little calmer on the pier. The athletes check in, then move out of the light and make their way through the long rows of bicycle racks to find their equipment and check it—slide a pair of water bottles into the cages, hang a helmet on the handlebars and pump up the tires. The sky is getting gray and the athletes move like shadows through the long lines of bikes. Some of them are too busy, looking for things to do. This can't be all, they think, there must be more, I can't be ready now. They leave their bikes and then come back, once, twice, three times. The only sound is the soft rustle of nylon as one of them moves close, still dressed in warm-ups, and the sharp hiss of pump nozzles being released quickly from high-pressure tires.

By the time it's light enough to see, there are athletes in the water warming up, or simply standing, knee-deep, waist-deep. Above and behind them, the crowd flows from the bleachers and legs hang over the sea wall. Mothers, fathers, boyfriends, girlfriends, sisters and brothers look for their triathletes and point. Some of the competitors wait on bleachers of their own along the edge of the pier, sitting capped and numbered and serious, watching nothing, staring. Finally, the entire field of 1000 is in the bay, a raft of orange and yellow swim caps drifting back and forth, up and down, with the swells. The tension, drawn long and tight before, is now sharp and quick. Helicopters circle above, their rotor blades smacking. The sun rises above the trees across the water and backlights the steeple of Moknaikna Church. The public address system blares the annual warning against the annual false start. "Ten...nine...eight...seven.... Everyone back! Back behind the line! We will not start...six...five...four...three.... Move back, move back."

But the front line of swimmers is moving, their heads down, their arms coming up, elbows high. The entire mass of caps begins to drift forward. "Two...one...." The cannon roars and shudders the air. The smoke from the blast drifts across the impossible sight of more than a thousand swimmers stroking and kicking at once, each fighting for space that isn't there, the leaders pressing hard for a good line to the first buoy.

Exactly 1.2 miles away, straight out south from the pier, the big, red-sailed catamaran sits at anchor, riding the soft swells. The swimmers will turn there and head back. The first mile.

Only 139 to go.

The Gates of Heaven, the Ironman finish line.
There's no place quite like it in the world.

The Ironman finish line is a strange and wonderful brew of raw emotion. You are here what you are. Few people have the energy to fake it. It is mostly a place of sheer joy, of knee-buckling relief—a monument to lifelong goals fulfilled, of spirits renewed. But there is confusion, too (as in, what do I do now?), and every once in a while, anger—anger over what the race has done to you, or over what you have allowed it to do. I suppose the worst thing of all is to be so out of it that you don't remember crossing. Can you imagine? To not remember?

Paula Newby-Fraser (above) has just finished second at the 1986 race, and has not yet learned that Patricia Puntous has been disqualified. But the rumors are flying. Why had there been a second finish line tape? It was a strange scene—an odd beginning to the unprecedented eight-victory reign of the greatest female endurance athlete of all time.

Patricia Puntous (right) supports her sister Sylviane, who has had a terrible day, at the finish line in 1986. The sisters would proceed to the medical tent, where Patricia will learn that she has been disqualified and that Paula Newby-Fraser has been declared the winner.

On a nightmarish day, Joanne Ernst (left) walks away from the finish line in 1986. The defending Ironman champion had suffered during the marathon, but in retrospect she counted the race as a greater achievement than her victory the previous year.

Through the 1980s the marathon started in the parking lot of the Kona Surf Hotel, and the first thing you saw as you staggered out onto the course was the big hill leading up to Alii Drive. After 112 miles on the bike, it was an incredible sight —almost funny if you weren't the poor soul on the way up (right).

(Below) The glory days of team J David. The boys are out for a winter training ride in ritzy Rancho Santa Fe. From left, Scott Molina, Scott Tinley, Masters phenomenon Ron Smith, and former tennis pro Gary Peterson. Missing from this shot are team members Mark Allen and John Howard. Like a lot of folks, the triathletes were duped by the spare-no-expense J David scandal, but they still couldn't beat Dave Scott.

(Left) Diana Nyad interviews Mark Allen before the October 1982 Ironman. He had beaten Scott Molina and Scott Tinley convincingly at the Horney Toad Triathlon in San Diego two months before. Could he do it again?

(Below) Jeff Tinley, Scott's brother, the greatest long-distance triathlete who never was. A strange, still undiagnosed illness cut his career far short. He recovered, but by the time he had, the sport had moved on.

In the summer of 1982 the U.S. Triathlon Series was born in the wake of Julie Moss's dramatic Ironman finish the previous February. The Series featured much shorter distances than the Ironman and made it possible for thousands of people to enter the new sport—even ones who were slightly less-finely trimmed.

(Right) Ironman rookie Mark Allen climbed out of Kailua Bay on Dave Scott's toes and paused for a quick drink in 1986. There had been a lot of buzz that year about Allen's great talent, but what he would need on this particular day was a better bike.

There had been many doubts along the way, but at the October 1982 Ironman, Julie Leach came down the final stretch of Alii Drive in first place. She looked strong, but she was concentrating like crazy, unwilling to let herself slip until she crossed. Finally, enveloped by volunteers (below), she saw the tender smile on the face of her husband, Bill. It was over, finally. She had won.

(Below) Dave Scott alone on the Highway in October 1982. Alone that is, except for the ABC camera van. Drafting off the truck was always a topic of bitter debate. The men and women in front denied an advantage, those behind (and usually losing ground) asserted it bitterly. Finally, the riding at the front became so fiercely competitive that the camera van issue faded, replaced by complaints that the lead pack was working together.

The early Fiesta Island triathlons (above) were known for their chaotic purity, but they were the cradle of the Ironman and the birthplace of the sport. When future NORBA world champion Ned Overend (below) competed in Chuck's Triathlon on Fiesta Island in 1980, the modern mountain bike was still in the process of being invented.

After so much hard work, with the finish line in your sights, what can you do but run across and let the reality of a thousand small victories sink in? One thing's for sure, a friend you make on the Highway, is a friend you'll have forever.

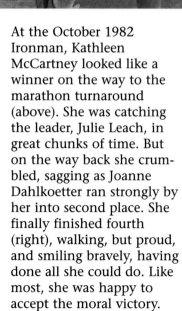

At the October 1982 Ironman, Kathleen McCartney looked like a winner on the way to the marathon turnaround (above). She was catching the leader, Julie Leach, in great chunks of time. But on the way back she crumbled, sagging as Joanne Dahlkoetter ran strongly by her into second place. She finally finished fourth (right), walking, but proud, and smiling bravely, having done all she could do. Like most, she was happy to accept the moral victory.

Triathlon pioneer Sally Edwards (above) at the October 1982 Ironman. Her racing style seems primitive by today's standards, but she was a relentless competitor, and she laid the groundwork for thousands of women who came after her.

Clare St. Arnaud, a Chippewa-Sioux blacksmith from Nebraska (right) couldn't swim before he came to Hawaii in 1981. But he would finish the race that year, and eventually graduated to longer events because he found the pace of the Ironman too fast, too "hectic."

If you can't remember breakfast at the Kona Ranch House (above), you probably haven't been to the Ironman. Walt Stack stopped for breakfast here in 1981 before moseying on over to the pier to complete his record breaking slowest-of-all-time Kona Ironman finish.

Mark Allen (right) raced wisely in 1986. It was Dave Scott's day, but in a way it was Allen's, too. His first victory in Kona was still three years away, but after '86, it was Allen who would haunt Dave Scott's dreams, not Scott Tinley. It was an important step in Allen's tortured Ironman apprenticeship.

At the pier (above, left, and facing page). The Kailua Pier is the site of the Ironman swim start, and where the triathletes, press, families and groupies hang out during race week. The morning scene at the pier is a must for everyone but the stars, most of whom shun the place like the plague. 1985 Ironman champion Joanne Ernst once referred to the pier as an "energy sink."

Scott Tinley on a mountain bike in San Diego (above). Tinley's love of the sport—his sheer joy in training—was unsurpassed. Give Tinley a dirt trail and a couple of hills and he's a happy man. His love-hate relationship with the Ironman was legendary.

Julie Moss looked hopelessly innocent at the Ironman in February 1982 (left). But later that same year she overcame frigid water, a treacherous bike course and pouring rain to win the $17,000 Malibu Triathlon. Moss was a whole lot tougher than she looked—and a fine athlete.

Even though some competitors
spend nearly 12 hours on the
course, they usually arrive at
the finish line smiling.

Triathlon legend Tom Warren (above) on the pier in October 1982. Warren pondered a lot. He might have been thinking about his swimming in this shot, but he might also have been thinking about real estate.

(Top left) Kathleen McCartney fit no one's image of an endurance athlete. But she was tough and talented.

(Left) Kathleen McCartney and Julie Moss. They played key roles (one could hardly call it a competitive battle) in the drama of the February 1982 Ironman. Who remembers that Scott Tinley outran Dave Scott that year? What they remember is Moss's dramatic crawl to the finish line and McCartney's ebullient victory just in front of her. It was an Ironman milestone.

Out of the water, out on the bike. The equipment in 1982 was primitive by today's standards, and the transitions were long, but the intensity of the swim-to-bike change was familiar—and just as frenzied. It's always tough to slow down and think—there's just too much going on.

Dave Scott, The Man, on the move (left).

At the October 1982 Ironman, Kathleen McCartney (below, back to camera) and Julie Leach passed within inches of each other. Moss was on the way out to the marathon turnaround; Leach was on the way in. Both women were sure that McCartney would lead before the day was done.

The Tinley brothers, Scott and Jeff (above) on the Highway in October 1982.

Mark Allen at the Nice Triathlon in France in 1983 (right). With a mile to go he staggered toward the finish line along one of the most glamorous thoroughfares, the Promenade des Anglais. Dave Scott was in second place and closing fast. Few people in the history of the sport could push themselves to the edge, and beyond, the way Allen could. His nickname, "The Grip of Death," referred to what he could do to others, but he caught himself in his own fist more than once.

At the ill-fated Malibu Triathlon in November 1982 (above) the world's best triathletes proved they could race three weeks after Hawaii—especially with prize money on the table. What they couldn't do was swim a mile-and-a-half in 59-degree water.

In 1984 the Highway was an oven. Foolishly Mark Allen forgot himself and rode away from the field. Dave Scott was 12 minutes down at the bike/run transition but he ran out of the Kona Surf parking lot as if Allen was right up the road. The look on Scott's face (left) was simply ferocious, and he'd changed so quickly that he'd put his singlet, with his race number pinned on the front, on backward. Thirteen miles later he was in first place.

Julie Leach (above) during the marathon
in October 1982. At this point she was
simply holding on, trying to ignore the voices in her head that were telling
her to walk off the course and go home. Almost everyone who has done
the Ironman has heard those voices. Almost everyone ignores them.

Dave Scott flashes the victory sign at the October 1982 Ironman (above
right). A one-man dynasty had begun. Always a favorite in Kona (below),
Scott heads down Pay and Save Hill toward the finish line in 1984.

Valerie Silk, the Mother of the Ironman. Her tender parenting of the race made it the great event it is today.

Tom Warren, sit-up king of the world and winner of the 1978 Ironman.

By 1986, Mark Allen had learned enough to know that Dave Scott's pace on the bike was probably the right pace for him, too. "The Grip" shadowed "The Man" all day, but then let him go with 10 miles still left to ride. The memory of his horrible failure two years before was too fresh in Allen's mind for him to risk a repeat performance.

Patricia Puntous (above left) begins to leave her sister, Sylviane, behind at the 1986 Ironman. The pair had raced together all day—too close for the comfort of race officials, who disqualified Patricia at the finish line, awarding the win instead to Paula Newby-Fraser. The French Canadian sisters (below, finishing the bike ride in 1984) were the dominant women at all distances through most of the 1980s. But their career was dogged by constant accusations of drafting on the bike.

The Ironman volunteers are part of the fabric of the race. Logistically the event could not happen without them. But they are of equal emotional importance. An iced sponge during the Ironman marathon offers temporary but welcome relief from the heat. An Ironman buffet—a couple of cold drinks and an iced sponge. But when you start looking forward to the next aid station before you've left the one you're at, you're in trouble.

John Howard (above), American cyclist of the decade in the 1970s and Ironman champion in 1981. He taught the sport how to ride a bike.

Scott Tinley (right) always a gracious champion.

Dave Scott (below) didn't race the Ironman, he attacked it. No one, before or since, could match his ferocious approach to endurance competition.

Joanne Ernst (above) could think herself into bad places during a long race, but when things were going right, she was as tough as nails.

On her way to victory in 1985 (above), Ernst shared the doubts of all the Ironman competitors who had gone before her. When she finished (left), there was nothing left but relief.

Scott Molina (above) at the Nice Triathlon in 1983. He tried many times, and even won the race in 1988, but he never mastered the Ironman. He led the Big Four throughout the 1980s—everywhere but in Kona.

The "Look" (top, right). There comes a time during the marathon when things have gone as badly as they could have gone. Only one goal remains: the finish line. When a triathlete reaches this point, nothing can stop him.

Julie Leach (right) struggled with the course, the heat, but mostly with herself in October 1982. She overcame them all.

In 1985, Scott Tinley (left) had the race won, and was on his way to a course record when he was forced to walk for a brief time on the way to the marathon turnaround. He recovered, but few who were on the scene will forget the image of Tinley's great rival Dave Scott watching the lapse from the ABC camera van.

The Highway (above). It's what makes the Hawaii Ironman the Ironman.

Mark Allen (right) during race week in October 1982. Built like a greyhound, he was perhaps the most naturally talented athlete the sport of triathlon has ever seen.

In 1984 Allen ignored the record heat and the better judgment of Dave Scott when he rode off on his own to a 12-minute lead going into the marathon (below). The decision cost him dearly.

Just prior to start of the race in October 1982, the athletes seemed to bless themselves with a cheer in the direction of a hovering helicopter. Moments later the tension returned, and then the race was on.

The Ironman start (below)—an epic sight, an epic sound. It's like a wave, hissing but never breaking.

9

ST MEETS THE MAN

When Olympic cyclist John Howard came to Hawaii for the Ironman in 1980, he brought with him his unofficial title of "American Cyclist of the Decade." He figured that his ability on the bike would be enough to overcome his serious shortcomings in swimming and running. The Ironman was still widely held to be a playground for a group of thick-headed, albeit incredibly fit, Neanderthals. "We didn't know that any of these guys were athletes," Howard said. "We thought that athletes either ran or biked or swam, but not more than one of those."

He was wrong, but not by much—he finished third. And he realized that his assessment of Ironman competitors had been too harsh. He was especially impressed by the man who won the race that year, a former competitive swimmer named Dave Scott.

"Scott was not a great cyclist," Howard said, "he was not a world-class swimmer, and he was certainly not a great runner. But he was *balanced*. He was a triathlete. In my book he was the first triathlete."

If Tom Warren represented the Ironman of the past—an eccentric, gritty, race-you-over-the-next-hill-for-a-beer kind of crazy man—then Scott was the look of the future: The cool, dedicated purist who took the rough edges off an oddball sport and redefined its limits in terms that could be appreciated by athletes competing in any area. He was the new man of the New Age of super fitness, handsome and glowing with health, friendly in public but never self-revealing. Rumors about his personal life and athletic philosophy became entrenched as fact and turned rapidly into clichés: the Dave Scott legend described a man who lived alone and trained day and night in mysterious solitude in Northern California, an aesthetic vegetarian who rinsed his cottage cheese to remove excess fat and who shunned personal relationships because they detracted from his Ironman mission.

Eventually Scott was revealed to be both bigger and smaller than the public perception, a modest, gregarious man with the aura of a saint, the person-to-person skills of a parish priest, and the neuroses of Woody Allen. By 1986 he'd won the Ironman five times, including twice, maybe three times, after he'd been written off as either too old or too slow. After his total domination of the October 1982 Ironman he became known as "The Man," but he'd been referred to in that context before. Back on the mainland during the summer triathlon season he was always the favorite, while in Hawaii he raced as if he actually derived strength from the lava fields, as if only under the worst conditions could he perform up to his potential, as if his big, strong body fed off the agony of his would-be peers. Scott was the Reggie Jackson of the triathlon world, the "Mr. October" of the Kona Coast. It seemed that no matter what kind of racing season he had going in, he was always ready when the cannon roared on the Kailua Pier.

As strong as Scott seemed to be on the Queen K, though, he let a lot of things bother him in other races. He acquired a reputation for being undependable in a promotional capacity. You didn't assume he was actually going to be where it had been announced he would be, until he was.

He let business interests interrupt his training schedule, then started to complain about that—publicly. And his stoic concentration at the Ironman contrasted sharply to the "sensitive" Dave Scott who began to appear in the media. A featured profile of him in a nationally circulated triathlon magazine used not a photograph of Ironman Scott as The King of the Kona Coast, but one of a domesticated Scott playing a piano at home. Another shot pictured him stretched out on the floor of his apartment with a glass of wine at his elbow. Instead of making him seem more like a well-rounded guy, as was intended, the piece made him look wimpy. Then in 1983, while racing on his bike against a top professional field in a triathlon on the island of Kanai, he explained to an astonished network film crew that he just wasn't feeling all that well. He hadn't been training consistently, Scott said. He'd been going through an emotional crisis with a girlfriend and it had been sapping much of his energy. He was having problems with his "love life."

Two years later, a film crew caught him waffling again, this time at the prestigious Nice Triathlon. On a nasty downhill section of the course Scott had suffered a flat and had dropped out of the race, admitting aloud his fear that a new tire might not stay on the rim during the rest of the descent and that he might crash. As rational as his decision might have been, it seemed frivolous at the time, hardly in keeping with the popular image of the triathlon as a romantically reckless activity. And in France, of all places! How the old French cyclists, bruised and scarred from hundreds of bad falls, must have laughed!

After each broadcast Scott's rivals scoffed, and his public blinked, confused. This was The Man? This is the guy who eats lava for breakfast and runs back-to-back marathons at 3 a.m. to warm himself up for a long bike ride?

Yet, despite the disarming demonstrations of his humanity, or perhaps partly because of them, the Dave Scott legend grew; his stature rose tremendously each time he returned to Kona and won the Ironman. The average competitors learned to love him, and so did the locals who had taken the race close to their hearts. To thousands of athletes new to the sport, Dave Scott *was* the sport of triathlon. Even in defeat, at smaller races back on the mainland during the summer, he always received the lion's share of media attention, the loudest applause at awards ceremonies; the lines for his autograph were always the longest. He became the average triathletes' hero, someone who could fail and fail and fail but always triumph when it counted—and in the face of overwhelming odds.

❖

The triathlete whom Scott always seemed to triumph over—at the Ironman at least—was Scott Tinley, or "ST." For the better part of six years, Tinley played the role of Rebel Prince to Dave Scott's Golden King. Handsome and tan, with blond hair and a dashing blond mustache, Tinley epitomized the Southern California super fit ideal. In public he was the antithesis of Scott: outspoken and controversial where Scott was diplomatic; cocky where Scott was humble; psychologically remote in difficult situations where Scott had learned to use a flashing smile and a rapid exit.

Tinley liked life simple, full of fun, but as the years went by his life became less of both, and his sense of frustration at that was palpable. He seemed to be more of a victim of his growing success than its instigator, happiest when the pressure was low and the spontaneity high. He appeared a reluctant villain who slapped himself mentally for making an offensive off-the-cuff remark while at the same time chiding his peers for not speaking out themselves. Tinley's feelings were in the right place, but his presentation and timing were often skewed. At the post-race press conference at Ironman in 1984 he accurately reflected a general feeling among the professional athletes when he said that being at the race was "like coming to a communist country." He was referring to the highly regimented structure of the event, a structure even many age-group competitors considered unreasonably impersonal. The statement was taken as further proof of Tinley's arrogance. His subsequent retraction was seen as self-serving. Petulant and moody, frequently misinterpreted, he was branded as a rebel and a malcontent, a guy who needed to be handled with kid gloves but who never wore them himself.

But Tinley was a superb athlete. Racing in the shadow of Dave Scott at the Ironman, often in the shadow of his friend and former training partner Scott Molina in shorter-distance triathlons, he was arguably the most versatile and durable triathlete in the world through the 1980s. He could win at all distances under any conditions, and he always did so dramatically, coming from behind. Often seen as being haughty and aloof by the average participant, he was at the same time admired for his take-no-flak attitude. He was certainly the easiest of the top triathletes for the recreational triathletes to identify with.

Like most of them, Tinley came from a running background and was a mediocre swimmer. He worked long and hard in the pool to become more competitive. In February 1982, he gave up 12 minutes to the fastest swimmers in Hawaii; by 1986 he had cut that gap to less than three, a remarkable achievement in a sport where progress is measured in terms of seconds.

The annual battles between Dave Scott and Tinley at the Ironman were epic. They turned each race into Hemingway-esque duels under the cruel Kona sun; *mano a mano* on the long black highway. Greatly respectful of each other's abilities, neither man promoted a rivalry in public (both in fact denied emphatically that one ever existed), but the competition between the two was always there. Even in the year of Scott's "retirement," 1985, when Tinley won the race and broke Scott's course record, The Man was watching closely—as a commentator from an ABC camera van.

❖

Scott's first Ironman appearance was in 1980, on the old course on the island of Oahu. McDermott's piece in *Sports Illustrated,* which had appeared the previous spring, had

boosted participation almost tenfold. It had boosted public interest, too. Cashing in on that was television's job;
ABC's "Wide World of Sports" was on hand for the first of
what would be many annual broadcasts of the race. It was
fitting that they were witness to the debut of the man who
would become a one-man Ironman dynasty.

ABC's commentary was being done that year by Jim
Lampley, who met Scott by chance the day before the race.
No one knew much about the event, and Lampley was
looking for favorites when he and a film crew walked into
the pre-race meeting at the Nautilus Fitness Center on King
Street the night before the event. Lampley knew Tom
Warren, and he knew John Howard. Hoping for a line on
other contenders, he sat and talked for a while to Rick
Kozlowski, a former University of Southern California
swimmer and water polo player who had competed successfully in multisport lifeguard competition. Kozlowski
could run and swim, but he was a little weak on the bike—
he'd trained for the Ironman on his mother's exercycle.

"So who do you think is going to win the race, Koz?"
Lampley asked.

Kozlowski jerked a thumb to his left, indicating a man
sitting in the next chair. "This guy right here," he said.
"This is Dave Scott."

Lampley leaned over and introduced himself to Scott.
"Hi, Dave, I'm Jim Lampley with ABC."

"Yeah, I recognize your face," Scott replied.

"Do you mind if we ask you a few questions?"

"No, that's okay," Scott said, nervously. Everyone in the
room had noticed when the ABC crew had walked in; now
Scott had suddenly become the center of attention. He
decided to strangle Kozlowski when the meeting was over.

"So who are you, Dave?" Lampley asked. "Tell me a little bit about yourself. Were you ever on an Olympic team?"
Lampley had a stack of profile sheets in front of him that
the triathletes had filled out previously. Unlike most of the
others, who had listed years of accomplishments, thousands of miles of training, runs to the top of this mountain
and across that desert, Scott had kept his self-promotion to

a bare minimum; he labeled himself an "average" cyclist and runner. The only achievements that he recorded were a pair of first-place finishes in the Master's division at the Waikiki Rough Water Swim in 1978 and 1979.

"I see you're a swimmer," Lampley said. "Have you gone to the Pan Am Games or anything like that?"

"No," Scott said, "none of that."

"Are you pretty good on the bike?" Lampley asked.

"Actually," Scott said, sounding apologetic, "I just bought my first good bike three months ago."

"How about running?"

"Well, I ran my first marathon a couple of months ago, and it didn't seem too bad."

Lampley was fumbling. There wasn't much to hang an interview on. He smiled and tried once more.

"So, ah, what's your claim to fame, Dave?"

Scott smiled weakly. He wasn't a famous person, how could he have a claim to fame? "Well, I really like to work out," Scott said.

Kozlowski, who had been giggling throughout the interview, almost fell down. Lampley turned and motioned to the crew and the lights went off, then he threw a glance at Kozlowski that made it clear there were now two people hoping to get their hands around his neck.

It was a good thing that Lampley did the interview, though, because he was talking to the right guy. The next day Scott was so far ahead of the rest of the field after the first half of the marathon that he could have stopped for lunch and still won. Howard was faster than Scott out on the bike course by 30 minutes, but Scott had beaten Howard out of the water by twice that. Then he outran Howard by 45 minutes, and won the event by an hour. He broke Warren's record by exactly 1:51:23. Ridiculous. Who was this guy?

Scott was 26 at the time, a Masters swimming coach in Davis, California. He'd been a swimmer and a water polo player at the University of California at Davis—a solid member of the varsity and a Division II All-American in distance freestyle—although, as he told Lampley, he'd never become a star. Even at UC-Davis there had been plenty of men who were much faster than Dave Scott.

"I was a much better water polo player than I was a swimmer," Scott said. "My forte was doing long workouts, just sort of grinding them out. On every team—high school, college—I was the coach's dream, a robot. The coaches would just love to stand there with their clipboards and say, 'God, Dave Scott did these 100s. Look at that: 1:02.5, 1:02.6, 1:02.4, 1:02.6.' We'd get to the meet and the guy next to me who'd been going 1:06.5, 1:13, 1:01, 1:06 would *clean* me. I *hated* my teammates.

"I'd get to meets and I'd be so tired! I'd get up to the block, and the guy would say, 'Take your mark,' and I'd just fall in! I'd say, 'Oh, man, I just swam about 5000 miles this week. My arms are *dead!'*

"I just don't have the right genes," Scott said. "You know, there are a lot of factors that make up a good swimmer. You look at triathletes who are really good swimmers—like Richard Wells or Djan Madruga—they have a nice stroke, tremendous body position. I don't have that. I know the mechanics; I just don't *have* it."

He might not have *it,* whatever it is, but he is a strong, solid swimmer, especially when it comes to swimming in the ocean. Scott's swimming in triathlon has always been a great strength; in every race he enters he is either in the lead or close to it by the end of the first event. But Scott is uncomfortable talking about his own accomplishments, so there is always a touch of modesty in his manner to cover that up. In this case he was simply being unrealistic, comparing himself to the wrong people. His style is not classic, but he can go forever at a pace that only the best can match.

Born and raised in Davis, a town of almost 50,000 people, Scott's calm, humble demeanor is a reflection of a stable upbringing.

His older sister, Patti, became an accomplished triathlete herself, racing under her married name of Patti Scott-Baier. His younger sister Jane would become involved in triathlons also—as a swim coach. Living in Boulder,

Colorado, she works with many of the best triathletes in the world during their annual summer migration to Boulder to train in the mountains.

Dave's mother, Dot, gets credit for teaching her son how to swim—in a neighbor's pool—but all three kids were involved in AAU swimming early. "We never missed a meet," Dot said proudly. "It's not that we ever felt we needed to; we wanted to be there."

Over the years his parents remained his biggest fans. His father, Verne, was one of the best over-age 60 triathletes in the nation before an operation in late 1986 on a bad knee made it impossible for him to run. And Dot, who is not an athlete, became the Great Chronicler of the House of Scott, maintaining a large collection of her son's awards and press clippings.

Scott was a good all-around athlete in high school. He played a little football, played basketball for four years, swam, of course, and was the star of Davis High School's first water polo team. He was named to the High School All-American water polo team in 1972, and was his high school's Athlete of the Year that same year.

Water polo was one of the things (besides the family ties, of course) that kept him close to home after high school. UC-Davis had a strong water polo team for years, and Scott made the most of the opportunity. He was twice voted a first-team All-American for his play on a squad that moved up to Division I and placed fifth in the NCAA championship tournament in 1976. For a while, Scott thought he might have a chance to make the Olympic team.

He graduated in 1976, and if anything, worked himself into even better shape, in part by making fitness his source of financial as well as emotional support. He founded the Davis Aquatics Masters. In a city where youth and fitness dominated the college-town mentality, the program had become a huge success—and a steady source of income for Scott. Hundreds of people signed up and stayed involved, and the team became a hub of masters swimming activity in Northern California. The program was an extension of Scott himself, for he was an active coach, roaming the deck and talking constantly when there were swimmers in the water. He pushed the swimmers hard, but was ready to prop them up when they failed. He had his detractors, of course—he ran the program Dave Scott's way and only Dave Scott's way—but the large majority were avid supporters of his methods and philosophy. "I think he's a better coach than he is an athlete," said one former member of the team who was well-acquainted with Scott's Ironman accomplishments. "That should give you some idea of how good a coach he really is."

Extremely conscious of his position as an example, Scott practiced his own teachings faithfully. With the benefit of a strong background in physiology from his days at UC-Davis, he had some well-founded convictions on how to maintain maximum fitness. He watched his diet like a hawk, continued to run—an activity he had taken up for recreation while he was still in school—worked out in the pool regularly, and became a successful Masters swimmer on the national level. And like almost everyone else in Davis, he rode his bike whenever he could.

"I didn't know where all the training would lead," Scott said, "but I liked being healthy. I liked feeling healthy. I took a certain pride in thinking that I was in tremendous shape, but I had no means of comparison. I couldn't compare myself with a cyclist. I couldn't compare myself with anyone else. But I lifted weights and I swam and I was doing a lot of running."

In that, Scott sounded a lot like Dunbar and Haller before their first Ironman. His competitive background was more extensive than theirs, and he was a much more naturally talented athlete, but the common ground is obvious, and it might point toward another clue to the appeal of the race. To men and women who drive their bodies to perform, the Ironman seems to offer an answer to a difficult yet inevitable question—the question a cyclist asks himself as he stares at the exceptionally developed legs of a fellow competitor; the question in the eyes of a marathoner as she glances furtively at the lean, well-defined arms of the woman standing next to her on the starting line; the question on the face of a swimmer who stops at the track on his way to the pool and watches the sweat glisten on the brown shoulders of the distance runners as they move smoothly, in unison, through a turn—How fit am I, really?

Curiously, the man who gave Dunbar and Haller a chance to answer that question also gave Dave Scott the same opportunity.

In September 1978, while Scott was in Hawaii to compete in the Maui Channel Swim and the Waikiki Rough Water Swim, he met John Collins, who was doing a personal, word-of-mouth promotion job for his "Iron Man," which had been held for the first time the previous January. Collins introduced himself to Scott during a briefing the day before the channel swim and handed him a flyer. Scott, preoccupied at the time, gave the flyer only a perfunctory glance, noting the distances and automatically assuming that the three events were strung out over three days. It was only later that he realized they were done consecutively.

"I couldn't fathom that," Scott said. "But Collins had said that 12 people actually did it. I thought to myself that here are 12 people who are in better shape than me! I was living in a little shell. I didn't know what was going on. Twelve people! It was amazing."

The "Iron Man" stuck in Scott's mind. He never seriously considered doing the race in 1979—there would have been only three months to train—but goaded by his curiosity, and with a little extra shove from Mike Norton, a runner and an old friend from Davis who at the time was attending medical school in Los Angeles, Scott decided to start training for the 1980 race.

"Mike and I would get together occasionally and train," Scott said. "He'd come up to Davis on the weekends and I'd drag him through a two-hour workout in the pool, then we'd lift weights, then we'd run 11 or 12 miles. We thought we were on top of the world if we could do that. We saw the article in *Sports Illustrated* about the race in 1979 and the splits that Warren did in establishing the record—11 hours and 15 minutes. Mike and I thought the times were terribly slow. He said: 'You'll obliterate 'em, Dave. This is an event that's made for you.'"

The article came out in May 1979. Scott had already done a couple of short triathlons and several biathlons in northern California, so he had one foot in the door. With Collins's invitation still sitting in the back of his mind, and Warren's times staring at him from the magazine, Scott decided to do the race. He began training seriously in June. Day by day, week by week, he gradually cut his social life down to the bare nub and whittled his list of priorities down to a single line that stretched from Davis, California, southwest to Hawaii. One of the casualties of his new preoccupation was his previously unrelenting devotion to the Davis Masters swimming program. Hundreds of swimmers trained with him, and now some of them grumbled when he had less time to spend than he had before.

"He had always maintained considerable intensity toward his physical fitness and training and competition," said Scott's father, Verne. "But it was apparent when he took this on that he took it on with even greater zeal and concentration and effort—at the expense of a number of different things. He sacrificed some support of the swim club, for example, because he was not as available as he had been before to people who had been accustomed to that kind of opportunity. He became the subject of some criticism as a result. It created some ill-feeling."

Scott was aware of the grumbling, but for the most part he ignored it. He figured he had paid his dues.

"I had coached Masters like a workaholic," he said. "I made sure I talked to everyone in the pool at least three times each session. The people were used to that; they wanted me out there the whole time. They couldn't understand why I was doing something for myself. And I couldn't understand why they couldn't accept it. Not all of them; a lot of people wholeheartedly supported me. When I won the 1980 race, there was a huge crowd at the airport, they greeted me with a banner."

Consumed by that same driving dedication he'd demonstrated in the college swimming pool, Scott swam and rode and ran, endlessly, without any idea of how much was enough, but taking no chances.

"He had a plan," Verne Scott said. "It was obvious to us that he knew what he was doing."

Emotionally he knew what he was doing. From a technical standpoint, though, he was as lost as every other would-be triathlete at the time. There wasn't a single expert around to ask for advice, so Scott wrote his own book, from scratch, on how to train for the Ironman. He was confident of his swimming. It was his business, after all, and he had the perfect place to train. The running was just a matter of putting one foot in front of the other; he had a good aerobic conditioning base to start with, and also the good fortune to be naturally durable. Swimmers who become runners often spend a lot of time nursing injuries instead of training. Scott would do that, but luckily not until after the race.

The cycling was more complicated. He had no formal background on the bike, although he had done a lot of casual cycling, and he knew he had some natural speed from the short triathlons and biathlons he'd done. Pat Feeney, who had been one of Scott's swimmers at the Davis Masters, had some experience in long-distance cycling, and offered to help. The two men were becoming good friends; now Feeney became his coach. They bought a new bike, a Raleigh Professional, and Scott started pouring on the miles, making up in distance what he lacked in expertise. He didn't buy a pair of cleated cycling shoes until December, six weeks before he flew off to Hawaii. He trained in tennis shoes, and bundled himself up in sweats when the weather turned cold in the fall.

In September he did his first marathon in Sacramento, running awkwardly, almost shuffling (his style is terrible to this day), but he ran it quickly. His time was 2:45, a remarkable first marathon for an ex-swimmer with so little running background. Then in late October he put himself through his own "mini-triathlon" as he called it: 5000 yards in the pool, a 105-mile bike ride, and a 20-mile run, and finished the day feeling "good." He knew then that the distances of the Ironman were doable, a tremendous advantage at a time when less than two dozen people in the world could honestly say that to themselves. He figured he was ready, and there were still two months to go.

❖

The 1980 Ironman (officially the Nautilus International Triathlon) itself was not only a Dave Scott show, it was a Scott family tour de force, with Feeney acting as consigliere. As had been the case in the first two Ironman races, all of the triathletes were required to supply their own support crew, but the Scotts refined the concept. Their level of intensity and sophistication took everyone by surprise. There was even a little ill will; some of the other competitors and their crews were mildly offended by Dave Scott's obvious desire to win.

Initiating a routine they would refine and then repeat again and again in the years to come, at long-distance triathlons and short, from the United States to Europe to Australia to New Zealand and Japan, Feeney and Scott spent the week before the race reviewing race strategy, driving the course, projecting times. On race day Feeney acted as driver and navigator; Verne and Dot took care of the logistics, handing food and water to Scott through the windows of their rented car. Between Dave's level of conditioning and his knowledge of his physical requirements and capabilities and his team's great attention to detail, the day went remarkably smoothly, especially when compared to the trials and tribulations of the 100 or so rookies stretched out for miles behind them.

The swim that year was held in the calm but dirty Ala Moana lagoon instead of the ocean. As had been the case the year before, high winds had whipped the ocean to a froth, and while the weather wasn't anywhere near as bad as it had been in 1979, there was more of a concern for the triathletes' safety because there was such a large field of inexperienced competitors to contend with—and ABC's cameras to consider.

With his long and successful experience as an ocean swimmer, Scott would have preferred the rough water; it would have given him more of an advantage, even over other strong swimmers in the race such as Warren and Tom Boughey of Costa Mesa, California. But he was ready for the lagoon, too. He came out of the water in 51 minutes, several minutes ahead of second place. He stood under an outdoor shower for a moment. Feeney handed him his cycling shorts and then he dashed into the women's rest-room to change. "Look out in there," he shouted as he went. "Here I come!" He was out again a few seconds later, sitting to pull on his socks ("Tube socks," Scott said, laughing. "Can you believe that? Big, heavy tube socks.") and his cycling shoes, then standing to pull on his gray UC-Davis basketball jersey while Feeney slapped a strip of duct tape over the backs of the shoes, which were loose in the heel. Before the second swimmer was out of the water, Scott was off, pedaling east toward Diamond Head. He would spend the next five hours pulling strongly away from the rest of the field. Only Howard gained time on him, but Howard had been so far behind when he emerged from the water, he would have needed a motorcycle to catch up. So Scott rode alone, unchallenged, with only his parents' rented car, the ABC camera van, and the normal Saturday morning traffic along the highway to keep him company. The only problem that he encountered during the ride was with his shoes. They might have been loose in the back, but they were tight in the front, and hurt him so badly during the ride that he was tempted to take them off and ride barefoot.

He came off the bike at the Aloha Tower in downtown Honolulu with a 30-minute lead. Actually, he *fell* off his bike. Wobbly after the long ride, slightly disoriented, he had to put on his brakes and stop in the transition area before he had loosened his toe straps. There was nowhere to go but down. The crowd was stunned, thinking for a moment that Scott was totally exhausted. Scott was tired but certainly not exhausted, and after a good cuss he changed clothes, stretched, took a long drink, and then was off again, running toward Waikiki. Feeney hopped on his bike; Verne and Dot followed in the car.

Scott had ridden the course much faster than he had projected. He had figured five and a half hours, maybe 5:40. But he came off in 5:03, and as he headed off into the run, Feeney was surprised at how tired he looked. On his bike it took Feeney only a few minutes to catch up, and when he did, Scott looked over, eyes tight with fatigue, face drawn, and said, "It hurts, it really hurts."

Compared to the men behind him, though, Scott looked terrific. His lead over Howard and Chuck Neumann, who was in third and gaining on Howard, was growing. The only direction from which a threat to Scott's win could come, it seemed, was from the race organization itself, and Feeney was ready even for that. Starting that year, and continuing through the February 1982 event, race officials at the Ironman checked the triathletes' weight at intervals throughout the competition. Anyone who was found to have lost 10 percent or more of his pre-race body weight would be withdrawn from the competition. Little was known about what an event as long as the Ironman, in conditions as warm and humid as Hawaii's, could do to the human body, but the Ironman wasn't taking any chances. And, of course, the event was still not considered a race, so the time lost at the checks was not seen as a problem. None of the triathletes, though, could imagine being pulled out of the race for so ridiculous a reason as sweating too much. Dave Scott was only the first of many to make extra sure it didn't happen. When he stepped on the scale at the 10-mile point, he put his hands behind his back and Feeney slipped him a full water bottle. It was a pound of insurance, just in case.

To the television people and the spectators Scott looked remarkably fresh during the marathon. None of them had the eye for him that Feeney had. What they had expected to see, especially considering the speed at which he had whipped around the island on his bike, was a mumbling, stumbling wreck of a human being, perhaps bumping into a car or two, *a la* John Dunbar in 1978. Instead, Scott was making the thing look almost easy.

"I had run only one marathon before that," Scott said, "and I was getting pretty weary by the 17-mile mark, but it wasn't the comatose state I've been in during some of my races. I crossed the finish line and felt reasonably coherent. I didn't have any measure of how far I could push myself, so when I finished, even a short time later, I said to myself: 'I know I can go faster. I know I can go *a lot* faster.'" Scott's huge margin of victory that year illustrated how well he had grasped the scope of the Ironman. As inexperienced as most of the other 108 competitors who started the event, he was the only one to catch a glimpse of the Ironman's potential, match it with his own, then drive both in the direction of the future, hard. As Howard said, Scott was a *triathlete.* Next to him, Warren, the defending champ, who placed a disgruntled fourth in 1980, was an aging pioneer, his one-year-old star already dim. Howard, in third place, was a world-class single-sport expert who, by being a year too late, had missed his only shot to be just that and win.

"I finished that race and there was a long, long lag before the second place guy came in," Scott said. "I said to myself, 'God, I've really found a sport, an event, that's built for me. After all those years in swimming, those long work-outs where I ended up being very mediocre, here's a test where you have to do aerobic work for an incredible amount of time, where I just out-persevered everyone else. This is pretty amazing!'

"Physically, I didn't feel I was any more talented than anyone else. I don't to this day. It's just a matter of having the mental fortitude and concentration and perseverance to go a little bit farther. I remember when Chuck Neumann crossed the finish line he almost fell over and his eyes kind of rolled back and he said, 'No way in hell am I going to do *that* again.' He said that on camera. It almost gave me energy. Here's a guy, he got second place, I beat him by an *hour,* and he's completely wiped out."

Scott had redefined the race. By challenging himself so relentlessly, he'd challenged the growing sport of triathlon to take itself seriously. Over the course of the next two years, many people would mourn the passing of the eccentric characters who had been a big part of the Ironman's infancy. Warren, with his superb athletic ability and grinding determination, would hang on longer than any of them. But the comedians and the professional characters, guys like Cowman Shirk, the Incredible Huck, and Born Again Smitty, all faded away or were pushed aside. After 1980 the issue at the Ironman was no longer how weird you were, but how fast and how tough.

❖

Scott intended to race the Ironman again in 1981, but a knee injury in the off-season, aggravated by his stubborn attempts to train hard despite it, cost him six months of conditioning. By the end of the summer he had grudgingly resigned himself to sitting the competition out. He gave the Ironman his official notice of withdrawal just three weeks before race day, too late for his name to be deleted from the official program. For Scott it was a bitter disappointment.

In his absence John Howard became a triathlon star on the brand-new course on the Big Island, having learned well the lessons Scott taught him on Oahu. Howard had spent months in the pool learning to swim, and months on the roads toughening up his legs, becoming a runner. In 1981 he came out of the water just 15 minutes behind the leaders (rather than an hour, as had been the case the year before), blew through the field on his bike, ran a 3:23 marathon, and won the race in 9:38:29. It was a slower time than Scott's, but the new course was acknowledged to be much tougher. Old Tom Warren was 26 minutes back in second place, 30 minutes faster than he'd been the year before. In third place, with the fastest run of the day, was a blond San Diegan named Scott Tinley.

Tinley still jokes about his lack of sophistication and organized training for that event, mostly about his heavy touring bike made even worse by the three-pound tool kit he strapped beneath the seat. A runner by preference, a cyclist only casually, and a swimmer for fun—for lifeguarding, for surfing, for climbing back on a sailboard, but never before just for *swimming*—Tinley was as surprised by his third place as anyone else. "I was a neophyte," he said. "I did everything wrong."

Not everything. What he did correctly was run well after cycling for almost six hours.

At the time he'd started to prepare for the event, at the urging of Tom Warren himself, Tinley was attending evening classes at San Diego State University, studying for a master's degree in education while at the same time working as a paramedic for the San Diego Fire Department. Since the job required his attention only 10 days a month, he had time during the day to train.

He trained mostly alone, although he rode sometimes with his brother Jeff and swam occasionally with his partner at the fire department. They'd take their equipment to the pool—hats, uniforms and radios—and listen for emergency calls between laps. They showed up for more than one call with hair dripping and the seats of their overalls plastered to their wet swimsuits underneath. Management considered that to be an unprofessional way to act and eventually ordered the swimming during on-call hours to stop.

Tinley's strongest event by far was the marathon. He'd been a runner in high school and had a marathon best of 2:30. He had no technical training at all on the bike, and while he rode regularly while training for the Ironman, he seldom rode more than 35 miles at a time. He remembered the bike ride in Hawaii that first year mostly for its discomfort.

"It was kind of long," he said. "My legs weren't that tired, but little things bothered me. My feet really hurt because I had these little touring cleats, and I had this big tank top that blew in the wind. I wore black wool shorts with a leather chamois in the crotch, and gloves, and a red Skid Lid. Everything was just sort of uncomfortable."

He got off the bike gratefully in 15th place. He wasn't used to running after riding that far, of course, so his legs were heavy as he headed out for the marathon. But then things started to feel better and better.

"My feet really hurt—ached—so I went slowly," Tinley said. "But then each half-mile little pains disappeared. All of a sudden my feet didn't hurt anymore, my hands didn't hurt anymore, my neck, my back. Within four or five miles it felt like I was just out running."

That was something; even Tinley himself could see that he was a special case. As he ran, picking off slower runners along the way, he was surprised at how tired everyone looked. And when he neared the turnaround and could see the men in front of him heading back the other way, his surprise turned to wonder at their condition.

"Howard looked terrible," Tinley said, smiling. "He had no shirt on, with that ungodly style. I couldn't believe that he was running like that. And Warren, I just laughed when I saw him. I remember running by people and thinking: 'God, it's not *that* bad. We're only running 26 miles, not a *hundred* and 26.'"

No one in the field that year could match him. He had a natural talent for the single most difficult aspect of the triathlon: He could run off the bike. It was an ability that would bring him face-to-face with Dave Scott the following February, and keep him there for years.

Curiously, facts about Tinley's upbringing and the forces that moved him in the athletic direction he took remained obscure, despite his long-standing and unshakable position among the top four triathletes in the world. He was treated by journalists within the sport like the too-pretty girl in high school who spends her weekend nights alone because all the boys assume she would refuse them. He never volunteered a lot of information; they never asked. Or when they asked, Tinley scoffed at the questions, as he is still prone to do, and they never pressed the point or asked again. "What you see is what I am," Tinley said again and again, pushing his image to the front, the kind of image the sport was looking for in the first place: Tinley the Stud, Tinley the Beachboy, Tinley the Golden Boy of the Golden Sport.

In-depth articles about Tinley in the national triathlon press were nonexistent. During the four-year period between early 1983 and January 1987, a grand total of two Tinley profiles were published in either of the two national journals of the sport (*Triathlon* first appeared in 1983. *Tri-Athlete* was introduced later the same year. The two finally merged and became *Triathlete* in 1986). The pieces appeared in back-to-back issues of *Triathlon*; the second one announced his selection as the magazine's Triathlete of the Year, but neither story went beyond the familiar Tinley-as-good-ol'-boy formula. Over the years there were numerous interviews with him and race reports of major events in which he figured prominently. He frequently wrote columns and articles, but nothing ever took the reader below the surface; it was always Tinley according to Tinley. The sheer number of column inches devoted to him were misleading; it was Tinley who was the triathlon mystery man, not Dave Scott.

There have been times during his career, though, when ST has offered glimpses of the man behind the face, but they were subtle glimpses presented only in context. More than any of the other top men in the sport, he has been the most apt to question both his motivations and those of his peers, to question the sanity of the level of effort and dedication required of the top triathletes. The most graphic example of the private Tinley popping to the surface was at the Nice Triathlon in 1983, when water for the competitors during the 75-mile bike ride and the 20-mile run was difficult to come by, despite the extremely warm conditions. Mark Allen won the race, but only barely. Dehydrated and overheated, he collapsed during the final stages of the run and barely made it to the finish line. Dave Scott was second and Tinley third. The medical facility at the finish, which was located in a bunker-like structure beneath the seaside promenade, resembled the aftermath of some terrible battle, with triathletes laid out like wounded soldiers in every corner, medics and doctors rushing back and forth trying to keep up with the flow.

"It's no good," Tinley said, surveying the scene. "You go to the bitter end, and you're doing it on balls alone; you're seeing *God* on every step. And you know, you're just...wasted! But you do it, you know? We do it on a bet. We do it in *practice*. I don't know how smart this is. But you lay that much money on the line and people are just gonna go for it.

"Somebody's gonna die!"

He was blond and tall and handsome, but he was much, much more than a beach boy.

Tinley, the second of eight children, was born in Santa Monica, California, in 1956. The family moved south to La Mirada in Orange County a couple of years later, and it was there that Tinley was raised and went to school. He became a runner at St. Paul's High School by default; when a minor back injury kept him from lifting weights with the rest of the football team, the coach assigned him to run laps instead. So Tinley ran—lap after lap after lap. Not only did he enjoy it but he had a natural talent for it. He was soon faster than anyone on St. Paul's cross-country team.

"I never liked team sports all that much," Tinley said. "Even in grade school, playing football and basketball, I was always second string. Of course, football and basketball were all there was at that time. The attraction for me came because even at a young age I realized that there were real good possibilities within sport itself to learn about yourself and to enjoy it—that it's part of the whole socialization process. You see so many people screwed up by the other things—like going out and hanging out with the gang, doing drugs, all that stuff. But it always seemed that the people involved with sports had their heads more together."

He was strongly influenced in that area by his father, Terry, a sales representative for a paper supply company. Terry Tinley was an exceptionally active parent, a good athlete who passed along his appreciation of sports and fitness to his children. Mostly, though, he passed along his concept of sport as fun, as a way of living. Tinley affectionately calls him "an old-time surf dog."

"He kept us all involved," Tinley said. "Not so much in organized sports but in activities, always doing something physical. I did a lot of modeling after my dad, seeing his friends, what they did and the fun they had. You see your dad get up and go surfing with his friends, then come back and play baseball with the kids in the neighborhood. He was literally out there playing with us. When you see your parents doing that kind of stuff, playing right there next to you, not just playing *at* you, that has an influence. He was one of the guys. He was 38, but he could act like a 15-year-old. Not in an immature way, but you know how some people can relate to people half their age? That had a bigger influence on me than anything else."

In all the years I'd known Tinley, watching his career expand, watching him race, annoying him at times by reaching for what I perceived to be his sensitive, spiritual self, I'd never heard him talk about his father or sound so affected by anything. I realized suddenly how successful he had been pushing that flip, public face of his to the front.

"How did your dad die?" I asked softly.

"Cancer," Tinley replied, cutting the syllables off sharply, getting the word out like it hurt him, physically. "Cancer of the stomach. It was real bad. He had it for a year-and-a-half. It was real discouraging because we just watched him deteriorate. We watched this thing just eat him alive—in 18 months he went from a specimen of health to just a shell of a person.

"That was a pivotal point for me," Tinley said. "I was at that very influential age—I was like 16—where you're deciding what sort of person you're going to be. There were a lot of bad influences. I had to make some decisions as to what kind of lifestyle I was going to lead. There was lack of motivation more than anything, I guess. Boredom. Lack of self-respect. People letting their bodies go, not really caring about things at all. You see that, and then on the other hand you see someone who has this incredible zest for life fighting the absolute worst thing that you can imagine, and there's a real contrast.

"I remember what happened to my dad being a major influence on me. I thought that as long as I was going to have to be alive for the next 70 or 80 years, I might as well go for it, you know, live a healthy life and be active and just try to do everything my father would have if he had continued to live."

His dad was just 39 when he died. Tinley was a junior in high school at the time, and he was crushed. He dealt with the situation mostly by denying it, by hauling a lot of his feelings inside himself and then closing the door, putting on his public face and "going for it." Perhaps he went too hard, too fast.

"He was at a very impressionable age," said Tinley's brother, Jeff. "At the time he was a big man on campus, he was running well, he was winning a lot of events, he had long hair—a full surf Nazi. He was into his own deal, and rightfully so."

Jeff, a successful sales representative for a major shoe company, is three years Scott's junior, although he seems at times much older, more mature. Despite their vast difference in temperament, the two men are close; Scott could never be as down-to-earth and sharply focused as Jeff, and Jeff has learned to roll his eyes and shrug his shoulders and not try too hard to understand his older brother.

"My mom was left alone," Jeff said. "We had a huge house, a huge yard, my youngest brother was eight months old, and Scott walked away. I was pissed, because there was no one else left to do it. The day after my dad died I went out and got a job washing tables at a little Chinese restaurant for a buck an hour. I was 13. That was just the way I wanted it; I wanted to help my mom any way I could.

"I think a lot of it was age and immaturity more than anything. When you're 16 or 17 or whatever Scott was, and you're a junior in high school, you've got a social life, you've got dates.... I didn't understand that."

Tinley moved to San Diego in 1974 to attend San Diego State University, right about the time the first triathlon was being glued together by Shanahan and Johnson down at Mission Bay. Tinley's formal competitive days as a runner were over, at least as far as school was concerned, but he raced frequently in local road races and stayed in touch with the San Diego running scene. Two years later he was running and cycling and swimming around and across Fiesta Island, chasing Tom Warren, Bill Phillips, and the

Buckingham brothers, all of them grass-roots pioneers in a fledgling sport. Triathlons must have touched a chord in Tinley, for they were exactly the kind of loosely organized, off-the-wall things that his dad would have enjoyed. And he must have been pleased with his life at the time, because he was studying hard, working as a lifeguard, and spending a lot of time playing his heart out, filling up his life, using every precious second, just the way he had promised himself he would. There was no way for him to know that the play would soon become serious business.

❖

Tinley's unexpected success in Hawaii in 1981 prompted him to give the Ironman another shot—despite what he'd promised his new wife, Virginia, whom he'd married the previous June, and his new boss at the Mission Bay Aquatic Center, a recreational facility affiliated with San Diego State that offered classes in sailing, water safety and sailboarding. Tinley had taken a management job there in December, two months before the Ironman, with the understanding that he could have two weeks off to do the race in Hawaii in February. He never thought there'd be a second time.

Things were different now, though. The possibilities were too intriguing to ignore. "If I could go over there as raw as I was and do as well as I did," Tinley said to himself, remembering what Howard and Warren had looked like coming back from the turnaround during the marathon, "suppose I really worked at it all this time?"

So he kept training, more out of curiosity than ambition, although it required a lot of thought because his schedule was getting tight. He had a staff of 100 or so people to supervise at the center, and a salaried position that required him to spend long hours there. Plus he was still going to school at night and at the same time trying to squeeze in the extra mileage he knew he needed now that he was going back to Hawaii. "My lunch hours kept getting longer and longer," said Tinley. "I was going nuts. I was literally doing something from 6 in the morning until 10 at night."

On the plus side was his brother Jeff, who was life-guarding at the time and had decided to try the race himself. A training partner was always welcome. Tinley was riding a better bike, too; a sponsorship deal had put him on a sleek Bianchi racer, a far cry from the massive touring machine he'd ridden at the previous Ironman.

While the hours he spent on his bike that year were far less than what he would spend later when his legs were better adapted, he was cramming into his hectic schedule what were then considered to be big miles: swimming every evening after work, riding 300 miles or so a week on the bike, most of them in the morning before work with Jeff, and running 60-70 miles a week. Lunch hours were running hours; weekends were for long rides—50 miles up the Pacific Coast Highway to San Clemente for lunch, then back. That summer he established a pattern that would remain a Tinley trademark: He raced as often as possible, racing himself into top shape, gearing his mind for competition, and focusing his training so that it maximized his ability to recover quickly from hard efforts. Without realizing what he was doing, Tinley was setting himself up to be a professional triathlete. When the prize money started to flow in late 1982 he would be ready; only he and Scott Molina would be tough enough to race and race again, plucking enough green off the prize money tree to establish themselves financially. It would take years, and a new generation of young triathletes, to catch on to the system. At the time, though, and despite the intensity of his effort, Tinley still didn't see triathlons as anything more than a time-consuming diversion.

"The aquatic center was hard work, but it was a lot of fun," he said. "I wasn't totally into triathlons; it was just another thing that I was doing. I was racing sailboats and hanging out at the beach and doing all that other stuff."

Meanwhile, 600 miles to the north, Dave Scott was driving himself hard, alone. Tinley might have been curious about his Ironman chances, but Scott wasn't curious about his in the least; he knew he had just scratched the surface of his potential. Frustrated because he hadn't been able to race in 1981, then irked by all the attention lavished on Howard, he trained with even greater focus than he'd devoted to the race in 1980. He even resigned his position at the Davis Masters so that he could train full time. "There was a lot more publicity around the event after the 1980 race," Scott said. "The sport was gaining momentum; there were more triathlons popping up all over. Even though he got third place, John Howard seemed to get as much publicity, or more, than I did, because he was a guy with great credentials who was destined to come back and win the next year."

Howard's legendary status in the American cycling community certainly didn't hurt. When he lived up to the expectations and won in 1981, the credibility he gave the new sport of triathlon was undeniable.

"His time was an hour faster than he'd done the previous year," Scott said, a hint of bitterness in his voice. "It was slower than my time, but it was like my time was completely erased because the new course was much, much more challenging than the Oahu course. It was if they were saying, 'Listen, this is the first year we're really going to establish the record. John Howard has just set the precedent for triathlons by going 9:39 and Dave's 9:24 doesn't mean beans.'

"It bothered me. I was irritated by the media and the race organizers for discounting my performance. Not that I trained out of spite, it just gave me a lot of energy and momentum to come back and place first, prove to myself that I could go much, much faster than 9:24, and second, to beat both records, mine and Howard's. Coming into that race I was like Howard had been. I was determined to do well."

And as Tinley himself would say four years later, "When Dave decides to get in shape, he gets in better shape than just about anybody." Neither man knew the other going into the race in February 1982. They'd never met. They'd heard stories about each other, but the sport was new, there weren't many races, so the rumor mill was not much of a source of information, accurate or otherwise. The book on Scott was that he was a prodigious trainer, secretive, driven, solitary. Tinley remembers only a vague impression that Scott was going to be the favorite—if he raced.

"I didn't know Scott Tinley beyond that I knew he'd gotten third in the '81 race," Scott said. "And he'd actually come up to Davis to the Davis Triathlon, which I'd won in 1980 [Tinley won it in '81; Scott didn't race]. He looked, you know, all right. He was one of the guys doing triathlons whose name kept cropping up, but I didn't feel as if he would be a threat. I did know that I didn't want to get into a foot race with the guy—he'd probably clean my clock."

Tinley shared Scott's view. "I knew at that point that I could outrun anybody in the sport, because nobody had a running background. I was the only one. I felt that if it came down to a run, it would be no contest."

Dave Scott was determined not to let it get that close.

❖

The Ironman had grown up tall since 1978. Considerable attention was being lavished on it by the media, and competitors were flocking to Kona in numbers that no one had ever expected. On the mainland, shorter-distance triathlons were being held all over the country, and the Ironman was seen as something more exciting and less frightening. The general level of triathlon ability skyrocketed. Several of the top triathletes competed as cyclists in bicycle races, outfitting themselves with top-of-the-line machines and wearing dramatic-looking, tight-fitting skin suits. When they raced in triathlons they brought both their new-found skill and their high-tech look with them. Soon everyone had a skin suit and a hot bike, too—equipment that made them want to train their brains out if only to be seen in public doing it. As February 6, 1982, crept closer, it was clear that the Ironman was going to be more competitive than ever.

Five weeks before the race, Scott came down with a tendon problem in his right knee. Panicky, he tried to push through it, training harder than ever, which was exactly the way he had turned his post-Ironman injury in 1980 into something serious. The knee got worse, until he could neither run on it nor ride. For a while it looked as if he might miss the Ironman entirely. He sat out for three weeks, then made a call the night before he and Feeney were scheduled to leave for Hawaii.

"Pat, I'm going to get up in the morning about four and try to run an easy four miles. If I can do it, then we're going."

The run was a success. Around five, Feeney got the message: "The blanket's been lifted! I'm gonna do it!"

It's impossible to tell how much those three weeks off affected Scott's condition, although an enforced layoff for as long as that has been known to help athletes who are prone to overtraining. But Scott had never had that problem; over the years he demonstrated an acute, consistent ability to bring himself into a race in top shape, aware of his body as few endurance athletes ever have been. His own analysis was that the layoff hurt him badly. Arriving in Hawaii only a week before the race, he proceeded to pack in the mileage, trying to make up the lost ground. He ran every day, biked the 40 miles to Kawaihae and back three times, and went into the race with just one day's rest.

The pattern of that first Scott/Tinley duel was to be duplicated again and again, year after year. At the center of it were the individual strengths of the two men, like chips of a long-running poker game in which Scott, the swimmer, always made the first bet. Tinley the runner then had to call the bet or raise it, using as much of his leg strength as he dared during the bike ride to get close enough to strike during the run. But how much to use? Without knowing the condition of the man in front, it was never an easy judgment for Tinley to make. In all the times that he looked darkly across the Ironman table at Scott, he never judged it so well as that first time, and he did it that time on bad information.

What threw Tinley off was the swim, which was slightly mis-measured, and choppy. He'd been counting on the lead swimmers, including Scott, to come out of the water at about the 50-minute mark, with his own time somewhere around an hour. But at the end of the 2.4 miles he climbed out of Kailua Bay, took a look at the clock, and gulped. 1:10! That meant an 18-, maybe a 20-minute deficit, a terrible gap. There was no choice but to throw caution and his pre-race strategy to the winds. He climbed up Palani Road and headed out onto the highway recklessly, with only one thing in mind: get to the front! Why save something for the end, Tinley figured, if what you've saved doesn't matter by the time you get there?

What he had no way of knowing was that the entire field had been slow on the swim. The leaders had come out of the water close to the hour mark themselves. Scott had come out at 58 minutes, not 50. Tinley's swim had not been the disaster he thought it was.

The panic helped though. It pushed him to ride much harder than he might have; it forced him to press the limits. And his legs responded. It was clear early in the ride that Tinley had learned the Big Lesson. He was a cyclist now, far more sure and conditioned on the bike than he'd been in 1981. He raced through the field with Howard-like efficiency. He made the turn at Kawaihae and headed up the hills toward Hawi, climbing hard. Pushing into the wind, he was able to get much closer to the turnaround than he'd let himself hope before he saw the leader, Kim Bushong, in his leopard-skin cycling outfit, flying back down the hill in the other direction, shepherded by the ABC camera van. Two minutes later Dave Scott followed. Tinley made the turn 13 minutes after that and headed grimly down, believing for the first time all day that there was a chance. Along the way he passed someone special. It sent his already rising spirits soaring.

"Warren was really surprised," Tinley laughed. "He looked at me as if to say: 'What are you doing here?! You're not supposed to be up here until the run!'"

Tinley was having a good day. His best. Scott, though, was having trouble. He felt he was not getting the support he needed from some of the aid stations, some of which were not ready for the leaders when they flashed by. It's a common problem at endurance events, but it's unforgivable at the Ironman, where the needs are critical and short-falls are relentlessly cumulative. In years to come, Scott would learn to carry much of what he needed to eat, but this time around he was helpless.

"I remember coming back I hadn't had any food until about mile 85 on the bike. I could feel myself getting hypo-glycemic and I told Pat, who I passed along the way, 'I gotta get a banana!' Finally this woman came up to me on a moped and asked me if I needed something. She got me the banana."

It was just about at that point in the race that Tinley caught him, having made up a tremendous amount of time over the second half of the bike ride. Bushong was still in front by a couple of minutes, but Tinley knew Bushong was not the man he'd have to beat. The man to worry about was right next to him. For the first time in his life he said hello to Dave Scott—in a way that Scott will never forget.

"He said, 'How are ya doing?' or something like that," Scott said, laughing. "There I was, with my teeth on the handlebars, and he says 'How are ya doing?' Like, 'Can I help you out?' I thought, 'What a sportsman!' I couldn't even remember my name.

"So he went around me and about that time I got the banana. I felt better instantly. I caught back up to him and we rode in together. I realized that if I'd had food, I would have felt a lot better; I probably would have held him off."

But Scott hadn't held him off. As anyone will tell you, "ifs" at the Ironman aren't rare, and they come cheap. The only thing there's more of is lava. The fact was that Scott's worst fear—and Tinley's greatest hope—had come to pass: The race had come down to the marathon. As both men had privately predicted, it was no contest.

"Good Lord," thought Scott, watching Tinley take off up the hill leading out of the Kona Surf. "I'll see you at the finish line. This is my pace today. If you die, I'll whittle you down. If you don't, then it's all over, because I can't go any faster."

Tinley didn't die. He passed Bushong at about mile 5 and won the race by a lopsided 17:16. His time was 9:19:41. In a film about the Ironman, produced by Freewheelin' Films and narrated by actor Bruce Dern, there is a long shot of Tinley during the marathon, running back toward town with a 15-minute lead, high-fiving another competitor who is running in the opposite direction. The scene perfectly expresses the cool, cocky, member-of-the-gang Tinley style. What the cameras didn't see, however, was Tinley's quiet walk with his wife, Virginia, after he'd crossed the finish line. Or his visit to the little church along Alii Drive to say thanks. And it couldn't catch the strange, empty-ish feeling of anticlimax or the puzzled look in his eyes that seemed to pose an odd question: "I'm supposed to be happy now, right?"

That was to be his triathlon fate. It would haunt him always. For Scott Tinley, a man who didn't like to lose, winning would never be as enjoyable as simply being in the middle of the game with no end to the fun in sight.

Dave Scott finished second, resigned and unchallenged, with almost 20 minutes to spare over Tinley's brother, Jeff. Scott's time was 9:36:57. True to his word, he had broken John Howard's record. Tinley, however, had destroyed it. ST had met The Man—and had whipped him.

10

THE KING IS
CROWNED

Dave Scott was mad. First Howard, now Tinley. "Good lord," he thought, "what next? Tinley's brother? His cousin? This is my sport. This is *my race*. And people keep stealing the spotlight."

On the other hand, he was encouraged, and the feeling had begun when he was running down that final stretch of Alii Drive on February 6.

"When I finished that race," he said, "when I came in second and saw that my time was 9:36, I couldn't believe it. It had been two years since I'd done the race for the first time and there was all that doubt—it was a different course, and people were saying that Dave Scott would never win the race again, all that kind of stuff. It actually gave me a lot of momentum. I'd just gotten second place and I was in really bad shape. I was just coming off a pretty severe injury. I told myself that with some training, no one was going to stop me.

"My theory was that there was no one else alive who was going to be able to do the volume of work that I was going to do. I didn't know—I wasn't going to call up guys on the phone and find out if they were riding or running more than I was—but I couldn't fathom that they would. I was too driven."

Scott was through being "the coach's dream." He wanted to be his own dream, Dave Scott's dream. Enough was enough.

Tinley's goals were not so well defined. He was pleased that he won the race, of course, but it had put him in an awkward position. Doing the race had been a lark in 1981, a natural step to take considering his marathon background and his participation in the recreational triathlons at Mission Bay in San Diego. The February race had been an extension of that; if he had placed 5th or 6th or 10th, then he might have ended his involvement with the Ironman right there. Didn't he have a new job with a substantial amount of responsibility that he enjoyed, a less-than-one-year-old relationship with his wife to nurture? Only now there was this damn race. He'd *won* the thing, for God's sake. He'd have to go back, of course.

From his first day back in San Diego after the Ironman, he agonized over his position. Not the going-back part but the level-of-involvement part. Something was telling him (had he sensed it in Dave Scott?) that the training was going to become more and more intense, that what he'd done to prepare for the last race was not going to be nearly enough for the next one. The day for hard decisions, for stating the priorities and then sticking to them, was coming. And while he pondered, his lunch hours got longer and longer, and the amount of time he spent at home was growing shorter and shorter. The Ironman, which he had always perceived as a challenging extension of his fun-in-the-sun Southern California lifestyle, was becoming his *life*.

Actually, it was becoming a lot of people's lives. Triathlons (most of them of considerably shorter than the Ironman) sprouted like mushrooms that summer. Everyone wanted to be a triathlete, especially in the wake of Julie Moss's dramatic loss to Kathleen McCartney in February. It was a spectacle that had stolen most of the thunder from Tinley's defeat of Scott, dooming his victory to a position on the shelf of triathlon trivia of the future: "Can *yyyouuu* name the overall winner of the Ironman the year Julie Moss crawled to the finish line? Nooo, I'm so sorry, the answer is not Dave Scott!"

Adding to the frenzy was the announcement that the Ironman was being moved permanently to October that year. Instead of being 12 months away, the race was coming around again in eight, and there was a mad rush for entry forms. The 850 places on the starting line were snapped up like Michael Jackson concert tickets, two months early, and there were hundreds of disappointed triathletes who had been pointing toward Hawaii in the fall and now were going nowhere. In San Diego, where being an Ironman veteran was just short of a social necessity, numbers for the race held by injured triathletes who couldn't compete sold like hotcakes, despite stern warnings by the Ironman administration that the practice was taboo, grounds for permanent disqualification. Pete Pettigrew, a commercial airline pilot who was the real-life model for the Viper character in the movie *Top Gun*, raced that year as Harvey Shapiro, the mayor of Del Mar. He did so well that he qualified to race the following year, but only as Shapiro, not Pettigrew. He petitioned for entry in 1983 anyway and was denied. The most public controversy occurred when a top female triathlete from San Diego, 21-year-old Gina Fleming, raced as 36-year-old Joyce Copeland, a mother of three from nearby Rancho Santa Fe. Fleming revealed herself to race officials prior to the competition, hoping for a rumored amnesty, but was told she couldn't race. She did anyway, finished sixth, and was disqualified. Somehow, though, Copeland-Fleming was not removed from the results sheet that was handed to the master of ceremonies at the awards ceremony, and "Joyce Copeland" was called to the stage. Flustered, unsure of the correct course of action, Fleming marched up and took her place among the top 10 women, where she was photographed and applauded while Ironman officials argued furiously in the wings about who was responsible. The following year, photo identification was required of all participants at registration.

Leading up to all that, the most significant of the new events that were held that summer was the newly formed United States Triathlon Series, a five-race, West Coast circuit that attracted large fields of athletes and a lot of media attention. The USTS held its first race that year on June 12, in San Diego, at Torrey Pines State Beach, just south of Del Mar. It featured a crowd of 800 mostly novice triathletes (there hadn't been many chances at the time for them to gain experience), $2000 in prize money, and a Tinley-Scott rematch. The distances were much shorter than in Hawaii: a 2km swim, a 35km bike ride, and a 15km run.

Scott unveiled the fruits of his new, or perhaps more accurately his renewed, competitive fervor at the San Diego event. He was relentless. He destroyed the field, winning by more than four minutes, a substantial margin in so short a race. In a news release after the event, the USTS press office used as the lead a quote from a local reporter who watched Scott cross the finish line: "The least he could do is look tired or pass out or something."

Scott felt as good as he looked. It had been easy. Tinley finished third, out-kicked in the final half-mile by a quiet, almost sullen kid from the northern California town of Pittsburg named Scott Molina, who had beaten Dave Scott at a bike-run biathlon near San Francisco a couple of years before. In fourth was a lean, wiry-looking lifeguard from Del Mar doing his very first triathlon. His name was Mark Allen.

The first San Diego USTS race was of great historical significance to the triathlon world, but in a more immediate sense it set the tone for the rest of the 1982 season. Scott had somehow conveyed the impression that the favored athlete had won, despite the fact that Tinley was the hometown favorite and the defending Ironman champ. It sent Tinley back to work at the aquatic center shaking his head, second thoughts raging more wildly than ever. "It's going to be a long summer," he said to himself. "Dave Scott was bad enough, now there's Molina."

Scott obviously meant business. He was thinking and training on a different level than Tinley, or anyone else in the sport at that time.

"Tinley gave a little talk in a gym before the race in San Diego," Scott said. "I was sitting in the stands and the last thing that he said was something about triathlons being a lot of fun, and that we should try to keep them low-key, and that he just wanted Dave Scott to hear that. "I remember thinking: 'No way is this low-key. This is *war!*' I mean it was a very nice thing that he said, but it added fuel to my anticipation of the race. I wanted to *win!*"

Win he did. As he had vowed, he won every race he entered that summer, often by wide margins, and the Dave Scott legend grew and became firmly entrenched, mostly because the Dave Scott legend at the time was pretty much the Dave Scott fact. He really did rinse his cottage cheese (to remove excess fat) like the stories said; he fueled his furious metabolism with prodigious quantities of fresh fruits and vegetables; and he trained, if not exactly day and night, then from early in the morning until after the sun went down. There were no distractions, but no social contact, either—something he began to miss as the season went on and the big race crept closer. Even if he had wanted to break out of his tight focus, there was no time, no room in his life for anything but his Ironman goal.

"On paper I had a very successful year in '82," Scott said, "but I think I just had a head start on the competition. They just weren't quite *there*. I don't think it was simply the volume of work that I was doing that made me one step higher than the competition. I think that probably hurt me by the end of the season. It was too much."

How much was too much?

"I'd ride the same route," Scott said, "at least to start with, out and back. I would ride either 67 miles or 78 or 82, with an occasional longer one. I would never go less than 67 miles. That was my short ride. And I was running about 9, 12 miles a day, somewhere in there, with one long run a week, 16 or 17 miles. And I'd swim about 5500 yards a day, which didn't really take that long. I was in the water about an hour and 10 minutes."

Davis is farm country, board-flat and windy. Inland from the coastal mountains, it is usually dry and hot in the summer, then dry and cool in the winter, occasionally cold enough that a thin coat of ice will form on the wet decks of the heated outdoor swimming pools that remain open year-round. It's not a bleak place by any means, but it was far both physically and emotionally from the Southern California center of the triathlon world in 1982. It was easy for the triathletes down south to see Davis as Scott's windswept citadel of pain—and in one sense he used it like that. Davis may not be the prettiest place in California, but with the wind and the heat and the long, flat, mind-numbing stretches of road, it might be one of the best places in the world to train for the Queen K.

It seemed to be Scott's destiny to win the Ironman that year, but he did more than just win. He took possession of it; he reached out and grabbed the race with both hands and shook it, unleashing the frustration of the previous two years with a performance that still ranks among his finest. It will rank among the best at Ironman forever.

Scott led the race throughout, recording the fastest times in each of the three events, an unlikely occurrence considering the growing sophistication and level of competitive experience of the other top men. He came out of the water in a tremendous rush, running up the ramp leading to the changing room so furiously that there was a kind of collective gasp from the spectators, then a fraction of a second of quiet before the cries of "It's Dave Scott!" "Go Dave!" and the applause began. At his toes, literally, was Allen, at that point still the great unknown. He was the man who had unexpectedly beaten Tinley and Molina in a half-Ironman-distance race in San Diego two months before and so was, suddenly, an Ironman contender.

Scott, the more experienced of the two, was out of the changing room first, then out of the transition area on his bike, and up Palani Road, heading for the Queen K, well before Allen. He rode alone for 35 miles, until Allen caught him at the far end of the highway, at Kawaihae, and the two men headed up the hills toward Hawi together. Surprisingly, Allen looked more relaxed; he was spinning his pedals smoothly and sitting squarely in his seat, his face a mask of calm concentration. Next to him, Scott was working harder, off his seat and standing on his pedals frequently to pump up some of the hills. He looked grim, a bit worried.

In fact, he *was* worried.

"I got a cramp in my right hamstring going up that first hill," Scott said. "Right off the pier. It knotted up really bad, and several times going out during the first three or four miles I would stop pedaling and just drop my leg down and try to stretch it out. I couldn't shake it. It stayed with me the whole race. All the way out to Hawi I couldn't even get down in a full crouch."

He tried not to panic, but he couldn't help but recall the image of eight months before and project the scenario: Tinley coming fast from behind during the marathon, with Dave Scott hobbling along on a bum leg. "Not again," thought Scott. "Please not again. I've worked too hard."

He concentrated instead on his strategic options. He looked over and inspected the gearing on Allen's bike, noting that it was not as well set up for pushing hard on the downhills as his own. Scott had one higher gear than Allen, something that could make a big difference under the proper circumstances.

The winds were strong that day and both men did a lot of hard pedaling up to Hawi. As they made the turn, Allen, in a gesture of deference to Scott, let him slide through and make the turn first. Then he reached for a banana and a water bottle, and his concentration momentarily lapsed. Sensing that, Scott shifted up and shot down the hill, pedaling as hard as he could, the strong wind now at his back. Before Allen realized what was happening, Scott had opened a gap of several hundred yards.

Allen pushed the pace over the next eight miles to catch up, and he gradually narrowed the margin: 200 yards, 100, then just 50. The winds were gusty now, no longer at the riders' backs, but blowing from the side, in strong puffs. The bikes felt unstable and sluggish. Allen pulled his shift lever back to make a gear change and he felt something snap. The lever moved too freely in his hand; the bike wasn't getting any easier to pedal. He looked back and saw that the chain was still on the highest gear, the smallest cog, and it was chattering, threatening to jump off the gear completely and lodge between the frame and the freewheel. Had he broken the cable?

Dazed, disbelieving, Allen steered his bike to the shoulder and got off to take a look. "This cannot be happening," he thought. But it was. The shift cable hadn't broken, but the flange that attached the cable to his derailleur had snapped off, which amounted to the same thing. Allen felt his face flush and his hands tremble as the implications of the problem hit him. He had only two gears to work with, both too high, too hard to pedal for the next 50 or 60 miles and still be able to get off the bike and run a marathon. He might be able to finish, but it would be a death march in any case, and that was not what he had come to Hawaii for. He wasn't sure whether to sit down and cry or throw his bike out into the lava. His day as a competitor was over.

"I was so mad," Allen said. "It was like waking up from a bad dream and finding out that it's real."

He had to hitch a ride back into town.

Scott, unaware of Allen's plight, was alone again—dramatically so. In his white shorts and shirt, with his shining black bike beneath him, he flashed through the lava fields like a jewel, his head down and his legs spinning. Where Tinley had been able to get splits from his wife the year before and watch the gap between himself and Dave Scott close, this year he watched it widen, mile after mile. It had been 10 minutes after the swim, then 12, 13, 16, and finally 18 minutes by the time Tinley finally got off his bike. Eighteen minutes! Tinley felt the same helplessness that Scott had felt eight months before.

"I knew there was no chance even then," Tinley said. "Even if I felt absolutely great, I would've had to run a 2:45 marathon to catch him. And after that bike ride...."

It looked for a while as if the race for second place, at least, was going to be dramatic. Both Tinleys, Molina, and another top triathlete living in San Diego at the time, Jody Durst, all ran out of the Kona Surf parking lot and charged up the big hill within a minute of each other. But that was the last of the charging. It quickly became obvious that none of the men were in any shape to think about catching the man in front; it was all they could do to hold off the guy behind.

The experts had predicted a close, down-to-the-wire battle between Scott and Tinley, perhaps with several others involved. Instead, it was a rout. Scott didn't exactly bound through his marathon, but he ran a solid 3:07 to finish in 9:08:23. Of the men behind him, Tinley was the best survivor, finishing second, eight minutes ahead of his brother. By the time Tinley crossed the line, an exhausted Dave Scott had begun to recover. He'd eaten several sandwiches, talked to the press. He'd won the race by more than 20 minutes, breaking Tinley's record by 11. He'd beaten his own best on the Kona course by almost half an hour, and turned the table Tinley had set for him eight months before. He was "The Man" now, for real.

❖

There could be no doubt in anyone's mind after the October 1982 Ironman that Dave Scott's single-minded approach to triathlons was the only road to success. And since Scott gave no indication that he was going to retire, all the other top triathletes either had to let Scott win it all again in 1983, or change their approach to the sport.

And change they did. In just the several-month period after the October race, three things happened that served to open the financial doors of the new sport wide enough to allow a select few to squeeze into a world they hadn't even dreamed existed just six months before.

The first step was the Malibu Triathlon, a half-Ironman-distance race that started on the beach in Malibu, California, on October 30, just three weeks after the Ironman.

Sponsored by Nike and pretentiously labeled the "United States Championship," the race offered a $17,000 prize purse, a figure so far beyond what the triathletes had seen up until that point that the race could have called itself the Folies-Bergere and none of them would have argued.

Unfortunately, the race was an organizational nightmare, a disastrous failure made all the worse by the dangerously low water temperature and torrential rains. Dave Scott, whose manager at the time was also the Malibu race director, wisely sat out the event, huddling with the rest of the spectators who watched in dismay as the swimmers staggered senseless out of the 59-degree water. Tinley raced, but broke his collarbone in a spectacular bike crash on a fast downhill corner. Allen competed, too, but he became so hypothermic during the swim he nearly drowned. He made it to the beach and his day ended there.

Aside from serving as a lesson in how not to produce a triathlon, the Malibu race started the top triathletes thinking in terms of recovering quickly and racing again soon after long events like the Ironman. That was an important step. And the $17,000 opened a lot of eyes. Was there indeed a future in this sport?

The second step forward was the Nice Triathlon, held in Nice, France, on November 20. Like Malibu, it was over-billed, calling itself "The Nice Triathlon World Championship," although once again a big prize purse ($17,600) served to validate the title. Nice was not much better organized than Malibu had been, but the environment made it easy for the invited American triathletes to overlook the rough edges. Produced and packaged specifically for NBC television, Nice was another indication to guys like Tinley that there was a future in the sport, and that maybe the Dave Scott method of training could be sweetened with money and plane trips and exotic locations.

Dave Scott didn't race in Nice that year, but Tinley did, broken shoulder and all, and he tied for third with brother Jeff, who took a slithering, screeching fall into a group of tables at an outdoor cafe at the top of the mountainous Nice bike course. Jeff was unhurt, but he seriously alarmed

NBC television commentator Bruce Jenner, who had been sitting at ground zero of the crash.

The third and most important milestone was the emergence of the ill-fated Team J David. As of October 1982, the group had already had a minor impact, but over the course of the next 12 months it would radically change the face of the sport, and therefore the face of the Ironman as well, at least as far as the top competitors were concerned.

The team made its first public appearance when Kathleen McCartney crossed the Ironman finish line in first place in February 1982. Few people took note of the name that ran across McCartney's running singlet. It read: Team J David. She was the team's first member, at least the first athlete to be offered financial support by the La Jolla, California-based securities brokerage of the same name. There were four other members of the team that year, but they were J David investors or future J David investors, and they all paid their own way. The team would return to Hawaii in greater force the following October, and would buy into the Ironman as a sponsor, the first step in a dizzying year in which team members set new standards of triathlon excellence while the company that lavishly supported them reached into every corner of the growing sport, stuffing pockets with cash at the merest hint that it was needed for this project or that. What no one knew at the time was that the J David Company was a multinational house of cards, a fraud, and that the funds were part of a $200 million pool of misappropriated money, some of it belonging to the triathletes themselves, a few of whom had invested their prize money in the J David trading fund. There were suspicions along the way, of course, thoughts that it was all too good to be true, but they weren't thoughts that any of the team members dwelled on for long.

"I remember sitting in my room at the Negresco Hotel in Nice," said Mark Allen, "thinking that it was all something out of F. Scott Fitzgerald."

And Tinley: "I guess all of us thought at one time or another that it was too good to be true. Once, during the height of the decadence, in mid-'83, I could tell that Molina sort of sensed that it wouldn't last forever. We were talking about the team and he said, half to himself, 'C'mon Nancy, I just need one more year until I can make it on my own.'"

The central figures in the J David episode were Jerry (J David) Dominelli, a dusty, bookish little man who was supposedly a genius at trading currency on the international exchange (he wasn't), and his partner, Nancy Hoover, a tall, athletic, outgoing former mayor of Del Mar. "Jerry and Nancy," as the triathletes affectionately called them, actively supported Dominelli's top salesman Ted Pulaski's fascination with triathlons—and with the Ironman in particular. It was Pulaski who led the team to Hawaii in 1982 while it was still nothing more than a small circle of friends. He would remain the unofficial team captain in the end, the cheerleader, the instigator of most of the wild spending in which the team indulged. Pampered like a favorite son by Dominelli (who gave him a new, fire-engine red Porsche 924 turbo for Christmas in 1983, just before the company collapsed), Pulaski knew that money was no object, and he used it to solve every problem that arose. Once at the Keahole Airport in Kona, just before the flight back to the mainland from the October '82 Ironman, he gathered up the tickets of the entire J David entourage so that he could deal with the ticket agent himself. To his fleeting dismay he found that he was one ticket short. "We don't have time to look," Pulaski said impatiently, reaching into his pocket for his wallet. "Just give us another one," and he pulled out his trusty American Express card.

Another time, there was some confusion among team members about which bicycle sponsor to choose, whether there should be a single sponsor or whether each athlete should be on his or her own. Neither, said Pulaski, who quickly commissioned a highly respected frame builder to construct custom frames for the entire team.

It was Hoover's 20-year-old son George who changed the focus of the team toward the elite triathletes. Mark Allen, whom George Hoover had met while the two were lifeguards together, was the first of the stars. The rest came on board shortly after him, shortly after the first Nice triathlon in 1982.

Nice was the first major European triathlon, a made-for-TV event designed to put NBC television in the triathlon business. It was packaged by Barry Frank of the International Management Group (IMG), in the hope that it would be able to stand against the popular ABC cover-age of the Ironman. World championship label aside, it was an American show from the beginning; there were simply no widely recognized (or capable) triathletes of any other nationality at the time. IMG brought over Molina, the two Tinleys, and the best American women, too, including defending Ironman champ Julie Leach. J David sent along its stars: Kathleen McCartney, Hoover, and Allen, along with Pulaski and several others. But the team sent more than people. It put up most of the prize money—$10,000 of the $17,600 purse, most of which went right back into the pockets of the American triath-letes, who captured all the top places despite being bat-tered after a full season of racing at home and being more than a little out of shape. The prize money had come as a result of some haggling over distances between IMG and the triathletes. IMG was insisting on a full marathon to end the Nice event. They were convinced it was what the American public wanted to see.

"The Ironman had a marathon," Frank said. "NBC wanted a marathon. They didn't want their event to come off looking like it was second-rate—a race for chickens."

Blood and guts was what they were looking for, an NBC version of the Julie Moss bit, although the American triath-letes weren't interested in giving it to them—not for free, anyway, or even for a trip to the French Riviera. It took J David's money to sweeten the pot and make the long run more palatable. Unfortunately, no one had mentioned how cold the Mediterranean Sea could get in November, and the swim bore a haunting resemblance to the Malibu race. McCartney was almost too cold to object to the French film crews stationed strategically but not at all diplomatically in the women's changing room. It was a generally miserable day for everyone except Allen, who took home the first of his five straight victories at Nice and $5000, which was a heck of a lot more than he'd ever made in one day as a lifeguard.

For Scott Molina, who finished second, and Scott and Jeff Tinley, the best part of the trip was that by the time they landed back in the States they were members of Team J David, with promises of steady incomes of $1500 a month, plus equipment and incidentals. In the months to come the incidental column would grow longer than any of them could have imagined.

In some respects, the short-lived Team J David corrupted and embittered the young sport. But the bottom line from a triathlon standpoint was that the team put a lot of talent in one place and allowed it to flourish, and in that sense it was not entirely an unhappy story. The elite triathletes who were enlisted were the best the sport had to offer. But after training together for a year, trading secrets, pushing each other through group workouts supervised at times by team coaches, racing with the best equipment available, they rose above the level of being merely the best to being unapproachable. They were called "Team Bitchin" and they lacked for nothing. They set a standard of triathlon living the rest of the sport envied, and standards of performance no one could match.

"It was like being in a training camp all year long," Molina said. "Everyone progressed."

While it is likely that Tinley, Molina, and Allen would have gone on to dominate the sport the way they did without their J David connections, there is a chance they wouldn't have. Allen, who was a lifeguard when it all began, might have ended up in medical school, where he'd been headed in the first place. Molina might have been cooking hamburgers at K-mart in Pittsburg, California, trying to save enough money to move his wife and baby out of the trailer park. And Tinley...he seemed to adapt better than any of them. The J David style fit him like a glove. Always cool, always confident, he never seemed visibly impressed by the change in his lifestyle. He settled in and accepted the situation as if he had been born to it. J David not only made it possible for him to quit his job at the aquatic center, it also gave him the chance to play with the boys, to live the good life for a year during a critical point in his career. It gave him both the means and the incentive to stay in the sport and to fight Scott again and again in Hawaii.

The dawn of Team J David was the dawn of the professional triathlete; an industry was created in the time it took to ruffle a stack of $100 bills. Not only did the J David triathletes receive financial and technical support that allowed them to train full time, the company directly funded the fledgling Association of Professional Triathletes (the APT), contributed to the prize money purses of some of the races that the APT promoted (and to the purses of some other races as well), and supported the original financing of the first nationally circulated journal of the sport, *Triathlon* magazine, which first appeared in the winter of 1982. By the time the various J David companies were revealed as fraudulent and the J David triathlon team had disappeared like the dream it had been all along, it was too late for anyone to turn around and go back. The sport had developed a momentum of its own.

Dave Scott, meanwhile, stayed in Davis, a recluse by comparison. He hardly raced at all, choosing the triathlons he did do carefully, the way an established Hollywood star might choose a script, with regard not just for the race itself but the long-term implications. Where Tinley seemed physically indestructible, Scott was rumored to be always on the verge of this injury or that, and his appearance at a triathlon swung upon the truth of those rumors. A tight hamstring or a twinge in his calf meant that he would not appear. There was more than once during that season when it was said that Scott was simply afraid to race when he wasn't at his best, that he was afraid to lose.

In fact, 1983 was a miserable year for Scott, emotionally and physically. His relentless commitment to training, which was being used as a blueprint by his competitors, was no longer working. It was clear that he wasn't as immersed in the sport as Tinley was, at least not in a way he could enjoy. True, there was an image he needed to live up to, but that didn't supply a hell of a lot of motivation.

And at what price the image? He could read about how the J David stars were living in luxury in San Diego, the mecca of the sport, training together without a care in the world. He knew what to tell the press about that: that it was keeping Tinley and Molina soft, that they were sharing their secrets, that Davis was keeping him nasty and ready for anything. But down deep there were doubts. Where Scott had been hungry and keen in 1982, quick to throw aside distractions, personal relationships included, he found himself less hungry now, less driven, lacking a clearly defined goal. He was a two-time Ironman champion, but as one triathlon publication headlined an interview with him a year later, "It's Lonely At The Top." Scott had made it lonely for himself; he wasn't sure he liked it. His own image was becoming downright depressing.

"I was irritated that everyone thought I was a loner," Scott said, "that I was living like a hermit up here in Davis. It's not like I lived in Butte, Montana, or out in the middle of a cornfield or something. Davis is not San Diego, but it's a university town, there are 50,000 people here, it's close to San Francisco. It's not like there was a fence around the city, a fence around my house!

"The connotation was that I didn't interact with people, that I didn't socialize with people, that I didn't do anything else but sit on my bike seat all day long. That's really contrary to what I am."

He had trained so hard for the October 1982 Ironman that it was hard for him to get going again in 1983. That was a normal reaction, especially considering the fact that Scott was a solitary trainer, a goal-oriented triathlete—not that Tinley didn't have goals, too, but in his case, all the training and the racing and the goals lumped themselves together into a lifestyle, something that Tinley *liked*. It wasn't that way with Scott.

"Toward the end of the summer before the October 1982 race I was getting tired of the rigorous routine," he said. "All I could think was, 'Wow, one more month of this before the Ironman.' I remember some days that I'd get up and drag my feet for a couple of hours."

Tinley had it pegged. In a droll but wonderfully accurate analysis of Dave Scott's roller-coaster cycles of motivation, he said, "Dave is so methodical. He gets to a certain point where he just says, 'Screw it,' you know? 'I don't want to train. I'm just gonna *eat!*'"

What snapped Scott back into focus that year, of course, was the Ironman. He couldn't imagine someone else being in the driver's seat in Kona. He began what has become his usual late-season rush, launching himself into a flood of training mileage. He had a good race in Nice on September 10, where he finished second to Allen, with Tinley in third, then had a disastrous day in Bass Lake, California, at the USTS National Championships. He finished 27th, a performance so poor, coming as it did on the heels of a terrible season—Nice notwithstanding—that reporters, even those within the sport, avoided him as if he had a strange, communicable disease.

Scott was hurt and confused at being ignored, even a little angry. He would gladly have explained about the night he spent before the race, suffering from some bad food or a stomach virus or something that sent him to the starting line barely able to stand, let alone race. But he never got the chance to explain, although he wasn't being so much ignored as avoided. The reluctance of the reporters to talk to him stemmed more from their respect for his ability and his position within the sport than from anything else. They were embarrassed for him. Assuming the worst, that Dave Scott really was on the skids, no longer a contender, they left him alone.

"I wasn't upset because I didn't get the press coverage," Scott said, "but I could sense that everyone was speculating that I really was over the hill."

Not even close. He had a bad year, but it was only that, a bad year. Perhaps the slight at Bass Lake gave him a little extra jolt of incentive, but he didn't really need it; the Ironman had always been incentive enough.

The Ironman that year was dramatic. Tinley and Scott pushed each other right to the edge. It was a race that Tinley kept refusing to believe he could win, and that Scott, believing that he could, won in a moment of sheer will. Where he had dominated physically the previous October, this time he beat Tinley with his mind—during the run, of all places—by mere seconds. For the first time, the race really was a duel between the two men, strength against strength, where all the "ifs" that lay heaped in piles along the Queen K really counted; where just one of those ifs might have made the difference at the end, giving the rubber match, the best two-out-of-three at Ironman not to Dave Scott, The Man, but to Scott Tinley, ST, the almost-legend who came so close. Tinley denies that he's been shaking his head about it ever since. He's better than most at shrugging his shoulders and walking away from a situation he's unable to change, but this one hurt.

It would be silly to say that Scott came into the race as an underdog, but it was close to that. First, there was his up-and-down season. Second, there was the multipronged assault of Team Bitchin', led by Tinley, and including Howard, Molina, and Allen. It was a tough spot, with Scott standing there like old Lefty Grove on the mound, pitching against Ruth, Gehrig, and Foxx in the 1927 All-Star Game. He was a star himself, surely, but what were the chances? *Somebody's* gonna smack one. Amazingly, no one did. Howard dropped out early in the bike ride with mechanical problems. Molina folded later with a bad back. Allen eventually finished third, but winning Nice had taken a lot out of him. He was so far behind that he was never a factor. It was almost as if the entire sport had suddenly taken a deep breath and stopped in mid-stride to watch the two men who mattered go at it, one-on-one.

Scott led with a strong swim. He wasn't first out of the water, but he was close, and he took the lead just 30 minutes into the bike ride, much sooner than he had dared to believe he could. Having missed too many days of training during the season, he was suspicious of his own level of conditioning.

"My training had been so sporadic," he said. "I went into that race with the loosest game plan I've ever had. I didn't know whether I'd get 10th or 1st; I really didn't have anything that was measurable in training. I was prepared for nine hours of total misery. So I was surprised to get out of the water when I did, and to take the lead that early. It spurred me on."

Tinley was only seven minutes behind coming out of the water—three minutes faster than he'd been in '82. He caught Allen about 40 miles out and the pair rode together up to the turnaround at Hawi, pushing through high winds that would get progressively worse as the morning wore on. To both men's surprise, Dave Scott had picked up two additional minutes.

Tinley at first thought the time must be wrong. Either he and Allen were dragging or Scott was flying.

Tinley looked over and asked his teammate about it.

"We're riding hard," Allen said, confirming Tinley's appraisal.

Which could mean only one thing.

"Dave wasn't that strong on the bike in Nice," Tinley said. "And I knew he couldn't have improved that much since. I knew what he was doing, the same thing he did the year before. He figured he'd just blow everyone away in the beginning and demoralize them."

It added up. Tinley figured he had Scott's number. Far from demoralized, he pressed on, leaving Allen to follow. "He'll come back to me," Tinley told himself. "He'll slow down."

Scott did indeed slow down, and perhaps if Tinley had just let the race happen from that point on, it might have ended differently. But instead of riding his own race, as experience and his own better judgment might have dictated, he played Scott's game, hoping to reverse the strategy. When the gap between the two men finally dropped below two minutes, Tinley decided to put something extra into the last 20 miles.

"The only way I was going to win," he said, "was to turn the tables, come off the bike in front of him. Make him think that he couldn't catch me. It was a gamble."

Cat and mouse. Scott realized what was happening. He was getting reports, too. They were riding south along Alii Drive, about three miles from the Kona Surf Hotel, when he eased off and let Tinley go around.

"It worked," Tinley thought. "I've got him."

"It worked," Scott thought. "I've got him."

One of them was wrong. Soon thereafter, Tinley's body began to tell him that it might be him. He had made up nine minutes during the second half of the ride—a tremendous amount of time, especially considering the way the wind had been blowing at the other end of the course. With his helmet off, his shoes off, and his shirt half over his head, he ran into the changing room, taking inventory as he went. The result was not encouraging: his back was sore, the bottom of his feet ached, and his legs were numb.

"I felt really, really bad," Tinley said. And Scott was 30 seconds behind.

What happened next is a function of the different ways Tinley and Scott perceive competition, not just that particular race, but competition in general. The two men are driven by entirely different motivations.

It went back to June 1982. Tinley had been talking about fun to the crowd at the first USTS race in San Diego; Scott was thinking about war. Not that Scott trained or raced out of vengeance, but he could get up for a race by singling out a motivating theme: a time he wanted to better, a person he wanted to beat. He could set his mind on a goal and forget everything else as he pursued it, something that Tinley had never been very good at. Years later Tinley would fill out a biographical information form and on the line that asked about his goals for the year he would write that he wanted "to continue to place in the top three of every race for the next 35 years." It's hard to imagine Dave Scott answering the same question that way. There was a driving need to race and win in Scott, but only a driving need to compete in Tinley. One race seldom meant that much to him; there was always another. For Scott, one race could mean a lifetime. The Ironman surely did.

So the tables turned for the second time that day when Scott burned by Tinley less than two miles into the marathon, right at the top of a short, steep downhill, just before Alii Drive turns sharply to the right and heads due north up the coast. Scott's head was high, his shoulders back, and he looked as if he could go much harder if he wanted to. "Don't even think about chasing me, ST," he seemed to be saying, "'cause I'm gone."

And Tinley, knowing it was all a game, let him go.

But the race wasn't over. There was a long way to go. Scott, having taken the lead, extended himself to stretch it out as far as possible. He ran much too fast up Alii Drive, and gained four minutes in seven miles. Then he began to crumble.

It happened slowly, agonizingly, one painful step at a time. Just outside of town, about nine miles into the run, Scott stopped to urinate and lost more than a minute of his four-minute lead. You can piss from the bike while moving along at a pretty good clip, but you can't while you're running. You have to stop. To Scott it seemed like it took an hour. Four miles later, thirteen miles into the run, he began to feel weak and light-headed. His control over his pace and his form began to slip, and his worries about Tinley began to grow: How far back? How fast is he running? How fast is he gaining?

Both men were getting information from their friends on the course. In Tinley's case it was his wife, Virginia; in Scott's it was Pat Feeney. According to Feeney, Tinley was gaining fast.

"Tinley made up 45 seconds on that last mile," Feeney said, trying to keep the worry out of his voice. "He ran a 6:15."

"Good lord," Scott said, "what's the guy doing?"

Tinley ran the next mile in seven minutes. Feeney calmed down. Then the next was under 6:30 again, and the next one over seven.

"He did that for about four miles," Scott said. "Slower, faster, slower, faster. Of course, psychologically I wasn't feeling good; I was too worried about him, knowing that he was capable of running a 6:15 mile. I didn't know if he was going to put two of those miles together. If he had, it probably would have made me crumble."

Curiously, neither Tinley nor his wife remember the pace fluctuating. It was obviously not a tactic. In fact Tinley remembers that he was gaining ground slowly, much too slowly for him to draw any encouragement from it.

Scott ran past the airport, made the turnaround, and then ran back, passing Tinley along the way. He stood as straight and tall as he could, putting on a show. But it was hard to do; he didn't have much left. His margin had shrunk to less than three minutes and he wanted the race to end. Oh, God, where was the end?

Tinley had no way of knowing what was going on in Scott's head. He didn't want to know, really. He didn't want to be told. He was getting times from Virginia, but it all kept sounding like the same thing he'd heard a mile or two before. "Three minutes, Scotty, three minutes!" That was with the airport and the turnaround in sight, with Scott running back the other way, trying to look like the race was in the bag. Then Tinley himself got to the turn-around, and he heard it again: three minutes. What was the point? "C'mon Scott, he's looking bad!" called Virginia. "You can catch him."

"Go to hell," thought Tinley. "Just go away. I ain't catching anyone today."

But he was. He couldn't help it. Endurance athletes often reach a stage when the fatigue has had time to sink in deep, where everything in the world becomes an annoyance, even people you love and who love you and are trying to help. It was like that for Tinley now. He stopped wanting to be helped. If he heard another split he was going to scream. Finally, frustrated by what looked like a losing cause, Virginia gave up. She headed back into town so that she could be at the finish when her husband arrived. That was right about the time Dave Scott began dropping the remaining pieces of his composure all over the highway.

"It was horrible with five miles to go," Scott said. "I had 2:25 on him at that point, and I could feel things slipping away. I was having trouble focusing on any other runners coming by. Then with three miles left Pat came up and said, 'You better move it, you're only 1:33 ahead. Tinley looks good.'

"There was nothing I could do. I just told myself, 'C'mon, get up to the top of that hill, that hill as you come into town, a long, horrible climb. It seemed like an eternity getting up there. If Tinley had gone around me I wouldn't have been able to go one second faster."

Tinley got word around the 22-mile point that the gap had closed again. He picked up the pace slightly in response, just to see, and was surprised to find that it felt pretty good, that after almost three hours of running his legs were starting to loosen up. He went faster and the gap squeezed tighter. Two minutes. Scott got the word that Tinley was finally coming hard and he pressed, desperately. Twenty-three miles. Tinley could finally see Scott at the top of the last hill. A minute and a half. Twenty-four miles. 'Faster, damn it,' Tinley said to himself, still not really believing.

"Even if I sprint now," he said, "I'm not gonna get him."

But he sprinted anyway, turning right off the highway and letting himself roll down the Pay and Save Hill toward the pier, then left at the intersection where the whistles of the police and the cheering of the crowd were only an afterthought. His vision had narrowed down tight, focusing on the asphalt in front of him as his legs moved faster and faster. It was as if someone else had control of them while the voice in his head kept asking the question that would never be answered: "Why didn't I start sooner, goddamn it—why didn't I start this sooner?"

Then he heard the roar as Scott finished and realized as he ran on that 33 seconds really was a long time when you thought about it.

❖

Scott announced that the 1984 Ironman would be his last. He said it early in the new season, then locked himself back up in Davis again. For the second season in a row he was rumored to be washed up, over the hill, burned out. Following his third Ironman win in October he had raced poorly in Kanai in December, a race that was covered and broadcast nationally by NBC. Tinley, burning a bit over having given up on himself at the Ironman, went by Scott during the bike ride in Kaui as if the Ironman champion were standing still. "I was going about 30," Tinley said, sounding a little embarrassed. "He was going about 20. It's the only time I've ever passed Dave without saying something to him."

Scott's poor race was understandable. His complaining publicly about his personal problems was not. It confused people. How could he be so depressed so soon after winning in Hawaii? Scott himself regrets the display—not because it was inaccurate, or because it expressed feelings that he is ashamed of, but because he was embarrassed about not being in good shape and expecting people to understand. They didn't. He should have known.

That summer belonged to Tinley, Molina, and perhaps most of all to Allen, who still wasn't racing frequently but was awesome when he did, winning by wide margins every time he stepped to the line. The exposure of the J David investment scheme fraud and the subsequent downfall of Team J David in the off-season hadn't put so much as a hitch in the strides of any of the three men.

Tinley pushed himself hard. For the first time it looked as if he was pursuing a single-minded campaign to rid himself of the Dave Scott jinx. In his workouts at the big outdoor pool at the University of California San Diego, he swam with a yellow cap on which was marked the magic number in bold, four-inch letters: "33 sec." On his swim paddles he marked his goal for the year: "BEAT DAVE SCOTT." And he made no effort to keep what he called his "reminders" secret. Both of the items were pictured in a big, four-color spread that accompanied an interview with him in the July 1984 issue of *Tri-Athlete* magazine. "My training program has been designed around one goal: winning the Hawaii Ironman," Tinley said. "Of course, I can't live in the past and I know it's not healthy to focus on something that has already happened.... Coming in second provided me with a year's worth of motivation. It's like *Rocky III*—you've got to go back. A year ago I had everything set [he was referring to Team J David]. Now I am scraping for money, I'm meaner than ever. I want to win. I am riding a rusty old bike and running in beat-up shoes."

In retrospect, the display on the cap and paddles embarrasses Tinley. It wasn't his style, any more than the interview itself was. He came off sounding brusque and cold, flip and full of himself. It reinforced his bad-boy image. Few saw it for what it really was: a self-parody.

"That was more of a joke than anything else," he said in 1986. "Losing was a real motivator, but I don't have any personal grudge against Dave. I respect his ability as an athlete, assuring that he's at his best for the races that count. He's also got a very strong background in exercise physiology that he's been able to apply to his training. He's become very methodical about it. That's his style and that's good. I probably should adopt some of his style, be more methodical about it, work with a coach who tells me when I'm doing too much. I probably should be more specific and systematic about my training. I know I could improve if I did that.

"And maybe Dave should be a little more relaxed about what he does, and a little more spontaneous, so he can avoid the kind of breakdown problems he had in '83."

By the end of the summer of 1984 Tinley had some breakdown problems of his own. He'd carried his style of racing in triathlon after triathlon after triathlon too far. He was riding the thin edge of total exhaustion. He'd beaten Molina at an Ironman-distance event in Minnesota in July, then bounced back into hard training too soon—the next day, in fact—and put himself in a deep hole. The Nice Triathlon rolled around in September and he finished third, behind Scott, who was fresh after another light season of racing, and Allen, who won the event for the third time, assuring himself of the position as the Dave Scott of the European triathlon scene. Tinley staggered back from France like a zombie, severely overtrained and overraced. When Curtis Alitz sprinted by him during the run to take second place at the USTS National Championship in Bass Lake two weeks later, it looked as if Tinley might serve himself best by skipping the Ironman altogether. If you asked around, you found that the best bets were on a Scott-Allen match-up in Hawaii. Tinley was shot.

Or was he? For one, the Ironman lure was too strong. He couldn't just let Scott have the thing. For another, the aura of the Ironman as a big race was beginning to dim. Valerie Silk, who was making the calls, stood steadfast against the idea of prize money, and the pros were grumbling louder than ever. There were too many other opportunities. Hawaii was too hard and too expensive. There was some talk that 1984 would be the last year that winning the race would be worth what it had been in terms of promotional value. Besides, overraced or not, Tinley had never seriously considered not going back. In that sense, at least, he was one with his great rival, Dave Scott. The Ironman had become too much a part of his life for him to skip it.

❖

Perhaps old Madame Pele, the ancient Hawaiian goddess of fire, had gotten a hint of all the negative talk about the race that year. Maybe all those bikes racing through the lava fields started to get under her skin. One thing for sure, somebody cooked up quite a stew. The weather for the Ironman in 1984 was cruelly, oppressively hot. The Queen K, bad enough on a good day, was an oven. The air temperature soared into the high 90s, with surface temperatures in the sun far above that. The race gradually devolved into a struggle to survive. Success was measured in terms of how close you came to quitting, not how quickly you completed the course. As women's winner Sylviane Puntous put it after she finished, "It was not a nice race."

It was a *terrible* race. The best triathletes in the world broke down during the marathon. Midway through the run they found themselves shuffling along the highway from aid station to aid station, not caring at all who was ahead of them or behind. It was left to Scott and Tinley (who else?) to march through the wreckage and pick up the pieces.

The day began by looking like another Mark Allen run-away. He'd been doing it all season, so when he started pulling away from the field on the bike, then kept pulling and pulling, 5 minutes, 8 minutes, 10, and finally 12, the experts nodded and admitted he might be for real.

But Allen was paying too much attention to his own superb condition and not enough to the environment. It was hot but also relatively calm in terms of wind, a lure that many triathletes would succumb to that day, seeing an opportunity for fast bike times. And the bike times were fast. Allen's was a course record. But they were all forgetting the marathon, which came back to hammer them all.

"I can't believe I did it again," Allen would say later, referring to the lesson about eating and drinking he'd thought he learned in Nice the previous year. Dave Scott had been behind him then, too. But the two men had been suffering from the same problem in France; they hadn't been able to get enough aid, although Allen got the worst of it. The problem had been forced on both of them. This time, The Man was in control of his own destiny.

Tinley, meanwhile, was having his worst bike ride of the year. The season had been going downhill since August, and it felt like this was the bottom. He was exhausted, not just tired in this race but tired forever, the way he'd been at the end of the race in Nice, the way he'd looked at the end of the race in Bass Lake. He'd gone far beyond his limits during the summer and was not of a mind to go any farther. He didn't want to be where he was; it wasn't any fun at all. Three hours into the bike race he wanted to stop, and what the sport of triathlon or Dave Scott or Mark Allen thought didn't matter.

That kind of thinking is not rare in the world of endurance sport; declining motivation is one symptom of the overtraining syndrome, and ST had it bad. The more he considered his position, the worse it got. He kept asking himself the same question: "Why?" He kept coming up with the same answer: "Don't know." He finally sat up in his seat, put his hands in the center of his handlebars, and coasted, turning his pedals slowly, waiting for the last little bit of the decision to take hold. He'd never dropped out of a race before, but that didn't matter either.

That was right about the time that Mark Evans, a triathlon coach from the San Francisco area, and Dave Epperson, a photographer working for *Ultrasport* magazine, drove up in a car. Both men knew Tinley well. Both were surprised to see him so far behind. He was in what, 14th place? They pulled around, and Epperson, sitting beneath the open hatchback, put his camera to his face and prepared to shoot. Tinley flipped a middle finger at him, wearily, as if to say, "Don't bother."

"How ya feeling, Scott?" Epperson asked sympathetically.

Tinley snorted. "Don't have it today," he said. "I'm fried. How're you guys?" He seemed glad to have some company.

"Doing okay," Epperson said. "Can I get some shots?"

Tinley responded by playfully reaching for the roof of the car as if to hitch a ride. He missed, but Epperson realized for the first time that ST was serious, that he really was about to drop out. It confused him. Still, there wasn't much they could do, except leave Tinley alone. No sense making it worse for him than it already was.

"I think we should get out of here, Mark," Epperson said.

Evans drove on ahead slowly, watching Tinley in the rearview mirror. Then he reconsidered and slowed.

"I can't believe he's giving up," Evans said. "That's not like Tinley. Something must be wrong." He leaned across and rolled down the window on the passenger side as Tinley came abreast of them again.

"Second place is not that bad, Scott," Evans yelled. "You've got to focus! There's still the run. Center yourself! Center yourself!"

Evans's words broke through. The verbal kick in the butt helped. The last thing Tinley needed was sympathy; he was giving himself enough of that already. He didn't say a word in response, but his hands slid forward to his brake hoods, his back flattened, and the fierce look came back into his eyes. He was back in the race.

"I knew if I dropped out I'd hate myself for a year," he would say later. And he made a point of looking for Evans later and thanking him at the finish line.

Allen, meanwhile, was still strong, his lead still growing. He finally rolled into the Kona Surf parking lot at about 1:10 in the afternoon, climbed off his bike, and headed for the changing room. The split clock read 4:59:21; Allen had broken John Howard's course record.

Allen had gained time on Scott on the way back into town from Kawaihae, but not as much time as he had gained going out. It was a clue to Scott that Allen might be tiring, that Allen's ferocious pace on the bike had been too much for him. Scott flew in and out of the transition area as if something big and mean was at his heels. He went past the aid station outside the changing room the way he'd come out of the water in October 1982—in a startling explosion of effort, with water and sponges flying in all directions. He didn't look at all as if he had resigned himself to second place. He was in such a rush he put his singlet on backward.

"It was funny," Scott said, "at the end of that ride I felt better than I did the whole race. When I got off the bike my legs felt like I hadn't ridden. My legs felt fresh.

"I knew that the only way I was going to break Mark," Scott said, "was to go very fast at the beginning to see if I could hurt him psychologically, to make him think that he had gone too hard on the bike and I had saved it."

Allen lasted about 45 minutes. He ran well enough past the condos along Alii Drive, but he started feeling a little wobbly as he got into town. Then he reached the Pay and Save Hill and fell apart. His hard bike ride came rushing back, wrapped itself around his chest and squeezed. By the 10-mile mark he was walking, and looking bad doing that. All he wanted to do was finish; he knew Dave Scott would be along any time.

Scott went by at the 13-mile mark. Allen was jogging right up until the actual pass, but as Scott neared him,

Allen stumbled on the seam between the shoulder and the pavement and almost fell for the third time that day. So Allen was walking when Scott passed him, and he continued to walk for a while afterward. He had been in first place for more than six-and-a-half hours; it took him a moment to accept the fact that it was gone.

"Somebody said, 'Here he comes,'" remembered Allen. "And boy, did he look good. He look springy. He looked like he weighed about half as much as he should for how big he is." Scott had run through town at around a 6-minute-mile pace, a level of effort that was, considering the heat, unthinkable. He was still doing 6:30s when he went by Allen. Nor did he slow down after that, at least not consciously. In fact, it was as if being in first spurred him to run even faster, as if the more distance he put between himself and second place, the easier it would be to forget the long summer of frustration and all the talk about him being over the hill.

He was racing so furiously that he almost ran into the ABC camera van at the 21-mile point, when it got in his way as he looked for aid. The tape was rolling and the van was close; Scott was coming hard, his gray shorts and white singlet plastered to his body, his deeply bronzed skin glowing in the late-afternoon sun. Each time his feet struck the ground, the muscles in his thighs exploded in definition. "Water," he screamed. "Water! Water!" The van moved to Scott's left, thinking that he was going to the other side, but Scott had spotted a table to the left and was going there, van or no van. The driver, confused, slowed, and Scott almost came in. "Get the goddamned truck out of the way!" he roared. The driver yanked the van to the right, and Scott went by without giving it a glance. "Water!" he shouted again. "Water!"

He finished with a 2:53 marathon, the first sub-three-hour marathon ever run at Ironman—on the day plagued by perhaps the worst conditions in the event's history. His total time was 8:54:20. That was a record, too, the first time anyone had broken nine hours. The next man to finish, 24 minutes later, was Scott Tinley, looking better than most of the men who finished after him. His poor bike ride had translated into a relatively easy marathon; he hadn't been able to ride hard enough to get tired. He'd started the run in eighth place and then picked his way through the line of ragged men in front of him until only Dave Scott remained. He'd run his first 13 miles in 1:21, but he slowed down after that. What was the point? ST never liked to make points.

"Don't hurt yourself," he said to Allen with sincerity and genuine concern as he went by.

"Once I caught Mark," Tinley said, "and Dave was still 16 or 17 minutes ahead or whatever, I told myself: 'Be real about the whole thing. Save yourself for a future date.' I could have run a 2:55, but it wouldn't have done any good to hurt myself. It was not the year to go for it. It's that last four minutes you try to gain that *destroys* you for months afterward."

As Mark Evans had said when Tinley had been out there on the edge: "Second place is not that bad." It wasn't. Still, Tinley couldn't really say what it was *good* for, either, except self-respect, which after all was said and done, had always counted for a lot.

Allen, who wobbled in at fifth place and then spent a good deal of time in the medical tent, hit that particular topic right in the center:

"For me it was more of an accomplishment to get fifth this year than third last year," he said. "Last year I didn't go as fast as I could have gone, because I didn't want to. I was just fried from Nice. And this year I went even faster than I thought I could."

"The conditions were extreme," Scott said the next day. "I wanted to go above and beyond. I wanted a chance to prove that I'm the fastest runner, that when it comes to a foot race, I'm a competitor."

He hadn't really needed to prove that, but he'd established it now beyond all shadow of a doubt.

❖

Scott would keep his promise not to return in 1985. He left the door wide open for Tinley, who took advantage of the opportunity and won by a wide margin over Chris Hinshaw, as everyone had predicted he would. In his 23rd triathlon of the year Tinley capped his best season ever by breaking Scott's record by four minutes. That winter he was voted Triathlete of the Year by *Triathlon* magazine and was feted by the magazine at a black-tie affair in San Diego in February.

And from Davis, where it gets a lot colder in the winter than it does in San Diego, Dave Scott watched it all and started to train, his breath puffing in the crisp morning air, the steam rising from his warm shoulders. The Ironman, which had been the focus of his life for six years, turned in his mind and he considered the possibilities. There was talk that the race would have prize money for the first time in 1986, that the old spirit would be re-infused and that the field would be stronger than ever. Mostly, though, he thought about that 8:50, the new record....

"One of these days," he had said after the October race in 1982, "we'll get a perfect day with no wind. It'll be overcast. It'll be in the low 80s and somebody will crack off an 8:40 or something. It just has to be right."

Tinley had put the thing on the table: 8:50:54. Dave Scott knew he was going to have to at least reach out and try to take it off, retirement be damned. "I can go faster," he said to himself, and as he said it he knew it was the truth. He felt the good, solid tingle of excitement in his gut as the new goal formed. "I know I can go faster."

Which meant, of course, that ST would meet The Man—at least one more time.

11

Big bucks and the end of the dream

Scott Tinley's win at the Ironman in 1985 was a spectacular achievement, especially when viewed in the context of the competitive season that had preceded it. Starting on April 19 of that year he had raced 20 times on three continents before the Ironman, an average of almost one triathlon a week. Only once during that time did he finish out of the top three; he was fourth at the Bud Light USTS National Championships in late September. During one stretch just before the race in Hawaii, he put together a string that only his former training partner, Scott Molina, could have comprehended, let alone duplicated: a win at the Houston USTS on September 1; a first place at the Ironman-distance Cape Cod Endurance Triathlon on September 8; a second place (to Molina) at the San Diego USTS; a tie for first with Molina at the Bass Lake Classic a week after that; then the fourth at the USTS nationals on September 28. Then he took a week off before the Nice Triathlon on October 12, where he took two bad falls on his bike and still finished a heroic second to Allen. That left Tinley two weeks to heal before the Ironman in Hawaii on October 26.

ST, clearly, was the state-of-the-art triathlete: durable beyond the belief of medical experts, fast beyond all reasonable expectations, and willing to try almost any technological innovation that might make him even faster. He resembled the gritty, guts-for-brains stereotype of an ultra-endurance athlete as much as a pilot in the cockpit of an Air Force F-16 resembles Wilbur Wright. He was the highest tech of the high-tech super jocks.

That fact was never more clearly illustrated than in Hawaii that year, where he was the center of attention in the transition area just before the race. Not even triathletes who were doing the race, and should have been too nervous and preoccupied to notice, could resist: "Hey, did you see Tinley's bike? You gotta come over here and see this!"

And there it was, racked in the number 1 slot (although Tinley wore number 2, his place at the Ironman in 1984), nearest the exit of the pier: a black Peugeot with low-slung, wing-shaped aerodynamic handlebars that looked like laser cannons on a *Star Wars* fighter. And there was Tinley, grim-faced, making last-minute adjustments to his equipment, wearing his ST signature swimsuit, attaching his shoes to the pedal shafts of his nonpedals, adjusting the color-coordinated stretch booties over the shoes so that he could slide his foot in, pull the booty up and reduce wind resistance still further. Even Tinley was sleeker than usual; at the suggestion of a friend he had shaved off his mustache before the race for a cleaner look. (Nobody liked it; the bare lip didn't look like ST at all. He grew the mustache back shortly after the race.)

It was a dramatic and glamorous display of technology's force, just as Tinley's ensuing 8:50:54 course record was an impressive illustration of his skill and conditioning.

The sport of triathlon had come a long way.

There were signs, however, that the Ironman itself had not come far at all. The absence of prize money in Hawaii had had its effects. The field of top men at the 1985

Ironman was weak. Dave Scott had retired, and most of the other stars had ended their seasons in Nice two weeks before, a race that was beginning to make its self-made label of "World Championship" stick by offering a $75,000 purse for the third year in a row.

By contrast, the Ironman, which had been calling itself the "Triathlon World Championship" since October 1982, cost a guy like Tinley several thousand dollars. None of his expenses were covered. The trip was worthwhile for ST because he was pushing his clothing line and his new book. In a promotional sense an Ironman win was worth a great deal. But he had to win; second place in Hawaii was like being vice president of the United States. Second place for Tinley, in the absence of Dave Scott, would have been a career disaster.

That year, the sport of triathlon was full of talk about Ironman and Nice, and it was widely acknowledged that the more commercially oriented European race, still promoted and packaged for television by IMG, had purposefully positioned itself two weeks before the Ironman to steal the competitive thunder from the American event. Premeditated or not, that was what had happened. If you subscribed to the war theory, and were gauging things from a purely competitive standpoint, then you had to say that Nice was winning big. There were certainly no doubts as to what drove the engines of that event.

"The elite athletes are the *essence* of Nice," said David Michaels, the producer of the Nice broadcast for CBS, which in 1983 succeeded NBC as broadcaster of the Nice event. "Because what we're attempting to do is to present triathlon as a real sport. To cover it the way we want to cover it, we must have the best in the world." That kind of talk was music to the ears of the top triathletes.

Officially, the Ironman denied both the "war" and the tarnish on its star. Valerie Silk had never felt close to the elite triathletes; she didn't feel they were an exceptionally important part of the race. If the field that backed up Tinley lacked strength, what of it? The Ironman still had that good strong human element as a base; it still represented the ultimate challenge for the average man, who didn't need aerodynamic handlebars to find what he had come to Hawaii to find.

When a question about the Nice Ironman scheduling conflict was asked at the post-race press conference in 1985, it was brushed quickly aside by the Ironman press coordinator, an action that so frustrated Tinley, who had gone into the conference determined not to get himself in trouble by speaking out, that he answered the question himself, giving the press much more of an earful than the Ironman had bargained for.

"They were saying basically that the Ironman doesn't care where Nice is," Tinley said later, "that they put on their race, publish the date far in advance and couldn't care less if the pros come or not. That made me mad; that wasn't the right attitude. The right attitude would have been to recognize that Nice was an important race and to make every effort to work with it so the two events didn't conflict.

"And I would have said amen, that's great," Tinley said. "Instead, what we got was: 'We're the best, screw everybody else.'"

But Silk was not a stupid woman. Clearly, the thrust of the sport was not in the conservative direction of the Ironman. The average competitors didn't need the top pros to race in their events, but it was nice. It added a level of glamour and prestige. And the triathlon media, which covered the stars all year long, could not help but view their absence as an issue—and a failing on the part of the race organization.

David Downs, a program director for ABC, recalled Silk's private fears: "Valerie was very concerned as the issue developed: Is the Ironman falling behind the times? Should it have prize money? Is it a race for freaks or a race for elite triathletes? And so on. There were some people who were trying to put some fairly heavy pressure on her to change her position. On a number of occasions she came to us and asked us what we thought."

Unlike CBS, however, ABC was not tied to the professional focus. "We told Valerie," Downs said, "that, number one, the race was her business; we didn't want to get involved in it. Number two, we felt that the key to the success of the Ironman from the ABC television standpoint was that it was the original, the most well-known, that it had the most interesting stories, etc., etc. We felt that regardless of whether she had any elite athletes or not, we would rather have the Ironman Triathlon on the air than any of the triathlons on the calendar.

"On the other hand, there is no doubt in our minds—and we said this, too—that the Ironman is a better race for having Scott Tinley and Dave Scott running up at the front."

That was the crux. If the Ironman was going to be the best, it had to have it all: the great stories, the human drama, but the best triathletes, too. Otherwise, as Swiss triathlete Carl Kupferschmid, who placed third behind Tinley and Hinshaw in 1985, suggested: "The Ironman will become a race for tourists."

❖

The controversy made the first two years back on Oahu— when men were men, when beer was served full strength, and when triathletes were fools and proud of it—seem remote. Prize money? Triathlons in France? Good God.

Not that you went home empty-handed back then. As Collins wrote in the original brochure, "Identical, distinctive, handcrafted trophies" were awarded to each finisher. The good commander made the trophies himself, brazing copper tubing together to form the arms, legs, and torso of a man, adding a nut for a head, then spray-painting the figure black. Wood base and all, the trophies stood about 7 inches high. Collins was up until midnight in 1978 screwing the things together, and he never did get them so they would stand properly. In 1979 he had spare parts left over from the year before, so he was able to "whomp" the trophies together well in advance. They stood up that year— all but one of them.

When Tom Warren got his little man the day after the race, one of the screws in the right leg was missing, a fact that delighted Warren because it reminded him of his bad right leg.

"He had the only one that was broken," said Barry McDermott. "So, naturally, he thought he had the best one. The thing about Warren is that he can figure out a way to make anything perfect."

You even got a T-shirt back then, too. "Bring your own light-colored T-shirt," wrote Collins the first year. "We will silk-screen it for you."

The second year, Nautilus picked up the tab for the shirts, except that at the last minute they lost track of the guy who was supposed to do the screening and the shirts never made it to the race. They did eventually show up, though. Seven years later, Collins was still trying to hunt down a couple of the finishers so he could make the presentations.

That was about it: T-shirts and hand-made copper Ironmen. Warren, however, like Tinley and Dave Scott, like Howard, Ernst, Puntous, and McCartney, was made aware of the promotional benefits of an Ironman win. People began showing up in his bar in San Diego and telling members of the staff that they'd like to talk to Tom Warren, that they were thinking about doing the race. They came from all over—Pennsylvania, Florida, D.C. Like McDermott, Warren found himself acting as an Ironman go-between, channeling information about prospective competitors back to Hawaii. His bar, which had always been popular, became something of an underground shrine of the fitness culture.

"I made a lot of money off that race," Warren said. "I wasn't an easy person to get along with, but then again I was a personality, so the press always wrote good things about me. And they always wrote about my bar. I mean, you put me on the Johnny Carson Show? With a Tug's Tavern T-shirt? How much do people pay for that?

"See, the Ironman wasn't organized that well in those days. The fact is that I was ultra-organized. So if you wanted to get in the Ironman and you lived somewhere, you contacted me. I'd answer every letter. It created business. People knew me and they went to my bar. And in a business like mine, say you're at 80 percent and then you go to 84 percent. That 4 percent could damn well double my salary! You don't need too many people spending an extra five dollars a day to make a whole lot more money."

But Warren's expectations of personal reward from the Ironman were low, and he was easily pleased. As McDermott said, he could figure out a way to make everything perfect. The same could not be said for many of the elite triathletes who came after him. Considering the investment they'd made in the sport—the time and the training, and the schooling or real jobs put on hold—you could hardly blame them. The Ironman was a tough freebie, especially since big prize money races in Europe and Australia had sprouted on both sides of it. Why sacrifice your body to the Queen K for nothing when you could be racing for money, or at least saving yourself for your next event—which was surely to be coming along in a week or two.

In short, by 1985 the Ironman was starting to slide. On an emotional level it was still the biggest race in the world. It was still the Ironman, the ultimate goal of every triathlete from Tokyo to Toledo. But it had not been a world championship that year, not even close.

Enter the Anonymous Donor.

The Ironman had been the beneficiary of charitable largesse in the past. Collins, of course, had founded the thing on a volunteer basis; he'd even taken a loss the first year. Anheuser-Busch's Bud Light beer became the race's (and the entire sport of triathlon's) benefactor in 1982, although no one thought for a moment that Bud Light was sponsoring the thing out of the goodness of Auggie Busch's heart. The demographics of the triathletes and the spectacular nature of the race made it a good promotional investment, pure and simple.

J David's sponsorship in 1982 and 1983 had more of a ring of charity to it. Disappointed at what the competitors were due to receive from Bud Light in the way of commemorative clothing, J David's Ted Pulaski committed his company to buy $15,000 worth of nylon running shorts and singlets, on which the Ironman logo was screened, for distribution in each competitor's race bag. It was a generous gift, one which the athletes appreciated all the more for the almost complete lack of sponsor identification that appeared on the clothing. In stark contrast to the aggressive Bud Light brand-name placement effort, the J David logo could barely be seen.

The arrangement was basically the same in 1983. J David was not around in '84 to make it three in a row.

But the gift of the Anonymous Donor in 1986 was unprecedented: $100,000, earmarked solely for prize money. In several strokes of a pen, the Ironman went from being a stodgy, near-anachronism to being the biggest prize money triathlon in the world. "As far as I was concerned," the Anonymous Donor said, "the race needed to maintain its premier position as the most sought-after goal for people in the sport. You can't just say that we have a wonderful race, and it's in Hawaii, and y'all come, 'cause that's not what's going on with the professionals. And in order to attract great amateurs, you need great professionals. The 1985 race was not a world championship, because all the world champions weren't here."

The Donor, who is firm in his desire to remain unidentified, made his offer to Valerie Silk soon after the race in 1985. She was stunned. One hundred thousand dollars!

"I knew that it would happen someday," she said. "I knew that it was something that we would do at some point, when funds became available. I didn't think the funds would be available so quickly!"

But even at that, Silk wasn't just going to take the money and run off to announce the salvation of her race. She still had to be convinced that it needed salvation in the first place.

"It took me probably two months of thinking on it before finally deciding that, 'yeah, maybe it's time to go ahead and take the step,'" Silk said. "Even after the money was available I still wanted to talk to a lot of people and do a lot of thinking about it. We discussed it among the staff quite a bit, talked to other race directors, other people in the sport, people in other sports."

If Silk had turned the offer down, and word of it had gotten out, she probably would have turned both herself and the Ironman into laughingstocks. As the anonymous donor pointed out, even the age-group triathletes wanted to see themselves as competing in a championship-caliber event. Such blatant disregard for that aspect of the race would have been unforgivable.

But Silk took the money, despite the fact that it scared her. Then, *because* it scared her, she hired Bob Bright, the controversial race director of the America's Marathon in Chicago, to administer its distribution. Bright, best known for his highly publicized and slyly orchestrated rivalry with New York Marathon race director Fred Lebow, had established a reputation as a man who could handle the volatile brew of world-class athletes and big-time money. Bright's official title at the Ironman was "Professional Athlete Liaison," but his job was much more complex than that. Suggesting first to IMG that they change the date of the Nice event (it was scheduled for October 4, two weeks before the Ironman), then directly challenging their ability to lure the best athletes to Nice in light of the Ironman's prestige, Bright traveled tirelessly to meet the movers and shakers of the sport and explain the Ironman position, disarming people with a level of candor the triathlon community had never before experienced. That community already viewed IMG, which played at the highest levels of international sport— packaging huge television deals, representing athletes, promoting events—as the Great Satan; now here was Bright, hardly a choirboy himself, taking IMG to the streets. Brash, outspoken, he soon became known as "Valerie Silk's hired gun."

A baby-faced, former combat Marine in Vietnam and two-time veteran of the Iditarod sled-dog race in Alaska, Bright billed himself as an expert in putting money and athletes together to come up with intense competition and record performances. Highly intelligent, as unafraid to ask questions as he was to offer strong opinions, he could be smooth and coercive one instant, then harsh and demanding the next. He didn't need to play the role of heavy, but he was willing to do so if that's what it took to get the job done.

For all of its rapid growth, the sport of triathlon was a community with a small-town mind, and it didn't know what to make of Bob Bright. He was seen as a shrewd wheeler-dealer from the world of big-time marathoning; he was not a man anyone was willing to trust right off the bat. Still, the professional triathletes liked much of what he said. He was interested in them, at least. Bright's big advantage was that he was dealing from the strong side of the table and everyone knew it. Nice could posture and bluster, but the Ironman mystique was worth 999 points in a game that was being played to 1000. The mere promise of prize money in Hawaii was enough to turn many of the right heads.

"To me," said 1985 women's winner Joanne Ernst, who had earlier contemplated a trip to France, "Ironman is worth more to win than Nice is, regardless of the money, from a psychological standpoint and a media standpoint. In the long term, being an Ironman winner is worth vastly more in terms of marketability than being a Nice champion. I have never once had anyone ask me whether I have done the Nice Triathlon. Never. And yet almost every single person I've ever met who knows anything about the word 'triathlon' at all asks me whether I've done the Ironman."

Bright's main objective for the Ironman that year was to have the top triathletes perform spectacularly. The ideal scenario in his mind was to have Dave Scott and Scott Tinley, with perhaps one other good but largely unsung competitor, make the final turn onto Alli Drive all within yards of one another, pushing to the end not just for the money but for the win.

"I'm a student of how you make them run fast," he said, "how to make them do things; how to get out of an athlete what he really wants to give you."

One of the tools to accomplish his goal was appearance money, a tactic that had become standard procedure in the marathoning business but which was looked on in triathlon circles with distaste. Since Nice, the shorter of the two events, came first on the schedule, Bright knew that the top guys would try to race in France, then turn around and race in Hawaii. He was unhappy with that scenario. He didn't want just the best names racing in Kona; he wanted the bodies that belonged to them.

"I feel much more comfortable," he said, "when key athletes *focus* on events."

So he set the prize purse at $85,000, added several performance bonuses, and, using money from the Ironman coffers beyond the $100,000 grant, offered the two key men, Tinley and Scott, $6000 each if they would race at Ironman—and only at Ironman. He offered Ernst $4300. Lesser deals (expenses only, no appearance money), with the same conditions, were made with a small group of other pros—top finishers from 1985, and past winners like Sylviane Puntous—with the understanding that along with the cash there would be considerations the top athletes had never before been offered in Hawaii: streamlined registration, an elite athlete hospitality suite, a special pre-race meeting, and a limited level of technical support on the bike course. (Because the athletes were paid to race, a breakdown like the one Allen suffered in 1982 would have hurt not just the athlete but also the Ironman's investment.) In short, the professional triathletes would be treated like elite performers, with a degree of respect to which they had long aspired.

Bright also made an offer to Mark Allen, but it was more out of courtesy than of expectation. Not that Allen wasn't interested, but he was being represented at the time by IMG and had strong commitments to the Nice event. Bright actually counseled him to stay where he was. Molina was approached as well; like Allen, his stature in the sport demanded it, although he had already made it clear that he wasn't interested in the Ironman, prize money or not.

Tinley was uneasy with Bright's maneuvering. He felt pressured—and he disliked being pressured more than anything in the world. What he preferred to do was pick up an appearance check and some prize money in France, then fly back and do battle with Scott in Hawaii. His record showed that he was capable of that, and others agreed.

"I think Tinley showed last year that Bob Bright is mistaken saying someone can't do both races well," Molina said. "He crashed twice and had a great performance in Nice, and then he came back and who knows how fast he could've gone at Ironman had somebody been on his butt to push him. No, there are definitely a few guys who could race well at both. It's not like marathoning; I don't think Bob understands that yet. Cyclists in the Tour de France do marathon stages day after day. If you're really fit, you can recover."

Meanwhile, Dave Scott signed on. He'd done some public waffling, some last-minute negotiating with Bright, making sure he was getting the best deal he could, but it was academic; he would no more have left the Ironman to Tinley than he would have grown a beard and walked off to live in a commune in Oregon. There was even less of a chance that he would have raced Nice and Ironman, knowing that Tinley was going into Hawaii rested and fresh.

As for Tinley....

"It is a tough spot to be in," he said, "because I'm one of only two or three people who can do both races 100 percent. And I have a chance at winning both, which puts even more pressure on me. It bothers me because the Ironman isn't paying me to do the Ironman, they're paying me to not do Nice."

There were too many "ifs" for ST. If he took the Ironman offer, then raced poorly in Hawaii, it would mean he'd made a big financial mistake, $10,000 worth, perhaps more. If he raced in Nice and crashed and couldn't come back and be competitive with Scott two weeks later, he'd be out again. If he and Scott both turned their backs on the Ironman, the race might suffer a big loss of credibility. Or worse, suppose it didn't even flinch? Suppose it was great without them?

"It's an odd position, Bob," Tinley said to Bright. "You're pulling me one way, the other guy is pulling me the other way...."

"Hey, Scott," Bright said softly, "you know what? Welcome to the big time."

Tinley, grumbling, finally signed with the Ironman. The race was on.

❖

The 1986 triathlon season leading up to Nice and Hawaii had been marked by tight, aggressive competition among the women and the continued domination of the Big Four in the men's field. Despite pre-season predictions of their demise, and challenges from a horde of tough youngsters, Tinley and Molina both competed as they had in the past: with awesome frequency and efficiency. By season's end, Molina's crown as short-distance king still sat on his head, undisturbed. Tinley, the defending Ironman champ, and therefore in great demand, raced everywhere at all distances, and won a hell of a lot more often than he didn't. One of his best races of the year came in early July, at the European Long Distance Triathlon Championship in Sweden. Over the metric equivalent of the Ironman distances, Tinley raced an impressive 8:27, finishing with a 2:49 near-marathon. The man in second place, six-and-a-half minutes back, was none other than Dave Scott. As for Allen, competing as usual in less than half as many events as Molina and Tinley, he was still showing signs of being the great talent. He lost only once all year—to Molina— although he did suffer through a spectacular disqualification for drafting after out-kicking Molina to the tape at the Chicago USTS in August. With a field of 3400 competitors, Chicago was the biggest triathlon in the world, and Allen's faux pas, which was more of a mental lapse than an attempt to gain an advantage, was hotly discussed on the national cable-feed television coverage of the event by Chicago's superstation, WGN. It was an unpleasant experience all around, both for Allen, who protested the decision unsuccessfully, and for the race itself. Unfortunately, the painful lesson was not taken as closely to heart as it might have been, and a scene similar to that which occurred in

Chicago would be played out in Hawaii two months later. The cast would be different, but the confusion and bitterness all too familiar.

What was different that season was Dave Scott. He raced more frequently than he had in years. Once again he had been written off as being over the hill. He was 32, which was too old, and he was too slow. That's what many of the experts said, at least. But as his racing showed, in a low-key, understated way, he wasn't too slow at all. In several major short-distance triathlons, none of which he won ("Dave Scott was fourth," they said. "Look at this, Dave Scott was third"), he recorded the fastest 10km time of the day, faster than any of the young Turks, faster even than Molina or Tinley. If he was indeed over the hill, then he was at least running, not walking, down the other side.

"In a lot of the races this year," Scott said, "I was really irritated while I was out there racing because I was mad at myself for not being in better shape, and the only salvaging thing that I could walk away with was to be able to say that at least I ran hard at the end. That was the redeeming event."

As the season progressed, Scott became faster and faster. Just before the start of the San Diego USTS on September 14, with the Ironman little more than a month away, he remarked to Anna, his wife, that he felt good, that he could win the race. But when he came out of the water in third place in San Diego and ran up the hill to the transition area, he couldn't find his bike. There'd been a numbering screw-up, and Anna had moved the bike, but the pair had miscommunicated on the new location. He lost several minutes, a huge chunk in a short-distance race. He was furious, and vented his anger during the run, working his way up to fourth place with a 32:26 10km. Tinley won the race, and had the second fastest run of the day, but it was a full minute slower than Scott's.

Two weeks later, at the USTS National Championships on Hilton Head Island, South Carolina, the final race before the Ironman for those receiving appearance money, Scott finally turned the trick. Molina, the Terminator, was in his best form, unbeatable, but Tinley and Scott were off the bike within eight seconds of each other, with Scott in front. Considering ST's short-distance competitive record, most people wouldn't have given Scott much of a chance to stay there. But stay there he did, and his 33:45 10km in the soggy Hilton Head heat was once again the fastest of the day. It was exactly the kind of note Scott wanted to fly off to Hawaii having sounded. Tinley was disappointed, of course, but there were three weeks of training and tapering to go before the big one. Anything could happen.

In Kona it was obvious that the $100,000 had made a big difference. The vague unease that had settled over the race in 1985 had been replaced by an aura of competitive tension and anticipation that surpassed anything the Ironman had known in its nine-year history. Never had the field been so strong. And with Bright's appearance-money restrictions, never had so many top athletes been so well-prepared for the event. No official world governing body had sanctioned the Ironman as the "world championship"; the title remained self-bestowed. But along Alii Drive that year, down at Dig Me Beach in the morning, the 10th anniversary Ironman felt like the championship of *something*. And the feeling ran straight through the ranks; the age-group triathletes were as sophisticated as the pros. The Ironman qualification procedures, the stiff competition between the age-groupers during the season back on the mainland, had had a cumulative effect. Only among the big block of Japanese competitors, whose largely unrestricted entry quota was sure to become an issue in the future, was the wide-eyed innocence of the triathlon novice the rule rather than the rare exception. Even before the majority of the sport had noticed it had slipped, the Ironman was back.

Then, suddenly, so was Mark Allen. He had the race of his life in Nice and won by 11 minutes; Molina was second. Rumors that both men would compete in Hawaii had been flying all over Kona the week before the race. The Molina rumors were pure fantasy; he had never seriously considered racing. But Allen had recovered quickly from

Nice and he was in top form. He was interested. His agent even tried to make an 11th-hour deal for appearance money, which Bright immediately rejected. With nothing to lose—he already had his fifth Nice title—Allen entered anyway. In so doing he reshaped the Ironman picture. Among the men, the race was still a Tinley-Scott duel, but Allen was playing a familiar role: the wild card.

Tinley was irked. Allen was doing what he, Tinley, had wanted to do all along: race in Nice, then race in Hawaii. And IMG had the nerve to ask for money! Somehow Tinley couldn't quite believe that Bright hadn't broken faith in that department and coughed up something. And even if he hadn't, Tinley felt betrayed. This was his show; Allen had already had his. And though ST was confident that the Ironman was still between himself and Dave Scott, there was in the back of his mind the incredible talent Allen had been showcasing all season. The guy was a threat, there was no doubt. The two men had been friends, J David teammates, but there had been tension between them all that year, even animosity. Now it was worse. They met inadvertently on the Thursday evening before the race at Dig Me Beach, where they had gone to take a swim before the sun went down. Tinley was coming out of the water with a couple of friends, Allen was just going in. No words were spoken, but the wall between them was thick, the ill feeling was palpable.

Tinley didn't need the added worry. He was having trouble enough coping with not having been able to race after Hilton Head. Focusing on a single event, even one as long and as important as the Ironman, was like locking himself in a box and having somebody shake it. He worried about getting stale, about resting too much, about having lost his fine competitive edge. Plus, in the week just before the race, he began having problems with one of his high-tech bikes. He ended up spending hours and hours trying to get the thing to work. It was a psychological drain. And the bike was just the tip of the iceberg. What he had started to do, and it was a crucial mistake, was worry about too many things that he could do nothing about—about Allen and

Scott, about whether Bright was taking advantage of him, and about the fact that maybe he should have gone to Nice after all.

"I almost hate to come to the races because of the pressure," Virginia would say just before the start of the race that year. "There's really not much I can do anyway, so it might almost be better to just wait and hear. Plus, Scott is hard to be with before the race; there's a tremendous amount of pressure at our house the week before."

Virginia, a tall, attractive blonde, had supported her husband faithfully in his racing since the beginning; she had been his most valued companion, but that year in Kona was harder than most. She looked down at him making final adjustments on his exotic machine in the predawn gloom and her mouth tightened. She had talked about her sense of pre-race helplessness.

"It's actually no more helpless for me than it is for him. The helpless feeling is if the bike breaks, if a jellyfish stings him.... Mainly it's if the bike breaks. If I didn't have to worry about the bike I'd be fine, because I know Scott's done his homework, and he's going to have a great race. I can't say he's going to win.... If I just knew that he could at least race his best race I'd be okay."

Dave Scott, in contrast, with his fifth Ironman title on the line, was loose and relaxed. The addition of Allen to the field was interesting; he would deal with it on race day. Scott was in better shape than he'd ever been in Hawaii, and he had ended the season on a high note at Hilton Head, so he was confident.

"I feel less pressure in this race than probably any of them," he said on Thursday night.

Why had he come back, since there was so much about the race he didn't like? He had his four wins. Was it just the money?

"I'm not going to say the money isn't an incentive," he said. "It certainly is. But it's the same thing that it was in 1980. I think the biggest thing is that I feel I can go faster.

"I'm like any athlete. I don't want to disgrace myself. I don't want to come in 15th or 20th and have people say,

'God, look at Dave Scott, he's 32 now, he was good once, but he's a step behind now.' I know a lot of people have said that already, at races where I have fallen off the pace and some of the young guys have clobbered me. I don't want that to happen; I want to be able to recognize it myself when it does. I know it will."

But Scott knew it wasn't going to happen for a while—and certainly not in 1986. He talked about watching Tinley from the ABC van the year before, giving him split times along the way, thinking that Tinley might go even faster than he did, 8:46 perhaps, instead of the 8:50. There were times during that race when Scott had wished he'd been out on the road himself, doing battle.

"I wished I was out there, pushing him, having him push me," Scott said, "because he *would've* gone 8:46. Or I would've gone 8:46 or 8:42 or something. I'm sure Scott thinks he can go considerably faster, and I feel the same way. I think that on this course, someone is going to pop off an 8:32 or an 8:33. And it might be this year. I want to do a fantastic race. If I can swim in 50 minutes, which I seem to be able to do pretty consistently, and then ride 5 hours, a little bit better, and then run 2:40, that would be a great race. And if someone beats me, well more power to 'em." Scott laughed nervously. "But I'm going to make them pay for it."

❖

The women's field was less defined than the men's. The biggest favorites had not raced much during the season at all. No one had dominated the way the top men had.

The defending champ was Ernst, who had abruptly stopped competing early in the season after a couple of poor races. She retreated to her home in Palo Alto, California, to train specifically for the Ironman. By October she was in tremendous shape, the best of her life, and after spending two weeks up the coast in Puako, away from the madness in Kona, she was calmer than she'd ever been in Hawaii.

Ernst's toughest competition was almost certainly going to come from the Puntous sisters: Sylviane, who had won the Ironman in 1983 and 1984, and her identical twin, Patricia, who had finished second both times. The pair had come out of the Montréal road-racing scene in 1982 and had dominated the women's side of triathlon through 1984. They raced less frequently the following two years, but they could still be counted on to delight photographers and spectators with their side-by-side first-place finishes. Unfortunately, their acceptance as sports personalities in this country was limited by an overly protective manager (they fired him in 1985) and by their thick French-Canadian accents, which gave the American press a lot of trouble. Worse, the twins were in the habit of giggling through interviews, thwarting the efforts of writers trying to portray them as serious professionals. They were simply cute. One Atlanta sportswriter, frustrated over trying to make sense of their tandem, light-headed chatter, dubbed them "The Stereo Sisters."

Unfortunately, some of their peers thought of the twins in the same way: in tandem, in situations where they should not have been. Not only was their practice of running together seen as unfair in a sport that centered around individual competition, they were also named a number of times in heated drafting protests by fellow competitors. With official enforcement procedures in a primitive state at best, the protests were never upheld, but the charges were never disproved, either, so the air around them stayed cloudy.

The twins usually claimed they had been victimized by male competitors who wouldn't allow themselves to be passed by a woman. Privately, however, they saw the protests as manifestations of jealousy, something they had seen in competition before they became involved in triathlons. Training and racing on a strikingly equal footing (Bright, after watching them run for the first time, said they were "connected"), they had been resented before; they figured this was more of the same. "Because we are twins," Patricia said, "it's like a team, kind of.

People are envious. For sure, we get people mad against us, but what can we do? It was like that in track and field and when we were in swimming. We have always had bad feelings from people."

They certainly seemed to make no overt attempts to correct the situation, an attitude that puzzled even those who were willing to think the best of them. "Maybe they just don't *know*" was the way some within the sport attempted to explain the recurring problem, thinking that perhaps the twins just weren't clear on the concept. But since no one ever seemed willing to find *out* if they knew—and then explain the problem to them if they didn't—the stigma remained, and the twins bubbled blithely on, winning and giggling together while the rest of the women tried to catch up.

Their penchant for getting themselves in tight situations, however, put them in direct conflict with Ernst, who saw the competitive arena as something almost sacred, and therefore drafting as an evil she could not tolerate. As she rose to prominence in the sport, becoming the first woman to successfully challenge the twins in competition, Ernst became an outspoken critic of unfairness at races, particularly in the area of drafting, growing less and less inhibited about citing names and specific instances. The twins were frequent targets of her wrath. At the Portland USTS event in 1984, Ernst was so enraged by what she perceived as their drafting that she not only protested the final results (she was joined by several other women), she also returned her third-place check to USTS officials.

"It is unfortunate that honest athletes following your formal protest procedures are made to feel like the guilty parties," Ernst wrote to the USTS National Series administrator Jim Curl. "It takes guts to file a formal protest, knowing that one is risking alienating fellow competitors. Unfortunately, I see no indication that your officials have the guts to carry out the established penalties for drafting, especially if protests involve famous athletes. In order to live by my word that fairness, not money, is my concern, I am returning to you my third place $500 check."

Ernst and husband Jim Collins hammered hard on the issue, and not just as it applied to the twins. They were soon viewed by many people in the sport as uncompromising malcontents. The uncompromising part they were willing to accept; it was a label they were proud of. But malcontents? Ernst, who was voted in a *Triathlon* magazine readers' poll as female triathlete of the year in 1985, did not consider her position extreme.

"All I want to do is *race,*" she said. "Go head-to-head with these people and may the best person win. But when I get into a situation, at least from my perspective, in which that is not being allowed, then I don't want any part of it. To me racing is about respect—earning the respect of your competitors and yourself. If you don't have that, it doesn't mean anything at all. *That's* why I get so irritated about drafting."

Sylviane and Patricia never responded, at least publicly. They were likable and pleasant, their innocent demeanor belying any controversy and baffling their critics. But they never came to terms with Ernst and her husband. Indeed, the situation continued to erode. The twins saw Ernst as envious and vindictive; Ernst came to view the twins as unrepentant cheaters. Negotiating Ernst's Ironman contact with Bob Bright in 1986, Collins requested a guarantee that the twins would be watched with extra diligence during the bike ride. Bright could not agree to that, of course. He assured a skeptical Collins that the situation was under control.

"I thought they were whining," Bright said. "I thought Joanne needed to think about more important things—like the *race.*"

The twins were not Ernst's only concern. Liz Bulman, the strong marathoner who had almost run Ernst down in 1985, was also in the field. So was the mysterious Erin Baker, who was undefeated in competition but had never raced on American soil.

Baker, from New Zealand, was a solidly built, pleasantly soft-spoken, freckle-faced 25-year-old sensation who all season long had been beating the best Americans in races outside their own country by embarrassingly wide margins. She had been unable to race in the United States because while taking part in an antinuclear demonstration back home, she had hurled a firecracker, been arrested, and subsequently labeled a terrorist, which made it impossible for her to obtain official permission to enter the United States. But much to everyone's pleasant surprise, months of delicate work through diplomatic and political channels by Earl Yamaguchi, the Ironman's director of international operations, paid off, and Baker was granted a visa so she could race in Hawaii. Bright did not offer her appearance money, but he did offer to pay for her flight from Nice, where she was scheduled to defend her 1985 title, to Hawaii. No one questioned his circumventing his own Nice prohibition in Baker's case; her presence in the field was too exciting, and none of the other women had wanted to attempt the Nice/Ironman double anyway. As for Bright, who had seen Baker race in the European championships and was enormously impressed, he figured that if she was a little tired, it might make the women's race in Hawaii more competitive. He thought she was that good.

As it turned out, neither Baker nor Bulman figured in the race for first place. Bulman had a good day, but not the great day she needed. She finished fourth. And Baker, jet-lagged and still suffering psychologically from having won in Nice and then being disqualified for receiving illegal aid, was overwhelmed by the Queen K. She dropped out during the bike ride in front of her condominium on Alii Drive, four miles from the Kona Surf.

It was left to Ernst to set the pace for the day. The Puntous twins were to be her biggest competition after all, along with a South African expatriate named Paula Newby-Fraser, who had placed a forgotten third behind Ernst and Bulman in the 1985 race.

Like Tinley, who she admits has been a role model for her, Ernst entered the sport as a poor swimmer. But she worked hard in the pool, knowing that to be competitive, she couldn't keep giving up huge chunks of time in the water. In 1984, the first time she did the Ironman, it took her 1:04 to cover the 2.4 miles. The next year, the year she won, she cut that to 1:01. In '86 she was out of the water in 57:36, an amazing improvement that put her less than a minute behind Bulman and the twins, just seconds behind Newby-Fraser. A strong cyclist, perhaps the strongest in the sport, Ernst was as close as she needed to be. Firing out of the transition area and up Pay and Save Hill, she passed all of the serious contenders early in the bike ride and was in the lead well before the turnaround at Hawi. She had set herself up for either a big win or a nasty fall.

While the leader in the men's race at Ironman has the advantage of being the center of a lot of attention, that's less true for the first woman. There is an ABC camera van for her as well, but it moves around a lot more—up and back to see where the other women are, pausing along the route to get shots of other triathletes. With the rest of the women behind her, Ernst spent much of her day pedaling through the heat alone, with only her assigned drafting marshal nearby. There was a certain comfort in the solitude—Ernst does much of her training by herself—but at the same time she started to lose touch with the race, and with herself, too, mostly with her need to take in enough food.

Complicating Ernst's problem was the decision taken by the Ironman to restrict the movement and actions of the friends and spouses of the top triathletes out on the course. In the past, people close to the competitors—Scott's right-hand man, Pat Feeney, or Virginia Tinley, for example—would wheedle press passes and then hitch rides with authorized vehicles so they could be out on the course and give progress reports as their athletes whizzed by: "He's four minutes back," "You're up two minutes on Allen," and so on. That system had been eliminated. In its place was a leader board, on which were written time differentials between the top men at various points along the course. The board was transported by car and displayed to cyclists as they rode. Once everyone on the leader list had been covered, the car moved to a new location and a new set of splits was taken.

It was an adequate solution to the problem, although no one was under any impression that it was going to work perfectly the first time out. What was difficult was that the system had been adopted close to race day and so no rehearsal of the procedure was possible. Even worse, there was no leader board for the women. "It's an experiment," race officials said. "We're going to have to see how it works."

From almost the beginning of the ride then, when she passed the twins and Newby-Fraser, Ernst had no idea where any of her competitors were. Finally, after almost five hours, she asked the marshal on the moped to find out.

"Four-twenty-two, Joanne," came the word. "Paula Newby-Fraser is in second and she's 4:22 back. The twins are 5:44 back."

Ernst seemed to flinch a little. She'd hoped for more.

"They must be tired if they're riding that hard," she said, trying to sound confident and brave. But there was a hint of panic in her voice. *She* was tired, definitely.

Newby-Fraser, whom Ernst knew to be a strong runner, had been lurking back there all day. She had pedaled away from the pier with a group of the top women, watched Ernst go by like a shot, then took off herself, riding most of the way to Hawi with Sylviane Puntous. Patricia caught them at the turnaround and the three women continued on together, overtaking other cyclists on the way back. By Sheraton Waikoloa Resort, 75 miles into the ride, Newby-Fraser had taken control and led the twins by 7 seconds. That margin lengthened, slowly; she was 8 seconds ahead 30 minutes later, 1:18 ahead a half-hour after that. By the time all four top women were on Alii Drive, pedaling toward the Kona Surf, Ernst had almost a 5-minute lead over Fraser and was 6:20 ahead of the twins.

Ernst had never liked to lead in a race, especially during the run. The only good thing that could happen to her when she was in first was that she could stay there and win; the menu for potential disaster was much longer, and Ernst was the kind of person who could convince herself that each disaster would, indeed, occur—if only she was out there long enough.

"It's a very hard position to be in," she said. "Even when I was running track in high school, my favorite thing to do was to sit on people and outkick them down the final stretch."

Nevertheless, there she was, running out of the parking lot at the Kona Surf, worried about the cramps in her legs that had twinged when she got off the bike, concerned with how tired she felt, hoping that things would loosen up once she'd put a few miles behind her. Along the way she watched Newby-Fraser come in, then the twins. It had been a long day already; it was going to get a lot longer.

She ran strongly through town, losing a little ground to the twins, but not much. The Canadians had run down Newby-Fraser easily and were in second and third places, five minutes back, by the time Ernst ran up Pay and Save Hill and headed out onto the highway. Once again she was alone, and this time the aloneness (not the loneliness; her mind didn't have time for that just yet) became a terrible enemy.

❖

At the pre-race meeting for the professionals, Dave Scott had argued against the prohibitions the race was placing on the triathletes' information sources. He argued so strongly about not being able to get split times and distances that some of the other pros seemed genuinely surprised. They threw looks back and forth between one another as if to say, "Big Dave sounds a little worried."

In fact, Big Dave *was* worried. In the past, his information sources had always been the best; he was proud of Feeney's fine ability to deal with figures during a race, and adamant about the fact that Feeney had always offered times to Tinley and Allen and the other top guys, too. "It just makes for a better race," Scott said. He might have sounded like he was whining a little in the meeting, but most of the people were missing the point. More than any of them, Scott treated even ultradistance events like head-to-head races, and a split time that said the competition was gaining meant that it was time for him to dig down deep; a split that suggested his opponent was crumbling meant it was time for him to turn the screws. All of the men and women pros used splits, of course, and were aware of their usefulness, but most treated them primarily as either good or bad news, period.

But even those athletes who did not depend on splits as heavily as Scott suffered from their absence, the women especially, since they were getting even less information from race officials than the men. Reports received only after many miles and long periods of time had elapsed could be psychologically devastating. In Ernst's case, they were. She was stunned when a marshal on a moped finally rolled up next to her just past the 12-mile point in the marathon and said: "They are one minute behind you."

"I'd lost five or six minutes, but I didn't know where," Ernst said. "It turns out I lost almost all of that time once I hit the highway. I can ride without information. I just have more self-confidence on the bike. I know when I'm riding the right pace. Whereas in the run, when I'm tired, I can't judge my pace. And because they don't have mile markers at the Ironman, it's even tougher. I'd run almost half a marathon in a vacuum."

Finally, about 13 miles out, Patricia Puntous ran strongly by, and Ernst's first place was gone. Sylviane passed her just seconds later. A half-mile after that, Newby-Fraser went by, too, although Ernst barely noticed her, for she was walking at the time, light-headed, sleepy from hypoglycemia, having nothing to do now but find something to eat as soon as she could and then run on, hoping to control the damage and stay out of fifth place. It took a special effort for her even to finish; she would say later that getting to the pier in fourth place in 1986 was a finer personal moment than winning the race in 1985.

Newby-Fraser was having her finest hour as well. Running through town along Alii Drive she had been on the ropes, had even walked in between some of the aid stations. With the twins five minutes ahead of her, she had all but given up any thought of being a contender. But once she got out of town and onto the highway, she started running well. Through the last half of the marathon, the twins both came back to her, slowly, yard by yard, second by second. Sylviane gave up second place at around 22 miles. Newby-Fraser went by without a word, looking for the sister. She got to within less than a minute of Patricia, but by that time the leader had crested that last long hill at 23.5 miles and was headed down, while Newby-Fraser had just begun the climb. It was too much, there really was no hope.

Meanwhile, a tremendous controversy had been brewing at the finish line. Back at the Kona Surf, marshals director Dennis Haserot had received word from the bike course that Patricia Puntous had been cited for drafting on the way up to Hawi. In fact, word of the incident had somehow already spread to the competitors. Both Newby-Fraser and Sylviane Puntous had heard someone yell something about a disqualification as they neared the bicycle turnaround; both thought that it might be them. Reassured at the time that such was not the case by the marshal who was following them, Sylviane heard the same rumor as she began her run, and was under the impression that she had been officially eliminated. Despite that, she continued her marathon.

But it was not Sylviane, it was Patricia, and according to the procedures that Haserot had instituted, disqualification was the only penalty that could be assessed for such an infraction. A time penalty of 20 minutes for a first offense during an ultradistance competition like the Ironman was provided for in the rules of the Triathlon Federation USA, the national governing body of the sport, but Tri-Fed was still solidifying its power, and the Ironman had been able to incorporate some of the Tri-Fed rules into its own system and discard others. Haserot had painted himself into a corner; he had no options at all. Adding to the problem was the fact that there was no provision for notifying an athlete at the time of the infraction. Haserot, in fact, had instructed the marshals not to make their calls out loud, but rather simply to record the number of the athlete, fill out the required form, and submit a report. This last provision was curious, because it seemed to contradict an existing Ironman rule that said course marshals did, indeed, have the authority to disqualify participants.

The situation was a mess, and Haserot was unsure as to how it should be handled.

"I would guess that I first knew about the disqualification when the girls [the twins] were well into the run," said Haserot, who is a longtime and successful bike racer himself. "See, we had played with different ways of handling this kind of thing, but frankly, naive as it sounds, it had never occurred to me that one of the top athletes would do that [draft]. And going back to my personal feeling—which is not necessarily the right way to judge something—if I trained for a year to come do this event and was in a situation that caused me to be disqualified, I would rather not know until it was over. I'm there to find out how well I can do against these other people. I wouldn't want to find out at the end of the bike that I'd just screwed up a year of my life. I'd just as soon hear about it afterward, deal with it, but at least I can look at my time and say, well, here's how I fit with all these people."

Haserot was indeed naive, even with respect to his own event. In October 1982 there had been the furious drafting controversy involving the women's winner that year, Julie Leach. Several protests against Leach were filed, and while none were upheld, the bitterness lapped over into a cover story written by journalist Lee Green for *Women's Sports* magazine titled "Trouble In Paradise."

Haserot was also handicapped by the fact that, like the majority of the Ironman staff, he was remote from the mainstream of the triathlon world. That partly had to do with geography; Hawaii was a long way from the mainland. But it had also to do with an almost institutionalized Ironman chauvinism. The race had been reading its own press for too long; it was still the emotional heart of the sport of triathlon, no doubt, but it was no longer on the cutting edge of the sport's growth and painfully developing maturity. Had Haserot been keeping up with just the biggest of the hundreds of triathlons that had been held the previous summer back on the mainland, he would have known that the top triathletes, increasingly competitive among themselves, had been repeatedly involved in drafting controversies, with penalties and disqualifications in the professional fields being thrown around like popcorn.

Nor would many of those professionals consider running the Ironman marathon just to see where they fit in the field. The point Haserot was missing was that most of the elite triathletes no longer trained a year specifically for the Ironman. That had been the case for most of them in 1982, but in 1986 they were training year-round for 10, 15, 20 triathlons, and doing so because it was their profession; the ability to recover from one race in order to race well in the next—and take home another paycheck—was critical. Running "just to see" was a luxury (or an agony) that few of them could afford.

All of that aside, however, Haserot was faced with a woman in first place who had run a good portion of perhaps the most grueling marathon in the sport, and had unwittingly done so for naught. Whether Puntous should have been pulled from the race or informed of her problem at the end of the bike ride was moot. The question was, should she be pulled off the course before she finished her run, sparing the race the messy situation of having a non-winner break the tape?

Bob Bright was strongly in favor of the latter option. Upon learning that Patricia Puntous had been disqualified but was still on the course, oblivious to her own predicament, Bright immediately recognized the public relations jam the race was in. Puzzled that no action had yet been taken, he approached Ironman media coordinator Jeanette Foster and asked if Puntous was, indeed, irrevocably disqualified. Foster said that, yes, she was. Bright then sought out Valerie Silk, who was at the finish line, placing leis over the heads of the exhausted triathletes as they crossed.

"Valerie," Bright said, "we have a problem here. Patricia Puntous is in the lead, it looks like she's going to win the race, but she's been disqualified. I think it's a liability and a bad PR deal for this event if she crosses the finish line as the winner and we disqualify her."

Silk agreed with Bright. He then asked her if race director Kay Rhead was available to make the decision to remove Puntous from the course. Unfortunately, Rhead, who had been diagnosed recently as having cancer, was exhausted and taking a nap. Bright, accustomed to being in command, stepped into what he perceived as an administrative void. He located Haserot and suggested a way to resolve the issue. Haserot had been considering the same solution but had apparently rejected it.

"I asked Dennis whether Patricia was unequivocally out of the race," Bright said. "He said, yes, she was out of the race, disqualified. It's done, there was no appeal. I then suggested that he go out on the course and talk to her, tell her she's disqualified and request that she leave the course. There was some discussion on how that ought to be done. Dennis was uncomfortable with having to do that. Finally, it was decided that he would go out and find Jim Bates [the Puntouses' agent and manager], whom he'd seen earlier out on the course, and get *him* to tell Patricia that she had been disqualified. I said, 'Well, however you think it ought to be done, why don't you do it?'"

In explaining the situation, Bright was careful not to be too critical of his employers. He'd been outspoken already about the incident and had been criticized for having overstepped his authority that day. An article about the race in *Outside* magazine (interestingly, by the same Lee Green who had written the "Trouble In Paradise" piece in 1982) had said that Bright had "dispatched" Haserot to take Puntous off the course, a term that rankled the Ironman leadership because Bright did not have the authority to dispatch anyone. Careful or not, however, the twinge of impatience in Bright's voice when he reviewed the chronology of that afternoon was unmistakable. He is comfortable with being in charge, fidgets when he is not, and enjoys the process of having to make hard decisions quickly, on the spot. He'd been annoyed at being caught in a situation where no one seemed to be doing anything—to the detriment of the public perception of the race. He was also embarrassed because a situation had arisen that he had been warned about; he would later apologize to Jim Collins for not having had the enforcement situation as firmly under control as he had assured Collins that he would.

Convinced in his own mind that he should *not* remove Puntous from the course, Haserot zoomed off on his motorcycle to find Bates, while Bright notified ABC of what he thought was about to happen, that Patricia Puntous was going to be pulled from the course. He figured that if they chose to tape it, fine; the Ironman would come off looking firm and decisive in a tough situation.

Bright is sure that Bates, the good agent, played for time with Haserot, hoping that he'd be able to find some way to salvage Patricia's win. Haserot believes that Bates was simply concerned, anguished over the situation. In any case, Bates convinced Haserot that there might have been a mistake, considering that the twins, who looked identical, had been competing in matching outfits and on matching bikes. "Suppose it wasn't Patricia?" posed Bates. "Wouldn't it be terrible to remove the wrong woman from the course?"

Haserot, still undecided, took Bates back to talk with Bright. Meanwhile, Patricia Puntous ran on, heading back toward town along the Queen K. If she was aware of the controversy that was swirling around her, she gave no indication. Twice she had been second to her sister in this race; if she felt anything it was the anticipation of her first Ironman victory, and the third win for the Puntous family in four years.

Back at the pier Bright pressed his point aggressively with Bates. "I was trying to intimidate him," he admitted. "Although, frankly, if I had been in his position I'd have done the same thing: Get Patricia across the finish line."

Bright, proud of his ability to create exciting competitions, had been enraged at the sight of the Puntous sisters running together out on the Queen K. He saw it as a blatant display of teamwork—a violation, as he put it, "of the spirit of the individual nature of the event," with the victim being Joanne Ernst. Bright was on shaky ground here, though, because the twins' actions were not strictly in violation of any Ironman rule.

Beyond that, Bright viewed a potential tie for first between the two sisters with special distaste. Before he had learned of Patricia's impending disqualification, he had wanted to send someone out onto the course to tell the twins that if they crossed the line together they would be able to split only first-place prize money, not first and second. It seemed an unfathomable position to the Ironman people; they couldn't know that Bright's America's Marathon in Chicago, which featured a $250,000 prize purse and paid the world's best marathoners appearance fees of up to $50,000, had just such a provision written into its official rules. Runners in Chicago judged by a three-member finish-line panel to have tied intentionally would split first-place money only. To Bright the thinking was simple and straightforward: He was protecting the race's investment.

Under pressure from Bright, Bates finally agreed that Patricia should be informed of the disqualification and asked to leave the course. "I won't tell her, but if you want to tell her...." he said to Bright. So Haserot headed out onto the course again—with a thought but not a mandate. He decided to take no action.

"I was concerned at that point because the camera was on the girl," he said. "I'd have to run out there and do it on camera. That to me would have been far worse a thing to do to her, to us, than to let her finish the race and deal with it as a disqualification then. I think she'd have gone to the ground if I had said, 'You're disqualified.' She was too far into the race, she would have just gone down, on camera. And then along would come Sylviane in second place [she was actually in third by this time] and see her twin sister there. When I ran the whole thing through my mind, I just decided that the best thing was just to let it happen, let it go on the way it did."

But it went terribly. By letting Puntous run the marathon in ignorance of her position a cruel ending was assured. Patricia crossed the finish line in 9:47:14, breaking her sister's course record by an astounding 35:59. She had become the first woman to break 10 hours on the Ironman course. Having run the fastest marathon of the day, having broken the course record and crossed the finish line first, she was in line for $16,000 in prize money and bonuses.

But something was amiss. Officials hurriedly reset the finish-line tape for Newby-Fraser. Puntous at this point had still not been notified of her situation, so media coordinator Foster had to convince photographers in the press bleachers to stay and get a shot of "second" place without actually telling them why. "I think you'd be real happy if you stayed," she said. "Trust me, you'll be glad that you did." Most stayed, and so ended up with photographs of a winner they could file. Newby-Fraser finished 1:30 after Puntous and played the scene well, raising her arms and smiling as the tape stretched across her chest. After being in such bad shape early in the marathon she was overjoyed that she had been able to come back and run so well. Second place, in her mind, was marvelous.

Sylviane Puntous crossed the line four minutes after Newby-Fraser, exhausted. Patricia, her face red and swollen with tears of concern for her sister, whom she knew had been having a bad time during the marathon, greeted Sylviane at the finish line and the pair walked together to the medical area, arms around each other. It was there, hidden from most of the reporters and photographers but not from an ABC telephoto lens, that Haserot informed Patricia of the disqualification. She was stunned. No one could have watched her reaction—and millions did on television—and not been convinced of the woman's utter disbelief that such a thing could have happened to her.

"I couldn't believe it," she said. "I was so tired, physically and mentally. I had nothing left for fighting. I was just exhausted."

"I think we realized more in the morning," Sylviane said.

When she was informed that she had been awarded first place, Newby-Fraser too was stunned. All she could do was shrug her shoulders at Puntous's misfortune.

"I just feel that I have no control over the situation," she said. "I feel for her, but I have no control. I'm pleased that I've won now—but that's just the way it goes."

It had never gone quite like this, however. A half hour later, as they walked up Palani Road from the pier on the way back to their hotel, the twins vented some of the anger and hurt that the long day—perhaps even the years—had created. Neither Joanne Ernst nor Jim Collins had anything to do with the drafting call, or with any aspect of the Ironman administration, but it wasn't clear in the twins' minds that there hadn't been some connection, no matter how remote. Their words would tear at the hearts of Ernst and Collins, who stood unjustly accused, but all the same could not help but feel that at some point over the past three years they could have done something to prevent what had happened. Indeed, the twins' words would tear at the hearts of many people within the sport, people who had refused to believe that what was happening out on the Queen K was not, as they so innocently supposed, just good, clean, friendly fun. It was serious business. It meant a lot, sometimes it meant too much. Patricia Puntous, the athlete, had broken the rules and so had failed, but to a far greater extent the system had failed the athlete. A sad but simple disqualification had turned into a tragedy whose final act had been played out in the very spot where so many personal triumphs of spirit and will had been celebrated—were being celebrated—even as Patricia Puntous spoke. It seemed obscene, a desecration. The dream of innocence at the Ironman was finally over.

"I'm so sick and tired of...." Patricia Puntous sobbed, her heavily accented English, for once, eloquent. "They are so jealous. When you don't have a good race or when you lose, God, you don't try to take that from the winner. You look at yourself and you say, well, what I do wrong? Or what I should do better? You don't try to take away from the people who do good. And she (Ernst) always do that. Always when she lose. And that's true. I'm so sick. Always the same people who complain.

"Since the money for sponsorship [prize money], it's just not the same anymore. And what's the money? Twelve thousand bucks instead of $100,000 like in Chicago [America's Marathon]? We fight for *that?* I feel sorry for the sport. Because it don't do good for the sport, that's for sure."

Coming on the heels of Baker's controversial disqualification in Nice two weeks before, Puntous's ill-orchestrated humiliation was indeed destructive. When both incidents received national television exposure in February, it looked bad, as Bright had known it would, presenting a public face of pettiness and confusion. Two things saved the day: First, the power of the Ironman event continued to be bigger than any one incident, even one with such impact. Second, nothing could take anyone's mind away too long from the men's race. Bob Bright had not gotten his down-to-the-wire, head-to-head battle for first; instead he'd gotten history.

12

KINGS OF
THE KONA
COAST

It was 10:30 or so at night, so quiet on the highway you could hear cars coming down the road from a mile or more away, their headlights glowing brighter and brighter from behind the next hill, then splashing rudely over the lonely figures that wobbled southward on foot along the shoulder of the road, heading for home. The sound of cars when they passed was almost painfully loud.

But they passed infrequently. In the long intervals between cars, the darkness was soft and warm. The full moon overhead was so bright that the white line marking the shoulder seemed to glow against the black asphalt, so bright that when clouds drifted across its face their edges gleamed and continued to light the way for the remaining handful, the last finishers of the 1986 Ironman World Championship Triathlon.

The race, and it was a still a race in some respects, was in its 15th hour. For those still on the course, there was one-and-a-half hours to get back into town, make those last few turns and run down Alii Drive to the finish line by midnight, to beat the clock to 17 hours and earn a T-shirt, be an Ironman, fly home a hero. In the eerie darkness of the long night, there was a wealth of lonely self-determination. True, the glory was long gone; the public kings and queens of this race had already been crowned. Most of them were already back in their hotel rooms, asleep. But there were heroes left on the highway even at this late hour, people still moving in the right direction—people of no particular athletic talent who were just too damn stubborn to stop. From the beginning, when the cannon boomed over Kailua Bay that morning, their goal had been simple: finish, just finish.

"Well, I'm thinking that I can finish," growled 63-year-old Max Burdick. He'd just left a brightly lit aid station at the 23-mile mark. "These blisters on the balls of my feet are hurting like crazy, though. They bandaged them and retaped them and all that, but that don't stop the pain."

It wasn't going to stop Burdick, either. He couldn't run anymore, but he was walking fiercely, leaning forward and swinging his arms, as if he was angry and wading Popeye-like into a brawl, the fluorescent green chemical light stick after-dark Ironman finishers are required to carry, bouncing at his hip. He was tired and he hurt, but he was moving.

"I thought somehow I'd get finished today," he said, "having done a couple of them. I was here in '83 and failed the swim [he missed the two-hour cutoff time that year and was disqualified]; I was here in '84 and failed the bike [he was 20 minutes behind schedule when they closed the bike course at the 10:30 mark]; made it all in '85. Had a great swim this morning: 1:48. That's knocking it down quite a bit from 2:02. Too bad I couldn't hook the bike up with it."

A lean, wiry little man with a gravely voice, Burdick has been a contractor for 40 years and a marathoner for 20. He owns his own contracting firm in Salt Lake City. It's a large firm, but after listening to Burdick speak just two or three sentences, you know he started at the bottom. He was Ironman material all the way.

Over the previous summer, the business had demanded all of his attention, and he wasn't able to train effectively. So he hadn't put in near enough miles for the Ironman, especially on the bike. His friends thought he was crazy for even trying to do the race, but Burdick came to Hawaii anyway, a month early, in the hopes that he could catch up. Now he was wishing he'd done more.

"I was in good shape last year," he grumbled. "I did 1000 miles of training on my bike after I got over here. This year I did about 500. Didn't do any century rides [100 miles]. Last year I did three. Just didn't get started this year until it was too late."

He was out of sight of the aid station now, around a corner and into the dark again, still following the white line. He hunched a bit more and seemed to pick up the pace as he walked away. From behind, in the moonlight, you could barely see his head, just the hump of his back and his two elbows sticking out sharply, side to side. Three miles to go.

It had been quite a day. Doggedly stalking his own humble goal, Max Burdick could have appreciated but not really comprehended what Dave Scott had accomplished some seven hours before. The Man had been magnificent. The best ultradistance triathlete in the world, on this course anyway, had the day of his life, the race he'd been talking about since 1982. "Someday," he'd said, "somebody is going to."

Somebody, hell. He'd been figuring all along it would be him, and now it was. Eight-twenty-eight. Tinley's course record going in had been 8:50.

❖

The Kailua Pier that morning, an hour before the start, was a trade show of triathlon talent and technology. There was not a single competitor in the ranks of the top professionals in the world who should have been in attendance but wasn't. Nice, in the battle for world championship legitimacy, was dwarfed. The Ironman had attracted even the best Europeans. And while Scott Tinley's bike had been an object of great curiosity in 1985, the long pro bike rack in 1986 was filled with machines that were as radical as his or more so: wild handlebars, strange-looking frame geometry, reduced diameter wheels. Even John Howard, whose mind has run through a fair share of radical designs, was impressed. Shooting a television spot on the pier the day before the race, he'd thrown a leg over one competitor's bike, crunched himself down in a racing position—the only position possible to assume on the new designs—then looked up and laughed. "Boy that's something," he said, flipping the tiny brake levers tucked beneath the reverse curve of the handlebars. "Will these things actually stop you?"

Interestingly, Dave Scott's bike was standard stuff, nothing fancy at all except the purple and yellow paint job. It looked almost stodgy that morning standing in the number two spot in the rack, between Tinley's machine in number one and Chris Hinshaw's in number three. The Man would ride simply too, in just a pair of bike shorts and an ordinary running singlet, nothing at all like the sleek, fashionable suits of the others. The legs had gotten a lot stronger since 1980, but Dave Scott hadn't changed the basic package.

"First, I hadn't been exposed to those bikes," Scott said, explaining his conservatism several months after the race. "I'd never had the opportunity to try one. Secondly, I don't like to be in that position; I think it's really an uncomfortable position to be able to get off the bike and run. I stand up a lot, so those cow-bars [the new handlebars were shaped like the up-sweeping horns of a cow] would really be horrible for me. Look at the times on the run; they're slow. Two guys ran well, the rest of them ran horribly. I think the position they were in on their bikes was a contributing factor. If your hips and your back and your neck are taking up an extra load because you're more aerodynamic on the bike, you may be suffering on the run.

"The race is won on the run, not on the bike."

Obviously, there were triathletes on the pier that morning who were not completely convinced of that. By the end of the day, they would be.

The swim, as usual, was a scramble. Drafting is legal in the water, and while it is nowhere near as effective as it is on the bike, where it isn't legal at all, it does make a difference. Some of the better swimmers strike out immediately for the front; others work hard to find groups of swimmers who are faster than they are, and latch on, swimming literally at their feet, moving more quickly and expending less energy than they would if they were alone. Scott, with his long experience as an ocean swimmer, usually finds himself being followed. Tinley, who over the years has became cagey in the water, as well as much faster than he was when he started, works hard at finding the right group to trail. Allen, one of the fastest swimmers, does a little of both; in February 1982 he greatly annoyed Dave Scott by swimming in Scott's bubbles for most of the 2.4 miles, letting him do the lion's share of the work.

In 1986, with the two Hinshaw brothers, Brad and Chris, far in front, Scott found himself fighting for open water all the way to the turnaround boat with Dirk Aschmoneit, the top German triathlete. The pair did not have the best line on the turn, and a pack of seven or eight men slid ahead. Scott was forced to work his way back into third place by swimming through the pack, and he ended up leading it to the pier, which frustrated him. It was during the second half of the swim that Allen picked up the scent. He began to focus on Dave Scott and would not lose that focus for the next five hours.

Feeling especially strong over the last 1000 yards, Scott climbed out of the bay in third place. He'd swum the 2.4 miles in 50:53, slightly slower than he was used to, but it had been a good effort. Up ahead, 21-year-old Brad Hinshaw had broken Djan Madruga's swim course record with a 47:39. It took Hinshaw slightly less than four minutes to change, hop on his bike and climb the steep, half-mile to the top of Pay and Save Hill. His brother, Chris, was 2:30 behind him. A minute later, the rush: Rob Barel, from

Holland, perhaps the best European; Aschmoneit; Bruce Silvano, an American from Florida; then Scott and Allen, with a string of riders following. Tinley crested the hill just two minutes later.

No one was prepared for the pace during the bike ride. Just two miles out, Scott went around Barel as if the Dutchman were standing still, surprising both men. Barel came off his seat and followed, along with Allen, who was several bike lengths in back of Scott, matching his pace. It wasn't until 10 minutes later that Scott noticed Barel had hung on. He saw Allen for the first time, too.

"I looked back and there was Mark," Scott said, "like a shadow. It surprised me when I first saw him there, but I wasn't shocked because we're always close on the swim and I knew I got out of the water third, and I presumed he was in that big pack." Scott laughed. "I was irritated. 'Damn it,' I said, 'none of these people have the balls to take the lead. Here I am again pulling this whole pack. And they know darn well who's pulling it, too.'"

Scott, Barel and Allen soon caught Chris Hinshaw, and the four men continued on together. Barel's pace was uneven. He surged back and forth; he'd spend a mile or two, 50, 60 yards in front, then the next mile or two in back, almost off the pace entirely. One of the few Europeans who had been able to compete with the American men, Barel had been third at Nice in 1985, behind Allen and Tinley, one place ahead of Molina. He was a strong, all-around triathlete, but he'd been nursing a leg injury in Hawaii and had serious doubts about his ability to run. Before the race, he had announced that he needed a go-for-broke bike ride to be competitive. The problem was that his go-for-broke pace seemed to suit Scott and Allen just fine.

"I pushed myself hard the entire time on the ride," Scott said, "but I was in control. It was fun for me to watch Chris Hinshaw and Rob Barel ride. I was worried about Barel, because I knew he was a strong cyclist—Chris is, too—but they gave me a lot of cues that they were struggling too much. About 35 miles, I remember watching Barel; he was squirming around on his seat a lot. And Chris Hinshaw would bait off everyone else. When someone would make a move, he would make a move. He would accelerate too many times. You do that and you start using the glycogen in your muscles and it wears you down. I knew he wasn't going to be able to do that forever."

As for Allen, his mission was obvious. He was, indeed, shadowing Scott, staying three, four, five bike lengths behind him at all times, matching him pedal stroke for pedal stroke. It was as if he were replaying the 1984 Ironman, only not as it actually had happened, with him flying off self-destructively alone into the terrible heat, but as he should have played it—keying on the guy who knew the race and the conditions better than anyone. "I knew before I went into the race," Allen said, "that I was going to try and stay with whoever was stronger on the bike, Tinley or Dave. It happened to be Dave. I figured that he wasn't going to do anything stupid; he wasn't going to blast his brains out and fall apart on the run. And if he did, then I would, too. It's better to be out there walking with Dave than to be walking by myself."

The pace seemed to increase as the four men passed the entrance to the Sheraton, 25 miles out. Barel was in front, then Scott, Hinshaw and Allen. As they rode toward Kawaihae, it became more of a group effort. They were staying far enough apart to keep the drafting marshals happy (who were easily pleased; one of them mentioned that they really weren't worried about drafting, because there wasn't any wind to speak of along the course that morning—a ludicrous statement coming from someone who should have known that drafting is a huge factor, wind or not), but they were moving back and forth, gracefully exchanging positions, flying along as one, pushing the same gear, their pedals moving in identical rhythm. The catalyst was Barel, who kept rabbiting to the front, then dropping back. Scott would follow and Allen would follow Scott, while on the outside, feeling the pressure of a pace he knew he could not maintain for long, was Hinshaw. It all looked relaxed, even to the point of Allen and Hinshaw chatting as they went through the right-hand turn in Kawaihae at 2:16 into the race and began climbing toward Hawi.

But it was not relaxed. The pace was fast, way over Hinshaw's head, and he had ridden the course in 4:57 the year before. It was out of sight for Barel, too, although it took him too long to admit that. Perhaps with his bad leg he figured he had nothing to lose. Scott and Allen were comfortable, though—and the four men were pulling away from the field.

"There were several times on the bike where it just felt really easy," Scott said. "I knew I could go harder, but we were pulling away; each time we saw the leader board the margin was greater. I said to myself: 'This is it, this is the race right here.' I worry about Scott Tinley all the time, don't let me deny that—he's ridden the second half of that course faster than anyone else, and he runs well, so I was worried about him—but I told myself to hold back and ride easy."

Tinley. Where was Tinley? He'd been just two minutes behind at the top of Pay and Save Hill. It had looked as if it might finally be his day to get to the front with Dave Scott and Mark Allen early, instead of having to play his usual game of catch-up on the return trip to town. But instead of gaining on the leaders on the way out, he'd been losing time steadily, and not just to Scott and Allen but also to lesser athletes back in the pack—good, solid competitors, but men he should have easily left behind. They went by him almost tentatively, as if to say, "That's Scott *Tinley*. Should I be doing this?"

Tinley was either having a bad day or he was waiting, marshaling his resources. If he was waiting it seemed a questionable strategy, since the only two men in the world who could run the way he could after 112 of riding were in front of him and gaining. And as he dropped farther behind—five minutes as he made the turn at Kawaihae and headed up—it seemed less and less likely that was the case. He was either being frustrated by a pair of legs that wouldn't respond, or being incredibly patient. Which? From his face, shielded by a white, aerodynamic helmet and a pair of big, diamond-shaped sunglasses, there was no clue.

Six miles outside of Hawi, as the group finally overtook Brad Hinshaw and the worst of the head winds began, Barel made a final stab at gaining an advantage. He broke recklessly away from Scott and Allen and headed hard for the turnaround. Chris Hinshaw dropped back, appalled that the already senseless pace was getting even faster.

"It was nuts!" said a wide-eyed Hinshaw after the race. "The first 25 miles took 58 minutes. When Barel took off I said to myself, 'This is nuts. I'm going to do what I have to do at my own pace.' And people kept coming by! I hit 100 at 4:28 or 4:27, and by that time I was in eighth place. The speed of everyone was overwhelming. I didn't imagine it would be so fast."

With lots of Ironman experience, including a second place to Tinley in 1985, Hinshaw would be able to hang on despite having ridden himself nearly into the ground in the early going. He would finish 19th. His brother Brad, though, after leading the race for 45 miles, slowed drastically over the second half of the ride, and would shuffle through an agonizing 4:19 marathon, finishing in 179th place. But it had been a heady morning.

So Rob Barel was the new race leader. He turned first and headed down. Scott was next, 45 seconds back, with Allen close behind. Tinley came through less than four-and-a-half minutes later, riding with Aschmoneit, both men having gained a little ground on the leaders coming up the hills. Was Tinley finally moving?

For the next 27 to 28 miles, Barel continued to confuse the issue. Scott and Allen caught and passed him coming out of Hawi, but he was back in front a mile later and held a small lead for the next 10 minutes. Confident that the Dutchman had already signaled his own demise, Scott maintained his pace and let Barel play games in front. Four hours and fifteen minutes into the race, Barel, a blur of blue, whooshed past the entrance of the Sheraton, moving south. Fifteen seconds later came Scott, then Allen.

Five miles later, Barel was gone, in third behind Allen and fading, this time for good. Tinley lost the time he gained on the way up to Hawi, and much more. Dave Scott was once again at the head of the Ironman pack and the race was in his hands.

Through it all Allen stayed relentlessly behind, through the heat and over the rolling hills of the lava fields, which Dave Scott calls "bumps." Scott was feeling better than he ever had on the bike at the Ironman, and he was deriving tremendous satisfaction from that.

"I've never had a good ride in that race," he said. "And I had always felt that my cycling was...well, for a while it was stronger than anyone's. And then everyone caught up to me; all of a sudden Molina was riding faster than everyone else, and Tinley was getting faster, and I was falling farther and farther behind. But I always felt that cycling was the event that I could really lean on, particularly in a longer race."

It had always been thought that as a rider Scott was merely smarter than his peers, not faster. Every year his bike time in Hawaii had been the same: 5:10:16 in October 1982; 5:10:48 in 1983; 5:10:59 in 1984. People looked at those splits and figured Dave Scott knew what it took to win.

But that wasn't the case at all. Those 5:10s had been bothering him.

"It's coincidental that it's come to that every time," he said. "Look at the conditions each year; they're completely different. I've been disappointed in my cycling. There's never been a year when I've ridden strong. I knew that eventually, if I got in good shape, I was really going to knock off some time on the ride."

He was doing that now, riding faster than anyone ever had. It was starting to worry Allen, who had had enough of scraping himself off the Queen K during the marathon. After haunting Scott from 15 to 20 yards back, mile after mile, he began to have second thoughts as they rode past the airport and headed for town. He'd raced spectacularly at Nice just two weeks before; how much of that race was still lurking in his legs? And while he'd been feeling smooth and loose all the way, handling the speed as well as Scott, it was beginning to wear on him now.

Incredibly, Scott remembers feeling *better* once he hit the airport; he felt stronger over the last 15 miles of the ride than he had all day. Allen felt him surge at that point, forcing the pace up still another notch. Allen followed, but he was pondering. Finally, at the infamous mile 99 marker on the highway, with 13 miles left in the ride, he let Scott go.

"I just didn't have that go-for-it-at-all-cost attitude at the end of the bike," Allen said. "I really wanted to make sure that I had something left for the run because it was such a disaster last time. I didn't feel that I had that little 5 percent extra that it would have taken to stay with Dave."

❖

It was the day after the race. The Kona Surf parking lot was still the center of a lot of activity; triathletes were picking up their bikes and bike gear left in the transition at the end of the ride the day before. The booth where they were selling photos of individual competitors taken during the race was predictably jammed. Allen was a little stiff, but he was in good shape. Three weeks before he'd won the Nice triathlon, now he'd raced well at the Ironman. It was a good month's work.

"I had a tremendous race in Nice," Allen, "a kind of out-of-your-head type of race, where you have that ultimate desire to win the race, knowing that you pointed all your training and energy into it, and then doing exactly what you need to do. That was the way I went into Nice this year. Consequently, I had a really fast time and it wasn't that hard. That's the way Dave was over here. To have beat him yesterday would have required the kind of commitment where you're willing to push your body to the maximum limit. Once I hit that run, I just had these major, heavy-duty, scary flashes of the last time I was here. I thought, 'Oh, my God, I don't want to go up that hill out of town and just turn into a marshmallow again.'"

When Scott was told of Allen's remarks, he downplayed his own superiority. "I've struggled out there," Scott said. "Don't let anyone fool you. It looks on paper that I've done okay on the run, but I've had some unbelievable runs; I've been at the physiological and psychological limit lines in a couple of races."

But Scott lacks perspective on his own reputation in Hawaii. Everyone knows he's been on the edge at times. They also know he's won, regardless. The physiology that enables him to deal with the conditions in Hawaii is a given. His focus on the race, his preparation, his knowledge of the course—all those are recognized. Beyond that, however, is the fact that over the years he's been able to intimidate the competition, to stand toe to toe with them, look them in the eye and make them blink—even on days when he wasn't at his physical best. In 1986, Allen was willing to come out of the Kona Surf and run hard, with the thought in his mind that if it was Dave Scott's turn to fall apart, then he, Mark Allen, would be there to pick up the flag and move on. What he was not willing to do was stay with Scott and suffer the punishment he knew he'd suffer, especially for the first 45 minutes of the marathon. If that isn't intimidation, there is no such thing.

"I don't think anything can compare to how I felt in 1983 at the finish line," Scott said. "But I said to myself that I didn't die; I'm willing to do it again, I'll do it one more time if I have to."

Who could doubt it? Scott roared into the transition area in a fury, whirled through his change of clothing and blasted out again, leaving the volunteers at the Kona Surf a little dazed. What had happened? That was Dave Scott, right? Or was it God, Godzilla, Attila the Hun? Allen followed almost 1:30 later and he seemed almost calm by comparison, although Allen was simply exhausted. On obviously weak knees, he wobbled out and headed for the first hill. He looked bad. If Tinley was close....

Tinley wasn't. He was four more places back, in 6th, almost 11 minutes down. He hadn't been waiting to make his move on the bike, after all. He hadn't been preserving anything; he was just having a lousy day. On the other hand, Tinley having a lousy day at the Ironman is like Gale Sayers running for only 95 yards against the Giants. Lousy in this case was a relative term, and the fact that Tinley had not been his best on the bike might mean that his legs were still fresh for the marathon. It had been that way with him before. Neither Scott nor Allen took anything for granted.

"Even with Tinley 10 minutes back," Allen said, "I knew it was a totally distinct possibility that he could pass me. Because if I had to start walking, there's 10 minutes right there in just one mile."

Scott, true to his consistent strategy in Hawaii of hammering through the first six or seven miles of the marathon, thereby deciding the issue before anyone has a chance to think that it might not yet be decided, gained six minutes on Allen before he reached the base of Pay and Save Hill. While he slowed a little once he reached the highway, he was still running steadily at well under a 6:30-per-mile pace. The Ironman had come to many things from a social and organizational standpoint, things that might be debated and argued over, but Dave Scott on that day was where the race had indisputably come in a physical sense. He had swum the 2.4 miles in 51 minutes, the third fastest of the day; he'd ridden the 112-mile bike course in an astonishing 4:48:32, almost 4 minutes under Tinley's record. He had started his marathon at 12:30 in the afternoon, with the temperature in the high 80s and the humidity close to that—and he was running 6:30 miles.

"I couldn't fathom it," he had said eight years before, when he first heard about the Ironman. "I thought, here are 12 people who are in better shape than I am."

Watching him in 1986, shuffling along relentlessly in a style that had become his trademark, his arms high, his chest stuck out and his head bobbing awkwardly, his long, lean legs churning, corded with muscle, you knew there were no longer 12 people in the world who were in better shape than he was. There wasn't one; there couldn't be. This was Dave Scott, The Man, not washed up at all at age 33, but in his prime, better and fitter than he or anyone else had ever been.

Scott was not a fool, though. He'd been up and down, and he knew how quickly things could change. He had buried Allen early, and knew that Allen's chances of coming back were slim. But there was someone else back there, someone who had been back there for five years, always a threat. Twelve miles into the run, drenched with sweat, pounding furiously toward the turnaround, Scott paid ST the highest compliment he could pay: "I want to know where Tinley is," he called. "How far back is Tinley?"

It was somehow sad that he needn't have worried. Tinley had run strongly along Alii Drive and pushed himself into third place, gaining fast on Allen. But while Allen soon found his legs and by 10 miles was running well, it went the other way for ST. Pay and Save Hill nearly killed him, although by that time he had already given up on the possibility of catching Scott. His goal, and there was a fine edge of anger to it, was to catch Allen. From what he heard of the other man's condition during the early miles, even considering his own, that still was possible, and in an emotional sense, it was all there was left to salvage from a terrible day. His bike hadn't broken as Virginia had feared, but he hadn't been able to do anything with the damn thing. His legs were dead—not sore or tired, because God knows he'd had enough rest—but just heavy, no snap. Bad day. "This is horrible," he had said at one point during the ride, sounding bitter and disgusted. But at least there was Allen. That would keep him going. "Tell Mark I'm on to him," Tinley called menacingly as he ran through the 12-mile mark.

It was a communications failure, really. Tinley *had* been gaining on Allen, but he was losing ground now, quickly. Unfortunately, he didn't know that. Two miles later, Dave Scott came pounding back toward town on the opposite side of the road, dragging with him an entire fleet of press vehicles, including the ABC camera van. Scott had seen the big clock at the turnaround; 07:21 it read, which meant that if he could get back to the pier without falling down, he was going to have a hell of a time. As Scott went by, Tinley, in a gesture that reflected five years of competitive respect and almost 700 miles of racing up and down the Kona Coast, slowed slightly and applauded. Scott, his mind focused tightly on his pace and the road in front of him, raised his left hand slightly and pointed his index finger in Tinley's direction, acknowledging the salute. The procession moved on, and Tinley turned his attention north again, to Allen. He would know where things stood when he saw the other man coming south. The trick was to run as strongly as he could for the next couple of miles, look as good as possible when Allen went by in the opposite direction, then make the turn himself and grind Allen down on the way in.

The problem was, Tinley would have had to run several back-to-back four-minute miles to make the plan work, and he was barely managing 7:30s. Shortly after seeing Scott, he got some applause of his own from some friends along the side of the road, and word came that Allen was just six minutes ahead. It was good news; it meant that he was still gaining, and that Allen must be feeling worse. But then, just half a mile later, with the turnaround still more than a mile away, there was Allen, running back toward town! It wasn't six minutes at all; it was more like 14 or 15. Allen was *gaining* ground, not losing it, and he didn't look that bad; in fact, he looked strong. The sight hit Tinley as if someone had punched him in the face. Even from behind you could see him crumble, feel his amazement and dismay.

A funny thing about the Ironman marathon: Even with the aid stations and the large field of competitors, there are times when it can be incredibly lonely, times when the only thing in sight is the highway itself, with maybe a figure or two moving in the distance through the waves of heat coming off the highway. The only sound is the pat of your own shoes on the asphalt. When Allen went by, Tinley looked up and saw nothing but road. What he felt exactly is impossible to know, but he stopped dead for a moment and put both hands on top of his head and then walked slowly for several yards, disgusted, frustrated. His anger, which had been driving him along, had been snuffed out. Over the years he'd been one of the Ironman's most severe critics, but of all the top men he was the most sensitive to the spiritual impact of the race, eloquent and emotional at times in its defense despite himself. For six years, seven races, he'd been so much a part of Ironman history, part of the race's growth and continuing sparkle; it seemed strange and sad to see him standing there on the highway, alone. Finally, and you could almost hear him exhale heavily and give himself the old ST pep talk, he started to run again, slowly, his bad day creeping back up into his legs until he was just shuffling, and instead of worrying about Mark Allen up ahead, he started asking about Klaus Barth, a 37-year-old West German who was having the race of his life, five minutes behind.

❖

When Dave Scott crossed the finish line, smiling, looking strong and in control, the clock read 8:28:37. It was his fifth Ironman win and a new course record by more than 22 minutes. He'd run a 2:49 marathon, the first man to break 2:50 in Hawaii—the only man ever to break three hours (he'd done it in 1984 as well) until Mark Allen finished 7:30 later with an 8:36:04 and a 2:55.

"You don't seem too tired right now, Dave," said a reporter at the finish line.

"Well, little do you know!" Scott replied, laughing.

But he really didn't. You could see that as he walked; his legs were firm, his stride steady. He stood with his arm around his wife, Anna and talked easily with a knot of reporters behind the finish line. His mother, Dorothy, stood nearby, beaming. A reporter complimented Scott on his record. "Not bad for an old man," he said. Scott laughed. Mom could restrain herself no longer. "You're beautiful, Dave," she gushed. And what the hell, he was—he'd been magnificent.

The finish line was a different kind of place for Scott Tinley, of course. Virginia greeted him and helped the volunteers hold him steady. He was very tired. He'd had some bad races in his day, but this was about the worst. And the timing was terrible. All those years without a cent of Ironman prize money—now the cash had finally arrived and two other guys were flying home with most of it. His time of 9:00:37 wasn't bad, but it was only good for third. It was the first time that had happened since 1981.

"I consider that race one of my gutsiest performances," Tinley said. "I had nothing. And to be able to still go nine hours on a day when you shouldn't even be getting out of bed. I'm not going to feel bad about it. I did everything I could. That marathon hurt more than any run I've ever done in any race."

That was something, a small victory. Sometimes you need those at the Ironman. Some days that's all there is.

"From now on," Tinley said, "it's merely a business deal. Of course, beating Dave would be a motivator for me—again. I'd like to go back and race Dave on my best day and his best day. That to me would be interesting."

Tinley paused.

"You know what it is?" he continued. "There's a lot of b.s. that goes down in that race. It's unavoidable. But the race also offers a lot of people a chance for self-knowledge, and nobody's immune to it, from the guy who finishes last to the guy who finishes first. That's the big draw for people. That's a big draw for me."

❖

The finish line at the Ironman is a special place. The bleachers along Alii Drive are full right up to the official end of the race at midnight—packed with hundreds of parents, friends, earlier finishers and spectators who stay to share in the reflected glow of joy, relief and sheer guts that comes rolling down that last 200 yards. Almost eight hours after Dave Scott's triumphant appearance, Max Burdick could hear them cheering as he made the final turn off the dark highway and walked down Palani Road at last. The steep descent tore at his feet, but it didn't dent his resolve. At least now he could see where he was going. Finally, looping around the final turn, he caught the glare of the lights square in his eyes, heard the announcer call his number, then his name. The big crowd roared as he crossed the line. The clock overhead read 16:08:39. He was the

5379th person to cross an Ironman finish line in 10 races. Piece of cake. Almost an hour to go before the cutoff.

"Feels great," Burdick said wearily, his face almost lost beneath the lei that had been draped over his neck. He was being all but carried toward the massage area by a female volunteer who was a head taller and 20 pounds heavier than he was. "Finishing feels great!" Burdick said. Then he growled back over his shoulder as they took him away: "I woulda been able to run in if I didn't have those blisters."

It sounded so familiar. See, it's easy to miss the point. It's not the pain of the Ironman that you enjoy, it's the potential that the pain opens up. And the potential is a variable, always out there a little beyond where you are at the moment and where you've been before. How far can you go, how quickly can you get there, how deep can you dig inside yourself along the way? The pain is a tool, that's all, like the heat and the highway and the lava. Tools. Looking back, Tom Warren saw it more purely than anyone. "I don't need to go back to a goal after I've failed," he said (although he always did, just for good measure), "because I've already got it figured out." That sounds crazy, but it makes sense. Warren was looking beyond the goal, beyond the pain. He'd learned what he needed to learn; he'd gotten better. Next challenge.

You can't ever do the Ironman just right. It's too big; there are too many places to fail. So you keep getting better and keep failing, and you correct this and fail at that, and all the while your potential keeps stretching way out there. And the funny thing is, right about the time you start to think that you will never do it right, you begin to realize you've already done it perfectly: You finished, once. The possibilities from that point on are endless.

Dave Scott won the Ironman again one more time, in 1987, in a race in which he used Mark Allen less as a foil than as a punching bag. Allen had tested a variety of strategies in previous races, but nothing had worked. In this one, on a day when he was not at his physical best, he tried running away from Scott after the two men had come off their bikes in first place, wheel to wheel. It was a disaster. Allen led for 13 miles, but his body betrayed him once again, and Scott's ferocious charge over the last half of the marathon featured a classic scene in which he passed his shattered rival using the ABC camera van as cover, just in case Allen had anything left. It was a move that was pure Dave Scott. He had never given quarter to a rival at Ironman, and it would have been completely uncharacteristic of him to cross the road and pat the struggling Allen on the butt as he went by.

But Scott needn't have worried because at the particular point, Allen was less concerned with chasing Dave Scott than with simply staying on his feet. He was—once more, for the millionth time, it seemed—a wreck. He finished second, 11 minutes behind Scott, but had anyone been close enough, he had been in no position to fight them off. He could have as easily ended up in third or fourth or 10th. He was barely able to stand at the finish line and was rushed to the hospital suffering from acute intestinal bleeding. He was released from the hospital to attend the award ceremony the next night, and I remember watching from the wings as he leaned, pale-faced, against the awards table for support as Dave Scott, the gleaming, golden champion once again, addressed the crowd. How much more can this man take? I wondered.

As it turned out, he could take—and give—much, much more. Scott's win in 1987 was his sixth in Kona, but it was also his last. But his best race ever—the race he always said was possible at Ironman, the race he knew he could one day run—would come two years later, in defeat at the hands of none other than Zen master Mark Allen, also known as "The Grip of Death," who after seven years of incredibly bad luck and crushing self-doubt, finally ascended the Ironman throne.

Perhaps the spiritual Allen appealed too much to Madame Pele, who thought him worthy of test after test, just to make sure he was The One. For some reason she had largely ignored Scott, leaving him free to zoom up and down the lava fields, year after year, with relative impunity. Perhaps she realized that Scott was usually harder on himself than she could ever be. Or perhaps he was simply the leading player in Allen's trial by fire. Besides, Scott was a great warrior, but he was bit too severe. Could a god really love a man who rinsed his cottage cheese?

Allen, on the other hand, had spent quiet, contemplative time in the lava fields. He had made the proper offerings, shown the traditional respect, ti leaves and all. In 1989, it paid off. Here, with only some minor edits, is how I saw that race at the time:

Finally, the seven-year monkey is off Mark Allen's back, and the last chapter of the triathlon's Big Four has been written. They've all won Hawaii now, Molina, in 1988, when no one expected it; now Allen in '89, years past the point when his great talent and will dictated that he might. What's next? Who cares? The blank page has been filled.

It was a joyous, unmitigated triumph. Allen told the audience at the awards ceremony on Sunday night that a vision of courage had sustained him, but that wasn't quite right. Allen has never lacked for courage. Indeed, it has been his depth of courage that at times has worried us all. Was he really a man who, like the greyhound he so resembled, could actually run himself to death, as he seemed ready to do in Nice in 1983, or in Hawaii in '87?

Courage? Of course. But smart, too. At last, smart. And with Mark Allen's smartest race, the Dave Scott era ended. Even if The Man returns to Kona in 1990 and wins for a seventh time, his long reign there has come to a close. He was magnificent on October 14, fulfilling all of our expectations—and most of his own is well. This time, though, someone else was everything Dave Scott was and more, a little more, 58 seconds more. It was enough.

The supporting cast included the 27-year-old West German, Wolfgang Dittrich, who led the field out of the water with a 48:13, then held grimly onto the lead for the next 112 miles, setting the stage for the Allen-Scott duel to come. How much do you pay a man for such a good day's work? Dittrich's last Ironman marathon, in 1987, was a 3:48; this time he managed a 3:12 and finished 10th. He earned $1600.

The battle started for real at the bike-run transition area at the Kona Surf Resort. Dittrich had been running for almost two minutes when Allen and Scott roared in. Allen ran out first, but Scott was right behind, and at an aid station still inside the parking lot he sprinted past Allen as if the finish line was 100 yards, not 26 miles, away. You knew then what was coming.

The two men ran literally shoulder-to-shoulder for the next 23 miles, and Scott would later praise Allen for a tactic that may or may not have been intentional: Allen ran to the inside, nearest the aid stations. Once every mile Scott had to drop back slightly to get aid, and once every mile he caught the aid station volunteers recovering from having just serviced Allen. And each mile, he had to surge a little to get back on pace. A drib of energy wasted here, a drab there.

The pace quickened at the turnaround, with nine miles left to run. The mile splits, which had been incredible, escalated toward the insane: 5:40s, 5:45s. Finally at the aid station at mile 23, Scott fell back five yards behind and struggled for three-quarters of a mile to catch up. He felt tired, he said, but was still strong—stronger, he thought, than Allen. Running abreast of Allen once again, he began to plot his two-mile strategy. "I'll idle with him here be patient," Scott said to himself. "I'll outrun him on the downhill."

But right then Allen made his move, a strong surge at the base of the low, almost non-existent uphill just outside of town that has broken thousands of Ironman hearts since the race came to Kona in 1981. Scott, caught off guard, was unable to respond. The master of the Ironman had been out-mastered by the Grip of Death himself, the man who had made all the mistakes and finally had learned all the lessons. "It was brilliantly timed," Scott said.

At the top of the hill, seven-10ths of a mile later, Allen had gained 31 seconds and the race was over. "I did it! I did it! I did it!" he cried to the shadowing ABC television van—or maybe just to himself. He crossed the finish line, exultant, waving a small American flag, washed of pain and fatigue and seven years of frustration by the thunderous roar of the huge crowd.

Allen's time of 8:09:15, a course record by more than 19 minutes, and personal best for him at Ironman by almost 30. "That was difference," Allen said, "between surviving and racing."

❖

Allen's 1989 triumph in what *Competitor* magazine called the "Ironwar," truly did mark the end of the Dave Scott era at Ironman and the beginning of the Mark Allen dynasty. It was the first of his six victories—the first of five wins in a row—and his 2:40:04 marathon (Scott ran 2:41:03, and lost) that year is still the best ever recorded in Kona. If you know what it's like to run a 2:40 marathon, you might begin to appreciate the madness of doing so—or being able to do so—at midday in Hawaii. You probably can't conceive of doing it after riding a fiercely competitive 112-mile time trial on a bike.

If you're not a runner, or you are not familiar with that kind of pace, go out the front door and run to the corner absolutely as fast you can. It's like that. Now jog upstairs and turn on the shower. Wait until it's good and steamy, then stand under it until you're slightly light-headed from the heat. Can you imagine keeping that up for 26 miles?

The 1989 battle between Scott and Allen was the sport's greatest race. But the greatest individual performance belongs to Paula Newby-Fraser, the ex-patriot former ballet dancer from Zimbabwe, whose career began with a humble third place in 1985, but who went on to match, then exceed, the achievements of both Scott and Allen. Her performance in 1988 was a masterpiece.

No one, least of all Newby-Fraser herself, foresaw her transition from worker bee to Wonder Woman. Indeed, her first few seasons on the Ironman stage were marked by predictions of greatness not for her, but for a succession of flashier rivals. For three years her remarkable endurance talent lay, like a raw diamond on the ground in her native Zimbabwe, disguised in plain sight. It was only after that talent had been tested under the hot Kona sun, tumbled, and polished and cut skillfully by the lava and the winds and the heat, that the finished gem emerged. When it did, finally, its brilliance was blinding.

What people did notice from the start was that Newby-Fraser was graceful under even the most trying circumstances. She marveled innocently at her own third-place finish in 1985 and was the calm at the center of the storm of Patricia Puntous's disqualification in 1986. Indeed, she was only one in sight that seemed to take the events of that frustrating, confusing afternoon in stride. Somehow, as the winner of the race by default she managed not to say anything foolish. Her attitude was strikingly matter-of-fact: she had raced well enough to benefit when the rules of the competition were enforced. End of story. In retrospect, her ability to rise above the fray might have been the earliest indication of her great talent for the Ironman, where the emotional fray stretches for 140 miles.

The following year, 1987, Newby-Fraser joined a chorus of pre-race praise for New Zealand sensation Erin Baker, whose brief, meteoric triathlon career was marked by her great talent and even greater penchant for attracting controversy. Talented, relentless and outspoken, Baker would become Newby-Fraser's chief rival and source of inspira-

·tion—sometimes not in the most positive sense. More than once, Newby-Fraser was spurred by Baker's confident predictions of victory and Newby-Fraser's inevitable demise.

Also in the field were the Puntous twins, Patricia and Sylviane. It still seems beyond belief that the pair would return to Kona after the debacle the previous October, but Ironman motivations have never been easy to figure. And it was not the last the Ironman would see of either of them. They would return in 1989, and Sylviane would close out the decade by placing second, capping a pair of bittersweet careers in a sport designed to celebrate individual achievement and that was never quite comfortable with the Canadian twin's interpretation of that concept.

Through nearly 22 miles of the marathon in 1987 Newby-Fraser held the lead, but it was tenuous grasp. Patricia Puntous had been dogging her footsteps throughout the run, not so much gaining ground, but more picking up the various pieces that Newby-Fraser was dropping as she went. The conditions were terrible. It was hot, it had been windy during the bike ride, and the pace had been furious all day. Talent was no longer part of the equation. It was a mental thing now, and Newby-Fraser had lost the edge. She was only hoping to win, hoping that somebody didn't catch her, hoping that the courage to continue would somehow well up inside and rush to her brain, because she had lost the ability to summon it herself. She had been racing for nine hours, and she had nothing left to give.

At 22 miles all hell broke loose. Puntous caught Newby-Fraser at almost the same moment Baker, who had been running in third but gaining on the leaders for miles, drove past both of them. Only Puntous could respond. Exhausted, Newby-Fraser folded up like a tent and embraced another third place finish.

Looking back, the last four miles of the 1987 Ironman constituted a pivotal point in the evolution of the women's competition there. For one thing, Newby-Fraser realized even before the finish line that in order to win this race she was going to have to devote her entire being to the process. That knowledge in itself proved fateful.

Moreover, running together now toward mile 23 was the old Ironman and the new, Puntous and Baker. Prior to the race, responding to a journalist's question about tactics, Patricia's sister, Sylviane, had announced that no matter what, the twins would stick with their time-tested strategy of walking through each Ironman aid station, even if running through them was what it took to win. ìWe will walk," Sylviane said emphatically.

It was the old way. And it's still the best way, even today, for a first-timer or a dedicated middle-of-the-packer to ensure a finish, or to soak up the legendary care and concern of the Ironman volunteers. It was, and is, a valuable survival technique, and it's a great way to absorb the full Ironman experience. But it is not a way to win. It had never been for the men, not at least since Dave Scott had begun manhandling the Ironman distance in 1980, and it would cease to be for the women in 1987.

As Baker and Puntous approached the aid station at mile 23, Baker was holding herself together by the barest of threads. She was by no means confident of being able to outrun Puntous, and she was sure that three more miles of hard racing were to come. Then, to her shock, Puntous slowed and began to walk, just as Sylviane had said she would.

In Baker's mind such an action was unthinkable. Could Puntous possibly be this determined not to win? "I couldn't believe it," Baker said. But she was not so surprised that she missed the opportunity. Known for her fierce, stone-faced competitive fire, Baker was suddenly refreshed. Puntous's stunning (and apparently premeditated) lack of resolve washed over her like a cool breeze. She surged and left Puntous to her ablutions. From that point on, you couldn't have taken the race away from her with a crowbar.

The day after that race, Baker was still in awe of what the competition had done to her, what it taken from her. She had never paid such a high price for victory.

"I had to concentrate like hell to get to the finish line," she said. "I didn't have anything left. I couldn't wave to people, I couldn't smile.

"Every year I see the pictures of Sylviane winning this race, Patricia even, last year. They're glum-faced, walking over the line. I always thought to myself, 'Can't they even smile?' But oh, shit, I didn't have the energy to do a thing."

But she'd had the guts to run, and on that day, the game changed. Baker had raised the bar. Either you ran the marathon, from start to finish, or you couldn't hope to win.

The lessons of the day were not lost on Paula Newby-Fraser. She forgot nothing. In 1988 she had a strong season, and was certainly considered one of the favorites when the triathlon world flew off on its annual pilgrimage to Kona. But Erin Baker had had a good season, too, and was coming off a spectacular race at the Nice Triathlon in late September. This would be the year, the pundits said, when Baker's talent and grit would combine and the world would truly see what could be done by a woman at the Ironman. Even Newby-Fraser seemed cowed. "After Nice, I guess we're all just racing for second place," she said.

I honestly don't remember even a hint of cynicism or irony in Newby-Fraser's voice when she said that. But it's been a long time. I can certainly imagine her responding dryly to the 13th consecutive journalist to observe that Erin Baker was "probably unbeatable, don't you agree, Paula?" But Baker had been truly impressive all season, and her marathon skills were formidable. On paper she really was unbeatable.

On the lava, though, it was different. For that matter, so was Paula Newby-Fraser. She was neither the humble novice who had wandered into third place in 1985, nor the sagging also-ran of 1987. On a perfect day, she simply turned her back on the rest of the women's field and rode away. She climbed off the bike with a six-minute lead and added eight minutes to that during the marathon, leaving not only Baker, but most of the men in the race, far behind. Newby-Fraser finished 11th overall, in 9:01:01, breaking Baker's course record by 34 minutes. Tellingly, the photograph of her at the finish line is a portrait of joy. As she crosses and breaks the tape, Newby-Fraser is off the ground. She is literally leaping over the finish line, her arms extended above her head and slightly to the sides, elbows locked tight, fists clenched. Her mouth is open; she is yelling like a cheerleader.

"Why can't they even smile?" Baker had asked. They can, Newby-Fraser answered. They can.

It is difficult to put Newby-Fraser's 1988 achievement in context, since the full emancipation of the female endurance athlete—measured against the inaugural women's Olympic marathon in 1984—was at the time less than a decade old. But considering the prestige, prize money and profile of the Ironman within the sport, her 11th-place finish was triathlon's equivalent to a woman playing first-string defensive back in a Super Bowl, or second base for the Yankees in the World Series. It had been only four years since Dave Scott himself had first broken the nine-hour barrier in Kona.

But Newby-Fraser was not finished. Far from it. In 1989, she returned to Kona and bettered her own record by five seconds, coming within less than a minute of breaking nine hours and silencing forever those few idiot-pundits who had maintained that her performance the year before had been a fluke—a mixture of good luck and ideal conditions.

For most of the next decade, Newby-Fraser was the undisputed Queen of Ironman, although Baker kept reappearing like a dark shadow, threatening with her great talent, predicting victory in interviews that journalists were only too eager to print.

Newby-Fraser was second to Baker in 1990, then rolled off four consecutive wins, including two sub-nine-hour performances. Her 8:55:28 in 1992 still stands as the Ironman women's course record. Indeed, in a list of the 10 fastest times by women on the Kona course, Newby-Fraser owns the top six. The other four (three by Baker), are second place times in years marked by Newby-Fraser victories. In all, she won the Ironman eight times—twice more than either Dave Scott or Mark Allen, each with six. (At the press conference following his great defeat of Dave Scott 1989, Mark Allen joked that his first goal "was to beat Paula." Everyone laughed, but there had been more than one top male pro who had considered with dread the possibly that Newby-Fraser might run by them late in the race. How do you explain that kind of thing to your sponsors?

Newby-Fraser's record remains, by far, the most impressive in the history of the sport. It's more than a record, it's a legacy. And it is almost certain that if she had performed comparably in golf, swimming, tennis or track and field, the mainstream sports media would have ranked her among the all-time greats of women's sports, along with Babe Didrickson, Margaret Court, Billie Jean King, Dawn Fraser, Wilma Rudolph and Evelyn Ashford. But who had the perspective to make the comparison—plus the voice or the platform to make it stick? As long as the Ironman itself is incomprehensible—and that's likely to be forever—the exploits of its heroes and heroines will remain incomprehensible as well.

Like Scott and Allen, Newby-Fraser was one of the few to have figured the Kona course—at least as much as such a thing was possible. Yet she, too, paid her pound of flesh—on more than one occasion. In 1995, at the height of her Ironman powers, she wobbled off the Highway and weaved into town with a one-minute lead, doubting her ability to even finish the race.

She had run, by her own later admission, a foolish marathon, wasting a huge lead off the bike by failing to show the proper respect for either the course or her own body. Always a careful, studied, immaculately prepared athlete, Newby-Fraser had grown careless. She hadn't lost an Ironman-distance competition in five years. Everyone said she was invulnerable—a sure bet to win her eighth race in Hawaii. Normally, Newby-Fraser would scoff at such talk; better than most she knew the risks in Kona. But at a critical moment—a few miles into the marathon and with a 10-minute cushion—she let her guard down. "I've got it," she thought. "I've won."

"I was so annoyed that year because everyone thought it was a big yawn—that I was just going to go out there and win. They took it for granted. I came off the bike with a huge lead, and I thought well, this is so easy. But it had been a treacherously windy day, and when I started going down the hole, I just didn't realize it. I was so focussed on winning, I didn't pay attention to the ground under my feet, to take care of the situation. I was in horrible trouble, and what I needed to do was pull up and get something to eat and drink. But all I heard from people along the way was, just keep going Paula, you've got it, keep going. And I listened to them. It was entirely my fault."

Finally, she sat heavily on a curb with two-10ths of a mile to go, as concerned spectators poured water over her head, lost in an Ironman nightmare that up until that point she had only witnessed as an outsider. One woman had already passed her. Two more would do so before she was able to walk unsteadily across that wafer-thin ribbon of real estate with which she was more familiar than any person on the planet. And yet it seemed, then, like foreign territory.

"I thought I was going to black out and die right there," Newby-Fraser said. "I really thought I was going to die— that if I passed out I was never going to wake up. Everybody was so moved by what they saw on television— the media glamorized the whole thing, but it was just idiotic. It was so...unprofessional. I was appalled at what I did to myself. The race was so mine, and I just gave it away.

"It broke my soul," she said.

Ah, well, what's one more soul among so many? That very night, 74-year-old Bill Bell, a long-time Ironman favorite and an annual fixture in Kona, collapsed and fell, senseless, just short of the finish line, yet as he did so, he reached out instinctively with one hand to officially record his presence there that day. His hand crossed the line, all right, but he was two minutes too late. The race clock read 12:02, and that meant Bill Bell was officially a DNF, as in Did-Not-Finish. In the darkness beyond the glare of the floodlights, Madame Pele chuckled softly to herself. Paula Newby-Fraser, who had recovered sufficiently from her own ordeal to return to the pier and watch the final finishers, did not.

The Ironman celebrated its 20th anniversary in 1998. For the record, 13,016 individuals (counting only once those people who have finished two or more races) are listed in the data as Ironman finishers. They all still get birth-

day cards from the Ironman organization, a practice started many years ago by Valerie Silk, who personally signed
every one and did not consider the practice to be a mere
public relations ploy. She never fully understood the
motives of the competitors, but she embraced them completely, and always seemed overwhelmed at their willing-
ness to share with her this immodestly transparent
moment of their lives. For Silk, the birthday cards were
thank-you cards, and she meant every one.

She now lives with her two dogs and two cats in Florida,
where she owns a small medical transcription firm. Aside
from a speech or an appearance here or there, she has little contact with the triathlon world, and she was never
tempted, even for a minute, to become a participant.
Unfairly (and inaccurately) criticized as a less-than-astute
businesswoman during her tenure as Ironman Race
Chairman, she is one of the few people to ever make a significant amount of money in the triathlon business.
Unfortunately, most of what she took away from the sale
of the Ironman in 1988 went to pay her lawyers, who
defended her against a series of post-sale lawsuits, including one by several of the original participants, who
claimed she had no right to sell it. John Collins, who put
together the original competition (not to mention the
original trophies), stood by her unfailingly. Retired now
from the Navy, Collins lives with his wife Judy on a boat in
Panama. He, like most others in the sport, see Valerie Silk
as a pivotal figure in triathlon history and the woman
who, with great love and true concern, raised the Ironman
from nothing into one of the word's greatest endurance
spectacles.

Tom Warren, whose lonely, wobbly victory in 1978
helped launched a sport (or a movement—it's still hard to
say which), still lives in San Diego, in a house high on a
hill overlooking Mission Bay. He has another home in the
mountains east of the city, in Cuyamaca, where the chance
exists that one day, on a run, he will be attacked by a
mountain lion—a fight he will no doubt win handily.
Fittingly, he has a wife now, Barbara, who, according to

Competitor magazine editor Bob Babbitt, "works out more than he does."

Scott Tinley never quite recovered from that moment on the Highway in 1986 when his hopes of catching Mark Allen were brutally dashed. Allen replaced him as Dave Scott's chief rival, and Tinley would appear only infrequently among the top 10 finishers thereafter—most notably in 1990, when he had a sparkling race and finished second to Allen by nine minutes. For a day, at least, it seemed like old times.

But he did not drift away. He will always race; if there is anyone likely to die on a race course in his late 90s, it is ST. To date, he has completed 19 Hawaii Ironman competitions. And his monthly column, "Tinley Talks" in Triathlete magazine has turned him into respected triathlon philosopher and historian ñ a role he plays with great humor and even greater sensitivity. To Tinley, triathlon has always been mostly about fun, a perspective that at times may have kept him from winning the really tough races, but has also kept him sane.

Scott Molina finally overcame his Ironman-averse physiology in 1988, sweating his way to victory in 8:34, then the second fastest time ever recorded in Hawaii. Unfortunately for Molina his performance was completely overshadowed by Newby-Fraser's historic 9:01, and complicated by a positive drug test in the wake of the Nice Triathlon two weeks before. Molina would marry Erin Baker and the pair would retire to her native New Zealand to raise a family and establish a gene pool of mind-boggling potential. The drug test did not hold up.

Mark Allen retired, graceful as always, in 1996, still at the top of his game. Now the former Grip of Death, he has been married for 10 years to Julie Moss, who brought the drama and occasional pathos of the Ironman into 20 million homes in 1982—the very year Allen himself entered the sport. The couple lives in Cardiff, California, with their young son. Allen, smiling his ever-present Mona Lisa smile, seems quite settled. But if he ever decides to come back, he will frighten the hell out of everyone, even the Germans.

At last report, Dave Scott is also retired. But a future Perfect Race on the Kona Coast no doubt still lingers in his mind. In 1994, he returned to the Ironman at age 40 and placed second in 8:24—his second best time in Hawaii ever and exactly one hour and one second faster than his premier Ironman appearance on Oahu in 1980. If you weren't counting, that's 14 years. They were victories in themslves greater than the first six. Coming back after not racing since '89. There were so many unknowns. I thought maybe I could competely fall on my face. When I caught those guys on the bike, it was a personal victory.

Scott's race in 1994 was certainly one of the most spectacular endurance performances ever by a Masters (over-40) triathlete, although Scott himself would regard with scorn the phrase "for a man his age." But even he admits a measure of pride in coming back so successfully after being out of the sport almost completely since 1989.

"There were so many unknowns!" he said. "I thought it was possible that I would go out there and completely fall on my face, so when I caught (the leaders) on the bike, it was a personal victory."

Sure enough, he was back again in 1996 to finish fifth, first among the U.S. contingent, with an 8:28. It was an odd race in which Scott went from has-been to holy-cow in the course of a single afternoon. For the first time in his long Ironman career, he was simply not a factor during the bike ride. "I actually thought I was in better shape that year than I'd been in '94," he said. "In hindsight I probably tried to do a little too much. I was pretty flat. At five miles I knew it wasn't there."

As men almost young enough to be his sons rushed by him ("in droves" as he said) on the way to the turnaround, his fears of "falling flat on his face" welled up, uncomfortably close to reality. When he finally came off the bike in 26th place, there were uncomfortable looks all around. Had he stayed too long?

What happened next was pure Scott—a mad dash out of the transition area, and a seemingly suicidal half marathon that moved him 13 places closer to the front. He passed seven more men on the way in, and ended the day with a 2:45 marathon—the second fastest of the afternoon.

"I figured that was one hell of a victory," he said. "I had wanted to pull of the road a thousand times. Of all the years I'd competed, that had never happened. It felt like the greatest race I'd ever done."

The race said wonderful things about Scott, but it didn't say much for the U.S. triathlon program, whose grip on the sport as a whole had slipped appreciably following the gradual departure of the Big Four. For 13 years, from 1980 through 1993, Scott, Allen, Molina and Tinley controlled the Kona Coast with a single exception in 1981, when the U.S. cycling star John Howard took the victory. How all that endurance ability—mental and physical— came to focus on so few for so long is unexplainable— especially in a young sport, when one would naturally expect a high rate of turnover at the top. Nevertheless, there they were, and for more than a decade no one else even came close.

The Australians and the Germans are the world triathlon powers now—at least among the men. Greg Stewart, a small, wiry, effervescent Aussie, broke the U.S. string at Ironman in 1994. He'd seemed destined to do so since his first race in Hawaii in 1987, when he placed third behind Scott and Allen and was so gleefully overwhelmed by the Ironman experience that he promised everyone he could find after the award ceremony on Sunday night, "I'm going to win this race! Someday I'm going to win this race!" Then Mark Allen returned the following year and won his sixth and final Ironman and Stewart ended up fourth, behind a pair of Germans.

A Belgian—Luc Van Lierde—won the race in '96, then the Germans were back in force in 1997 when Thomas Hellriegel, Jürgen Zäck and Lothar Leder finished one-two-three. Hellriegel, who had finished second in each of the two previous races, was only joking at the awards ceremony that year when he said that people at the Ironman had better start learning how to speak German, but he had a point. Peter Reid, from Canada, won the 20th Anniversary event in 1998, but there were three Germans in the top 10, and not a single American.

There is no similar trend among the women. Paula Newby-Fraser won the race as recently as 1996, and the vacuum left by her recent departure has not been filled. Her records have not even been threatened, but it's only a matter of time until a perfect day—low clouds and cool (In the 80s only. "Perfect" is a most relative term at the Ironman), with a tail wind on the bike coming back from the turnaround at Hawi—will coincide with someone's perfect health, perfect training and perfect state of mind.... Who knows what's possible? Hell, they used to think this race could kill you.

There can be, really, no epilogue for the Ironman, only periodic updates. Who won, who didn't, who fell down here, or there. The event itself never changes, yet it is a work in constant progress, an open-ended project to plumb the depths of our emotions, to measure our ability to transcend the moment in pursuit of the future, to laugh at ourselves in the midst of miserable failure and to move on, grimly, or with good humor—whatever works—to rise above, to cope, to challenge, to survive, to live.

In her last Ironman race in 1998, Paula Newby-Fraser struggled through a miserable day and finished 11th—among the women this time, not the men. Yet, like almost everyone who gets there, she was buoyed at the finish line, not humbled. "By the time I got to the run I had pretty much decided that this was a participation race more than anything else," she told Triathlete magazine. "I was going to put one foot in front of the other and get to the finish line. I definitely didn't want to DNF. When I came into the finish, the crowd was so supportive, it felt like I'd won the race."

But she had won, of course—perhaps in a more complete way than she had ever won before. The crowd at the finish line, which always grasps these things before the athletes do, recognized this immediately. Finishing first on a perfect day, when everything clicks...well, you can miss the point. Which is why you'll see the racers, the stars, like

Newby-Fraser, back at the finish line after dark, filling in the blanks, fleshing out the day's experience. The crowd roars for the first people to cross, but it cries for the ones who come after—the kind of tears you shed when a movie really gets you, or when you finish a book that ends so bittersweetly it hurts.

The last time I saw Max Burdick was at the Ironman finish line in 1986. He was grumbling about his blisters, about how they slowed him down and made it impossible for him for to run. Even before he'd gotten to the end he was thinking about the next time. He was 63 then, and when I called the Ironman office in early 1999 to inquire after him, I was little nervous. Hell, it had been 13 years. Burdick was 76 now and anything could have happened. But no, the office said, Max was still around. He had entered the race in 1997 and been back in '98, too—a DNF both times.

It was good news, and I couldn't help but smile. In my mind I could hear him grumbling still, growling like an old dog about going all the way to Hawaii for nothing. It had been the swim in 1997—he hadn't made the two-hour cut-off—and he'd missed the mark on the bike in '98. Or was it the other way around? Well, it didn't matter. It wasn't the blisters, at least. And he'd already seen the finish line, years before. He had that, forever.

—Mike Plant